American Indian
Reference and Resource Books
for
Children and Young Adults

American Indian Reference and Resource Books for Children and Young Adults

Second Edition

BARBARA J. KUIPERS

1995
LIBRARIES UNLIMITED, INC.
Englewood, Colorado

LIBRARIES UNLIMITED, INC.
P.O. Box 6633
Englewood, CO 80155-6633
1-800-237-6124

Library of Congress Cataloging-in-Publication Data

Kuipers, Barbara J.
  American Indian reference and resource books for children and
young adults / Barbara J. Kuipers. -- 2nd ed.
    xii, 230 p. 17x25 cm.
    Includes bibliographical references (p. 55) and index.
    ISBN 1-56308-258-6
    1. Indians of North America--Bibliography--Juvenile literature.
  2. Indians of North America--Library resources--Juvenile literature.
  3. Reference books--Indians of North America--Juvenile literature.
  I. Title.
  Z1209.2.N67K84   1995
  [E77.4]
  016.973'0497--dc20   95-10008
                                                            CIP

E
77.4
.299
K84
1995

Contents

Foreword vii

Preface ix

PART 1
American Indian Literature
for
Children and Young Adults

**1—ASSUMING RESPONSIBILITY FOR SELECTION OF
AMERICAN INDIAN BOOKS OF REFERENCE VALUE** 3

**2—UNDERSTANDING THE EVALUATION CRITERIA
FOR AMERICAN INDIAN LITERATURE** 5

Evaluation Criteria 7
Authorship 8
Value System of American Indians 13
Treatment of American Indians in the Literature 18
Summary 32

**3—USING THE EVALUATIVE CHECKLIST FOR AMERICAN
INDIAN MATERIALS OF REFERENCE VALUE** 35

4—PUBLISHING AMERICAN INDIAN BOOKS 41

Publishing and Purchasing 43
Publishers of Indian Books and Materials 43
Local Publishers of Tribal Culture 49
Building Blocks for Success 49

**5—INCORPORATING AMERICAN INDIAN RESOURCE
MATERIALS INTO THE CURRICULUM** 51

Social Sciences 51
American Indian Languages 52
Mathematics 52

5—INCORPORATING AMERICAN INDIAN RESOURCE MATERIALS INTO THE CURRICULUM (*continued*)

Computer Literacy 52
Science 52
Fine Arts 53
Physical Education and Health 53
Home Economics 53
English and Language Arts 53
Technology 54

REFERENCE SOURCES 55

SELECTED AMERICAN INDIAN BIBLIOGRAPHIES 61

PART 2
Annotated Bibliography
of American Indian Books
of Reference Value
for Children and Young Adults

INTRODUCTION: Preparation of the Bibliography 67

Rationale 67
Development 68
References 70

SELECTED, ANNOTATED BIBLIOGRAPHY OF AMERICAN INDIAN BOOKS OF REFERENCE VALUE FOR SCHOOL-AGE CHILDREN 73

000-099 General Works 73
100-199 Philosophy and Related Disciplines 76
200-299 Religion 78
300-399 Social Sciences 84
400-499 Language 114
500-599 Pure Sciences 118
600-699 Technology (Applied Sciences) 120
700-799 Arts and Recreation 125
800-899 Literature 143
900-999 Geography and History 152
920 Collective Biography 190
92 Individual Biography 200

Appendix: Publishers' Addresses 209

Author/Title Index 215

Subject Index to Annotations 225

Foreword

Barbara J. Kuipers is a sensitive, intelligent educator who moved to a remote, yet exquisitely beautiful area in southeastern Utah to administer a school library media program. She found the students with whom she was to work to be predominantly American Indians. Apathy and lack of self-esteem were characteristics she found in far too many of her students, which caused her to seriously consider, read about, and study the contributing factors. In the process of studying the collection of materials she had inherited as part of her media program, she found, to her total dismay, that book after book contained blatant stereotypes and misinformation, which could easily have contributed to the negativism she observed.

Simultaneously, in the process of withdrawing poor books from the media center, she began to search for bibliographies and evaluative criteria that would form the foundation for a new collection to help young people acquire accurate information and impressions of American Indian life, both historical and contemporary.

As an ingenious person will do, when she couldn't find what she needed, she created it. The bibliography in this book was meticulously developed. Hundreds of hours were required to locate, read, study, analyze, and evaluate each book to determine both the accuracy and integrity of the work and its value as a reference source.

In addition to the bibliography, the background information the author has included will help the novice in materials selection acquire valuable initial understanding and help the veteran add significant dimensions to his or her understanding.

I am proud to have worked with Barbara Kuipers and take this opportunity to say that her respect for young people and scholarship has manifested itself in this book, which is certain to contribute to improved understanding for each of us who uses it personally and with our patrons.

Brenda Branyan-Broadbent
Utah State University
Logan, Utah

Preface

During the last two decades, public and school libraries have experienced an increased demand for quality ethnic literature. School curricula are also being revised to include minority resource materials. Providing cultural enrichment for all children requires that accurate materials written by and about American Indian people be available. This book is concerned with the selection of quality American Indian resource materials by public and school library professionals. How important are American Indian books? The literature that was reviewed for this book suggests that quality American Indian books are crucial in the educational development of American Indian students. The primary purpose of this book is to assist public and school library professionals in developing competence for selecting quality nonfiction materials of reference value for young American Indian readers and for all young people who are interested in American Indian subjects.

Public and school library professionals and educators have generally tried to provide resource materials that appeal to American Indian students and others interested in the area of American Indian literature. However, this task is frequently one in which professionals have little expertise or experience. Consequently, two critical areas are reviewed in this book to assist those responsible for meeting the nonfiction needs of American Indian readers. First, the background needed to evaluate American Indian books of reference value is presented. School and public library professionals are encouraged to read the other materials about building American Indian collections listed in "Selected American Indian Bibliographies" (pp. 61-64).

Next, a discussion of evaluative criteria for choosing quality materials of reference value is provided. This section guides public and school library professionals in the selection of materials by providing carefully researched information on common problems, such as books with stereotypical or inaccurate information. Following this chapter, a two-page evaluative checklist is included for use in critiquing materials being considered for purchase. Using the checklist can promote the selection of materials that are meaningful, realistic, and accurately representative of American Indian culture. The checklist may be duplicated for use as an evaluation tool with any ethnic materials and textbooks, including fiction.

Because those responsible for developing or extending a collection will not be familiar with all the books published on American Indian life, this volume meets a second need. An annotated bibliography of recommended books, organized by Dewey Decimal classification area, is provided. Entries include bibliographic data, reading level, subject areas, and an annotation that suggests curriculum use. The selected bibliography is helpful in developing a basic American Indian collection of nonfiction books of reference value, especially for those without access to large collections. The bibliography can be a basis for selecting books for an initial satellite collection or for adding materials to an existing collection for elementary, middle, or high school-age readers.

Educators, as well as children and young adults, look to public and school libraries for materials to complement educational assignments. Therefore, library professionals also want to know whether materials they purchase will meet the instruction needs of American Indian students. The discussions in chapter 5 include suggestions to facilitate the use of the materials in the classroom by teachers as well as students. Not only is it important to provide materials, but use of this information should also result in more effective instruction.

Nineteen years ago I became the library media specialist for a school that served students in grades seven through twelve in the San Juan School District, located in southeastern Utah. The majority of students were (and are) American Indian, primarily Navajo and Ute youth. Despite this fact, the media center had only three nonfiction American Indian books. Most of the fiction books were the type that perpetuated stereotypical myths about American Indians. Within a few weeks I knew that there was a desperate need for resource materials about all facets of American Indian life. If the center was going to provide adequate literature for the educational and recreational reading of the American Indian students, some drastic changes were needed.

I studied bibliographies, searched major library reference tools, read recommendations, and purchased over 2,500 fiction and nonfiction books by and about American Indians. Today the library media center has a comprehensive collection of American Indian books. Many are used extensively and meet the needs of students and teachers. However, some were poor choices.

As a result of this experience, I designed my master's research for the Department of Instructional Technology at Utah State University with two primary objectives. The first was to create a concise, easy-to-use checklist that could be used by public and school library professionals to evaluate American Indian books for reference value. The second objective was to compile a bibliography of American Indian books of reference and resource value that met the criteria used in the evaluation checklist.

A review of the writings of educators, social critics, bibliographers, anthropologists, ethnologists, historians, and librarians provided the background needed to develop evaluative criteria for American Indian literature. An easy-to-use, short, evaluative checklist for American Indian books of reference value was created. The checklist was evaluated and accepted by a panel of four university educators and five educators from San Juan High School District. Five members of the panel were of Indian ancestry.

More recently, I recognized a growing need in public and school libraries for materials by and about American Indians for all school-age children. I updated evaluation materials that I had gathered, and reviewed and evaluated books for all school-age children. This book provides (1) the criteria that library professionals should understand to select books of reference value; (2) an evaluation checklist for American Indian printed materials that can serve as a selection tool for most minority literature; and (3) a basic, annotated bibliography of American Indian books of reference value, with suggested curriculum use for children and young adults, especially for Indian young people.

The most difficult task I faced was locating American Indian books of reference value for children and young adults. Very few nonfiction titles were available, and many of these were poorly written. Informational books for young readers should meet the same criteria as adult books. A table of contents, an index, a bibliography, and a glossary make a book valuable as a reference. Many nonfiction books for children do not contain any of these essentials. Students often look for specific information that can be found only if the book has a table of contents or an index. Young readers need to know where the author found the information so they can search further and know that the author's work has some credibility. Books of reference value for children and young adults should contain information written at an appropriate grade level.

Often when authors present information for younger readers, they tend to oversimplify or romanticize the subject. In many books, authors omit important facts and "imagine" the details of an event in an attempt to make it more readable. In these cases, students may find more accurate information in encyclopedia articles. The most important criterion in evaluating information books for reference value is to select only the books that present a clear, unbiased view of the American Indian.

No collection of books on the American Indian is complete without folklore, poetry, and mythology. Books on poetry and riddles are placed in the literature section of the library. Mythology and legends fall into the category of religion or social sciences. None of these subject areas are considered factual. However, they are a vital part of American Indian literature and culture and must be included as valuable references for American Indian studies. The cultural heritage of native peoples should be considered as a special genre. Poetry and mythology are an essential part of religious ceremonies and practices and reflect the fundamental belief systems of the American Indian. Books on these subjects deserve to be recognized as books of reference value in a library collection.

In the 1990s, books of folklore have gained a prominent place in library collections, with many stories being retold and illustrated by such Native American authors as Shonto Begay and Michael Lacapa. Many non-Indian writers have had legends published. Librarians and educators should be very selective when choosing retold stories. Books of folklore, mythology, and poetry should contain bibliographic information on their sources of information. There is still a vital need for good books of reference value for children and young adults, a shortage that American Indian authors are beginning to amend. Books about language, science, mathematics, and biography are still few.

The movie industry has had a profound impact on the proliferation of American Indian books being published. Although filmmakers still take liberties with historical facts, often failing to see the differences between tribal groups, the Native Americans of recent media releases have been transformed from inarticulate savages to intelligent, complex, humorous, and civilized individuals. Major publishing houses have capitalized on the public's interest in the American Indian and are offering more titles than in recent years. The novel that inspired the movie *Dances with Wolves* has sold millions of copies. Interestingly, many educators see little harm in this trend. They are willing to accept anything that is written as the truth if it presents the Indian in a positive context.

Evaluating and selecting quality American Indian materials is difficult. Changes are taking place as more books on the American Indian are published. Those who are responsible for providing children and young adults with literature will find more books written by authors who are part of the culture about which they are writing. Only quality books of reference value should be offered to children and young adults.

Although I continue to read and learn more about American Indian culture and history, especially from Indian children, young adults, and colleagues, I lack the "Indian" consciousness of a Native American person. If the reader encounters any lack of insight or errors in this book, I can only say that I continue to grow in awareness, knowing that the selection of these materials is very important to the self-image of Indian young people. The material in this book was compiled to serve as a guide for library professionals and teachers as they work with young people. The selection of resource materials to be placed in libraries and made available to readers remains the decision of librarians. This book's purpose is to serve as a useful tool in the selection of quality American Indian books of reference and resource value for children and young adults.

Making available an American Indian collection of reference value is one way library professionals and educators can provide exposure to American Indian culture. As we serve children and young adults, our goal should be to ensure not just that American Indian resources are used for information, but also that reading about American Indians will instill an appreciation of differences and promote an understanding of alternate ways of seeing the world and living in it.

Educational leaders should recognize the importance of providing materials on the American Indian that are accurate, authentic, and objective for all students at every grade level. Equally imperative is the need to provide Indian students with quality literature on their heritage and contemporary life. Because Indian students may view themselves as others see them, carefully selected literature can play a major role in improving the Indian student's self-concept and, consequently, achievement in school. To help attain the major goal of cultural pluralism, library professionals are challenged to develop an awareness of the equality and worth of all students, regardless of cultural and ethnic background. Public and school library professionals who provide American Indian students with material that specifically pertain to their interests and needs can positively affect the total educational environment.

I would like to acknowledge Dr. Brenda Branyan-Broadbent, of Utah State University, and David V. Loertscher, of Libraries Unlimited, who encouraged me to publish my research and offered helpful suggestions. My appreciation is extended to the Utah State Library Commission and the Salt Lake City public and county libraries, whose personnel spent many hours locating and ordering books. Colleagues and family have also provided assistance. For his invaluable assistance through his own expertise and detailed knowledge of American Indian people and their literature, I wish to thank my husband, Albert L. Kuipers, who read the manuscript time and time again, providing helpful comments and criticism, for his invaluable support.

My years of living among the Indian people have provided me with a strong commitment to this project. I dedicate this book to American Indian young people, who deserve well-written, accurate, and meaningful literature.

B.J.K.

Part 1
American Indian Literature
for
Children and Young Adults

Assuming Responsibility for Selection of American Indian Books of Reference Value

The powerful influence of books on the shaping of young minds has long been recognized by psychologists and educators. The responsibility for developing a well-balanced collection of books of reference value thus assumes major significance for the public and school library professional. One of the most demanding responsibilities of the library professional is the selection of appropriate materials that will meet the nonfiction reading and educational needs of all children and young adults who use library services.

Carefully selected American Indian nonfiction books of reference value that cover all subject areas on an appropriate reading level will provide access to information and ideas and promote lifelong learning. "The future of our society depends on developing the learning potential inherent in all children and youth, especially literary, reading, research and retrieval skills" (*School Library Journal* 1990, 34). A collection of quality American Indian materials, constantly evaluated and replaced as better materials are published or selected, will continue to make public and school libraries a vital educational force. Young readers can learn about today's complex Indian issues, delve into a repository of accurate and well-written information about native life, and promote better understanding of American Indian people.

Authorities in ethnic education state that media centers serving schools that enroll minority student populations should make an effort to provide materials that specifically pertain to the interests and needs of each minority group within the school (Haley, Hustleby, and McCormick 1978). When minority children and young adults do not have access to supplementary reading in their homes, public and school libraries have an opportunity to fill this void with suitable materials.

Culturally relevant materials on ethnic groups offer a stimulus to encourage reading, whether children and young adults are searching for leisure reading or seeking research materials for academic pursuits. When the readers are American Indian young people, public and school library professionals should take advantage of the opportunity to provide resources that can be used to develop pride in the American Indian cultural heritage.

What is the value of literature to American Indians? Literature is valuable not only because it is useful but the act of reading literature is enjoyable. A special interaction can happen between readers and books. Literature that appeals to a student can provide a vehicle for teaching second language skills if it succeeds as a literary experience (Pialorski 1974, 226).

When offered a choice, American Indian students will frequently select a topic on native life to study or research. This research can be either a satisfying or an alienating experience, depending on the quality and availability of materials.

Interest in the heritage of the American Indian has varied greatly, often depending on politics rather than on the needs of children and youth. American Indian library resources can provide readily available and accessible information on the differing and unique contributions of Indian people. Librarians and educators cannot assume that American Indian children and young adults are well acquainted with their heritage. While many are knowledgeable about the cultural traditions of their people and proud that they are tribal members, many other young American Indians have more in common with all American children and youth. They know more about television, junk food, and fads than about Indian customs and traditions. They need to be provided with quality American Indian nonfiction books that will help them become informed about their native heritage. Carefully selected American Indian materials can add an important dimension to the library's outreach efforts. The selection and purchase of accurate and well-written American Indian literature will encourage all youth to develop respect for the rights and dignity of American Indians, and also provide an understanding of cultural diversity.

2

Understanding the Evaluation Criteria for American Indian Literature

The pluralist ideal of adapting to the larger society of Anglo-Saxon America has not been accepted by most American Indians. Many have succeeded economically and socially, but many others still remain adrift between two cultures. They choose not to forfeit a values-laden heritage. Similarly, the history of Indian education is one of undetermined purposes and confusion. In spring 1989, Secretary of the Interior Manuel J. Lujan pledged that education would be "the number-one priority of the department, as far as Indian Country is concerned." If the needs of the American Indian are to be met, one of the most critical goals must be the education of non-Indians about Indians. Libraries, both public and school, can provide American Indian materials to meet this need. A well-balanced and accurate collection of American Indian resources will also serve Indian youth, whom one Native American tribe describes as "stuck in the horizon—part of neither the earth nor the sky" (*Education Week* 1989, 1).

Quality American Indian books of reference and resource value are crucial to the intellectual development of American Indian children and young adults. These books should be read by all young people as preparation for living in a multicultural world. A requisite for school libraries is building a satellite collection of American Indian books of reference value. In seven regional, grass roots "dialogues," members of Indian communities expressed the educational changes they want for American Indian youth:

> Drawing upon their impressive knowledge of Indian culture, history, and contemporary status, the participants presented positive formulations for revitalizing Indian life.... They wanted curricula to include Indian languages, world views, culture, concepts, values and perspectives.... Dialogue participants agreed that schools must begin to integrate Indian culture into the Basic Academic Competencies as well as subject-matter areas (American Indian Science & Engineering Society 1989, 2).

This report represents a consensus achieved at meetings of 150 Indian leaders, school administrators, teachers, parents, and students from eighty-seven tribes, with every major geographic region in the nation represented. Public libraries, more available to these young people during extended hours, can provide relevant cultural materials not available at home or school. As library professionals seek to broaden their ethnic collections, they need to emphasize the literature of the native people of America.

Developing an understanding of the criteria for selecting American Indian books is a difficult task, especially for the non-Indian library professional or educator. For this reason, a detailed explanation of the main points library professionals should carefully examine is presented in this chapter. A comprehensive understanding of the most important criteria for evaluating literature on American Indian life can benefit those responsible for selecting materials in two ways. First, they will be able to evaluate books more effectively. Second, they will gain an insight into the cultural background of the Indian students whose needs they attempt to meet. Of equal importance is the expectation that a knowledge of the evaluation criteria will enable librarians and educators to reject books that contain misinformation on American Indian life.

In addition, all adults providing materials to school-age children should understand the American Indian people's values and not attempt to impose the values of the dominant culture. The topics discussed in this chapter focus on the beliefs of educators, social critics, bibliographers, anthropologists, ethnologists, historians, and librarians. This information can promote an understanding of the concepts needed to effectively evaluate American Indian literature.

A general knowledge of American Indian students' educational needs and value system is vital to the selection of books for children and young adults. Bahr, Chadwick, and Day (1972, 140) suggest that examination of evidence from national and regional surveys shows that the most important factors that schools serving Indian students must confront are (1) language problems, (2) cultural deprivation, and (3) negative self-concepts. One way in which school and public library professionals can help American Indian students overcome these three factors is to have American Indian materials available that have been evaluated for accuracy, authenticity, and objectivity. Stereotypes, omissions, and distortions in these three areas have perpetuated stereotypical myths about American Indians and their culture. Reading good material can help students become familiar with the English language, gain cultural pride, and strengthen positive self-concepts.

Educational institutions, including public and school libraries, have the responsibility to contribute to the understanding and appreciation of many diverse groups in society. The availability and selection of valid cultural materials promote an understanding attitude toward all cultures.

> Children learn about cultures and values, their own and others, through the things they read.... The difference in achievement and attitude that good materials make will be well worth the effort.
>
> If Native American students are to build self-esteem, a feeling of personal worth, and a sense of their place in history, their reading must include adequate culturally and historically accurate material about their own people (Gilliland and Reyhner 1988, 93).

The achievements of American Indians have largely been ignored. The reasons for studying the American Indian and integrating the literature of the American Indian into the curriculum are twofold. First, the concept of respecting cultural diversity will be reinforced by teaching the literature, history, and values of this group, which is a part of American society. Second, students are provided with the knowledge and materials that can enable them to make intelligent decisions in a pluralistic society (Bataille 1979, 7). Public libraries can support the demands of a curriculum that includes American Indian culture by providing materials on the history and heritage of the native people.

If Indian students are to become productive tribal members, informed citizens, and problem solvers of the future, they need to start reading meaningful, realistic literature about which they can think and hold discussions. Reading textbooks can, at best, only provide an appetizer to encourage students to utilize classroom libraries, school libraries, community libraries, and bookstores. If meaningful and interesting stories are too difficult for beginning readers to read, then teachers need to read them out loud to their students (Reyhner 1988, 156).

Evaluation Criteria

Books of reference value to be included in a collection of American Indian literature should meet the same standards of evaluation required of any reference book. To determine the potential usefulness of a reference book, *The Encyclopedia of Library and Information Science (ELIS)* recommends considering the following questions:

I. Authority
1. Authorship: What are the qualifications in experience and education of the authors, contributors, and editors by reputation and as revealed in previous works?
2. Auspices: What is the reputation of the publisher or sponsoring agency?
3. Genealogy: Is the work new? If it is based on a previous publication, what is the extent of revision?

II. Scope
4. Purpose: To what extent is the statement of purpose in the preface fulfilled in the text?
5. Coverage: What is the range of subject matter and what are the limitations?
6. Recency: How up-to-date is the material?
7. Bibliographies: To what extent do the bibliographies indicate scholarship and send the user to additional information?

III. Treatment
8. Accuracy: How thorough, reliable, and complete are the facts?
9. Objectivity: Is there any bias in controversial issues?
(Shores and Krzys 1979, 146-47)

Broadus agrees with these criteria and adds three more requirements for reference books: (1) clarity in style is essential; (2) physical format should be easily readable, be sturdily bound, have quality paper, and contain good visuals; and (3) users should easily find answers to questions they ask and information they want (Broadus 1981, 171).

Authorship

The authorship (which includes illustration) of nonfiction books to be selected as part of a reference collection of American Indian literature needs to be carefully considered. Concern about the author's or illustrator's background is expressed in Slapin and Seale (1992). The authors all work with school-age children and are concerned with the materials on native peoples that are placed in school and public libraries:

> Is the background of the author and illustrator devoid of the qualities that enable them to write about Native peoples in an accurate, respectful manner? Is there an ethnocentric bias which leads to distortions or omissions?
>
> Is there anything in the author's and illustrator's background that qualifies them to write about Native peoples? Do their perspectives strengthen the work? (Slapin and Seale 1992, 264)

While research shows the need for American Indian materials that are readily available to school-age children, there are many differing opinions on the subject of authorship. Even bibliographers and educators who are of American Indian ancestry have divergent criteria for the authors and illustrators of American Indian resources.

James W. Ramsey, a specialist in Native American literature and professor of English at the University of Rochester, has expressed concern about the definition of minority literature: "What constitutes a Hispanic or an American Indian or an Asian American literary work: Is it necessary that the authors of such works be born into the ethnic groups about which they write?" (Coughlin 1990, A12). Among scholars this is a difficult question that has not been answered. To give library professionals an understanding of the many viewpoints, a discussion of many of the sources listed in the "Selected American Indian Bibliographies" (pp. 61-64) follows.

Many of the earlier bibliographies, such as Marken (1973), Hillyer (1969), Klein and Icolari (1973), and Idaho State Department of Education (1970), state no definitive evaluation criteria of authorship. The bibliography of books about American Indians by the Idaho State Department of Education (1970) includes all titles sent by publishers who responded to their inquiries. The reference volume on Indian books by Klein and Icolari (1973) is the largest bibliography located, and includes 2,000 books then in print, but lists no specific criteria for inclusion except that the entries were researched from questionnaires or gathered from reliable sources. The purpose appears to have been to compile everything the authors could locate in seventeen broad categories. Klein has since published new editions (1986 and 1990); both list 3,500 books in print related to the Indians of North America. No criteria for selection is stated. Marken (1973) includes all books by and about American and Canadian Indians and Eskimos in print in 1972.

Some bibliographic sources focus on one authorship evaluation criterion. The United States Department of the Interior (1972), Revai (1972), Hirschfelder (1973), and Byler (1973) selected books written only by American Indian authors. Although Hirschfelder (1973) acknowledges that American Indian authors can be as slanted, self-serving, and inaccurate as non-Indian authors of books on American Indians, her purpose in selecting only American Indian authors is to represent American Indians "as they are, through their writings, for all their human faults, and for all their magnificence." She advocates that American Indians "speak for themselves, unmediated by non-Indians" (Hirschfelder 1973, preface).

If the counsel of Vine Deloria were followed, schools for American Indian students would only include the three R's as tools for real educational experiences to learn the traditions, customs, and beliefs of the tribal community. He advocates that Indian young people not be concerned with names of the presidents of the United States but concern themselves with great American Indian chiefs, headman, and leaders. If this concept of education were followed, Indian students would study only those things directly related to Indian culture (Deloria 1978, 26).

The most insistent of the bibliographers who feels strongly about non-Indian authors is Mary Byler, a member of the Eastern Band of Cherokee Indians of North Carolina and editor of *Indian Affairs*, the newsletter of the Association on American Indian Affairs. She decries the image of the American Indian projected by non-Indian writers:

> Non-Indian writers have created an image of American Indians that is almost sheer fantasy. It is an image that is not authentic and one that has little value except that of sustaining the illusion that the original inhabitants deserved to lose their land because they were so barbaric and uncivilized.
>
> This fantasy does not take into account the rich diversity of cultures that did, and do, exist. Violence is glorified over gentleness and love of peace. The humanistic aspects of American Indian societies are ignored in the standard book (Slapin and Seale 1992, 84).

The mass of material about American Indians produced by the nation's major publishing houses, Byler believes, is distorted to some degree by non-Indian authors' concepts of things that are "Indian" (Byler 1973, 11). Sociologists and psychologists have determined the detrimental effects on children of negative stereotypes and derogatory images. Byler asserts that American publishing houses, schools, and libraries should take a look at the books they offer children and compensate for some of the damage they have done. "Only American Indians can tell non-Indians what it is to be an Indian. There is no longer any need for non-Indian writers to 'interpret' American Indians for the American public" (Byler 1974, 549).

A promising modern trend is that multiculturalism is broadening the horizons of children's literature. No one wants to eliminate the classics in children's literature. However, children of other cultural backgrounds often cannot identify with white characters in children's books. Traditional classics do not begin to reflect the complicated, diverse world of children today. "If black children or Native Americans or Asians don't see themselves in books," says Roberta Long, an Alabama professor who teaches a course in children's literature, "they won't see themselves as important people. And we will be sending that message to white children, too." By the 1990s, multiculturalism has become a well-established part of children's literature. The person most responsible for the high standards of these books is Harriet Rohmer, founder of Children's Book Press in San Francisco. Books published by this company are multicultural and authored by a person who shares the story's culture (Jones 1991, 64-65).

Other educators share the belief that only authors of the same racial background should write books about that culture. Educator and author of four children's books, Candy Dawson Boyd of St. Mary's College of California in Moraga insists that authors who are of a different cultural background than their subject matter "write from outside the skin." Referring to them as "secondary writers," she notes, "Their perspective is different and they have a much higher probability to make mistakes." She contends that people's good intentions and experiences cannot substitute for ethnicity.

The recent interest in Christopher Columbus created a unique historical situation. Who should be a "primary writer" for the Taino, the native people of San Salvador who were completely wiped out by the Spanish after Columbus' arrival? Can an Indian author with no intimate knowledge present a more accurate book than a non-Indian author? Should the quality of the book's content have more weight than the ethnic background of the author? Writer and editor Jan Yolan made the decision to speak for the Taino in her book *Encounter* (Harcourt Brace Jovanovich). If Yolan, author of many outstanding books for young adults, were pigeonholed by her ethnicity, she would be limited to writing about Jewish girls in New York City. Having written 120 books on a broad variety of subjects, she resists Boyd's attitude toward "secondary writers" (Donahue 1992, D2).

Naomi Caldwell-Wood, President of the American Indian Library Association in 1992, acknowledges that most Native American materials are written, illustrated, and edited by non-Indians. While some books are excellent, others have patronizing overtones. Anthropologists, travelers, and historians translated and interpreted early American Indian words. Other earlier information was gathered from the journals, letters, diaries, and paintings and photographs of people who had contact with Indians. Because native peoples have strong oral traditions, they didn't document their own cultures. Because history, culture, and religion are so interconnected in most native culture, many tribal groups did not and still do not allow recordings, photographs, or written documentation of ceremonies. Some groups are writing their own histories and establishing their own archives (Caldwell-Wood 1992, 47-48.) Many writers of Native American materials rely on printed documents and have little personal contact with the actual people they write about. As a result, although these books are often scholarly, they may lack a true understanding of Indian culture.

Caldwell-Wood notes that more native writers and illustrators are being published (Caldwell-Wood 1992, 48). Stensland (1979) and Bataille (1979) offer the names of some fine Native American authors—James Welch, Leslie Marmon Silko, Jamake Highwater, N. Scott Momaday, Wendy Rose, and Roy Young Bear—who write accurate American Indian literature free of the stereotypical images, and they reflect a sensitive understanding of the past and a hope for the future. Unlike some others, Stensland has regard for a growing number of non-Indian writers who have turned to serious American Indian themes and are treating them with accuracy and dignity. She includes both Indian and non-Indian books in her bibliography (Stensland 1979, 23).

Seale, a children's librarian of Santee, Cree, and white ancestry, also expresses strong concern about non-Indian authors in an essay in *Books Without Bias: Through Indian Eyes*:

> As a children's librarian, it is my obligation to see that the collection contains balance, that the Children's Room be a place where all children will feel welcome, and comfortable. As a Native woman, it doesn't seem to me a lot to ask that the books written about Indians be honest, if nothing else. That is not so simple as it sounds. Very few non-Native writers have bothered to acquire the knowledge to produce meaningful work about our history, cultures and lives—although this ignorance does not stop them from doing the books, and getting published.... In fact, Indians are the only Americans whose history has been set down almost exclusively by those who are not members of the group about which they are writing (Slapin and Seale 1992, 10).

Roessel (1979) is a strong supporter of the value of literature produced by American Indian writers. While in charge of Navajo education at Rough Rock Demonstration School for thirty years, Roessel has demonstrated his concern over the lack of Indian authors by establishing a publishing house for American Indian authors. He feels they should write their own volumes, especially the histories of the individual tribes, so that students can learn from firsthand sources about themselves and their culture. Every book published is written by Navajo Indians. Oral language interviews in Navajo, translated into English and later published, provide a background for many of the books.

Lass-Woodfin, of mixed Scotch-Irish, German, and American Indian background, created a bibliography to help librarians, parents, and educators make intelligent choices of Indian and Eskimo books. She includes books by Indian authors and non-Indian authors:

> If ... only those books on Indians ... were written by knowledgeable tribal members, that never used stereotyping, that contained illustrations showing in exact and minute detail the dress, life and environment of the group depicted, and that were, in equal measure, well written, well illustrated, and accurate in every word, the final collection would be small indeed (Lass-Woodfin 1978, vii).

An unusual aspect of her bibliography is that it includes books of varying quality and provides examples of inappropriate choices. Such books can be used by educators and librarians to illustrate critical reading skills, the detection of propaganda techniques, and recognition of author bias and assumptions. Lass-Woodfin offers this advice to other bibliographers: expect controversy because any choice will, in fact should, be debated. Books written by Indians, part Indians, and non-Indians are needed (Lass-Woodfin 1978, 2-3). Much Indian culture would have been lost had it not been for non-Indian anthropologists, writers, and ethnologists, because Indian writers had not at that time received sufficient education or achieved sufficient proficiency in written English to assume this work. Lass-Woodfin comments on the state of the art:

> The perfect world for some would be one in which authors write perfect books for perfect readers who understand perfectly what the author is trying to communicate. For the rest of us, the better world would have books of diverse opinions, against whose ideas we could compare our own, to include or exclude whatever we choose to make ourselves better people, thinkers and readers. Perhaps young people's literature on Indians ... will present in the future a wider diversity of geography, tribes, and ideas to help us adults help children do this very thing (Lass-Woodfin 1978, 16).

A review of the criteria listed in Gilliland and Reyhner (1988, 95) will focus the attention of the library professional on some important concerns when considering the author's attitude toward American Indian people. Although authors may be accurate in their presentation of historical facts, they may reveal attitudes of prejudice or superiority, resulting in material that will be damaging to the young reader. Stereotypes, prejudices, and loaded vocabulary are keys to the author's attitude. Innuendos missed by the non-Indian reader may harm the Indian child's self-concept or encourage prejudices in the non-Indian. (For example, "He was an Indian, but he was a very smart man.") Vocabulary also often brings out the writer's attitude, when descriptions such as soldiers' "victories" but Indian "massacres" and of settlers as "patriots" but Indians as "murderers" are used. Librarians should evaluate books for stereotypes of the Indian. Do they have many faults and few virtues? In addition, are minority people and their groups depicted as "different" in a way that seems inferior to the white middle class? As library professionals and educators read American Indian literature they will become more conscious of authors' attitudes toward American Indian people and choose books by authors who do not perpetuate stereotypes.

Perhaps the real test of authorship is best expressed in the words of Paula Gunn Allen, an American Indian poet and professor of ethnic studies at the University of California at Berkeley: "I was nearly 30 years old ... before I read a book that was about me, that spoke to me out of shared experience and knowledge, out of spiritual and social kinship" (Coughlin 1990, A7).

The recommendation for inclusion in a bibliography by an Indian group, publication, or individual is another guideline for selection mentioned by bibliographers of books about American Indian life. For the professional librarian, book reviews and bibliographies are additional sources for evaluating authorship. However, reviews will differ. Even reviews by Indian individuals or organizations may not agree, depending on their expertise and background. Bataille encourages recommendation by an American Indian organization or publication (Bataille 1978, 3). Smith reinforces this approach:

> The average librarian may experience some difficulty in applying ... guidelines, since many people are themselves not fully aware of Indian values and cultural contributions and may not yet have developed a full sensibility to materials which either offend or denigrate the American Indian (Smith 1971, 610).

She recommends review or evaluation by a person knowledgeable about American Indians.

Lass-Woodfin (1978) takes another approach. She has the books she selects for inclusion read by two reviewers, and in some cases retains both readers' comments (Lass-Woodfin 1978, viii). For reviews of American Indian books, Bataille (1979) recommends four American Indian publications: *Wassaha, The Indian Historian, The Weewish Tree,* and *Akwesasne Notes.* School and public library professionals will want to look carefully at materials reviewed by standard sources and should rely heavily on the recommendations made in bibliographies prepared by those of Indian ancestry: Lass-Woodfin (1978), Bataille (1979), Byler (1973), and Slapin and Seale (1988, 1992).

The National Indian Education Association developed Project Media (1975, 1978) to identify, acquire, review, and evaluate print and nonprint media materials pertaining to the American Indian and Alaska natives. All those working on the project are native people. Each evaluation of an entry is completed by an American Indian, then reviewed and evaluated by staff members. All entries reviewed are included in the publication, which has been updated once. Consequently, evaluations are printed whether the material was acceptable or not. The bibliography provides insight into why materials are objectionable to American Indians. The objective of the project is to produce quality evaluations, with a concentrated effort on involving local Indian resource people as well as individuals from tribes across the country. Paxton (1976) recommends Project Media as a good bibliographic source. Common selection tools of the school media specialist, including *Guide to Reference Books for School Media Centers* by Nichols (1992), *Recommended Reference Books in Paperback* by March (1992), and *Recommended Reference Books for Small and Medium-sized Libraries and Media Centers, 1993* by Bohdan S. Wynar, list a small number of American Indian books of reference value.

In conclusion, the best way to judge authorship is to read the book, check it against book reviews and standard selection tools as well as "Selected American Indian Bibliographies" (pp. 61-64), and when possible have an Indian person read the materials and make recommendations. A growing amount of resource material is being published by tribal concerns; many are excellent, while others contain errors and are poorly written. If a poor selection is made, the school and public library professional should not hesitate to discard materials that do not meet the standard of good writing and honest and creditable scholarship.

Value System of American Indians

American Indian students live between two worlds: (1) the traditional way of life represented by the culture of their people prior to the coming of white people, and (2) modern civilization, with its own distinctive patterns and sets of values (Roessel 1979). American Indian students face cultural conflicts in school environments:

> Being an American Indian in itself is no problem; however, being an American Indian and growing up and going to school in a non-Indian environment and society frequently is a problem. Children from the dominant American culture grow up experiencing and being influenced

by one predominant way of life while American Indian children grow up experiencing at least two very different views of the world they live in (Reyhner 1988, ix).

Education is the vehicle used by the American Indian young person to bridge these worlds. For educators to reach American Indian school-age children and instill within them a desire to learn, school and public libraries should have quality American Indian materials available to inculcate or reinforce a sense of pride. One of the major goals of our educational system should be to recognize and promote ethnic values and contributions and encourage a positive self-concept in Indian students. The mandate issued by the National Commission on Excellence in Education in *A Nation at Risk: The Imperative for Educational Reform* (1983, 9) states: "All, regardless of race or class or economic status, are entitled to a fair chance and to the tools for developing their individual powers of mind and spirit to the utmost." Public and school library professionals can be a part of this reform by developing multicultural resources for minority children.

Metoyer (1978) considers the first step in this monumental task of selecting quality American Indian literature to be the exploration of the image of the American Indian in the library resources through considering contemporary attitudes, aspirations, and lifestyles faced by young American Indians. In *Teaching the Native American* (Gilliland and Reyhner 1988, 96), Gilliland expresses concern about "values interpreted in terms of an Indian or non-Indian point of view. How is success described? Is a person respected only if he gets ahead in White society? To gain acceptance, does he have to get A's, excel in sports and make money?" Gilliland is concerned with how written material portrays Indian values:

Many stories which accurately portray historical events and the physical environment of the Indian completely misinterpret Indian values. The concepts of sharing and cooperative living are missed along with the differences in feelings about property, time, family relationships, the significance of nature and the importance of spiritual life. Authors who have not lived among Indian people are prone to give their Indian characters the same motivations and values as their non-Indian friends.... If you must use these books, discuss the misconceptions as you read with your students (Gilliland and Reyhner 1988, 96).

American Indian children usually begin their formal education as average achievers, but fall further behind the norm as they progress in school after the primary grades. According to "A Special Report on the Education of Native Americans" (*Education Week* 1989, 2), "Native Americans have the highest dropout rates of any racial or ethnic group in the United States." In a U.S. Education Department longitudinal study of 1980 high school sophomores cited in the report, 29 percent left school. Additional studies in the report on students from lower grades and federal Indian school students place the figure as high as 50 percent. Despite the problems of "at risk" American Indian youth, Indian people view education as one of the critical means of realizing their rightful place in American society: equality in every field of endeavor. They feel that self-equality means the opportunity to retain their culture while obtaining the full blessings of American citizenship promised them through treaties and federal legislation.

Native America has been undergoing a robust population growth. In 1960, the U.S. census counted only 551,669 Indians, Eskimos, and Aleuts. The total climbed to 827,268 in 1970, to 1.4 million in 1980, and to 1.9 million in 1990. The population quadrupled in only thirty years. An explanation for this dramatic increase, according to Jeffrey S. Passel of the Washington-based Urban Institute and other experts, is noteworthy. People are now more willing to identify themselves as American Indian on census forms. Passel also questions if those listing themselves as American Indian on the census form are actually enrolled by the tribes they claim as members.

Most of the unexpected population growth during the past decade occurred in Southern and Eastern states that historically have not had large Native American communities. Some demographers believe that urban Indians in these states opted for Native American identify for the first time in 1990. Newfound racial pride and cultural awareness may be a factor (Worsnop 1992, 389). The statistics also mean that educators may have more Indian students in their classrooms than they realized.

Despite the diversity and complexity of cultures and tribal affiliations, there are eight values basic to the social structure of most American Indian tribes. School and public library professionals should understand this basic value system to effectively select materials dealing with the American Indian because American Indian students in public, private, and government schools are the major consumers of these materials (Metoyer 1978, 16). These eight values, formulated by William Fire Thunder and Sam Akeah, are listed below:

Values Which an Indian May Lose

1. Being an Indian:
   Language, generosity, unity, respect

2. His land (home):
   Attachment to land vs. pressure to part with it

3. Arts and crafts:
   Indigenous skills such as beadwork vs. blue collar tasks

4. Health:
   Dissolution of healthy life vs. poor health in urban environment

5. Religion:
   Disappearance of religious priorities

6. Hunting and fishing:
   Respect for nature vs. killing for sport

7. Law and order:
   Tribal code vs. White man's judicial system

8. Commitment to community:
   Responsibilities undertaken without pay

(Metoyer 1978, 16)

These values or traits occur frequently among many different native people and are highly regarded. They are positive cultural characteristics of which American Indians are proud. While many values, customs, and characteristics are common to Native American groups, each native child lives somewhere between the traditional way and the middle-class Anglo way. There are also great differences between cultural groups, and not all of these values apply to any one group. American Indian values are continually changing, just as those of non-Indian societies.

Despite their great diversity, one value Native Americans share is a fierce attachment to the land. Only 46 million acres remain under tribal jurisdiction today. The loss of the more than 1.9 billion acres that Native Americans roamed for more than 500 years helps explain their outrage over the celebrations of Christopher Columbus's first voyage to the New World. In 1992, Representative Ben Nighthorse Campbell rode in the Tournament of Roses Parade as one of the grand marshals to make a point about the parade's theme—"Voyages of Discovery." Campbell said, "I saw 1992 as a time to reflect on and to mourn our tragic and unjust treatment for the past 500 years. I saw it as a time for lawful and hopefully nonviolent protests protected by a Constitution we did not write. And I saw it as a time ... to educate the non-Indian world about our lives."

Campbell, the only Native American in Congress, relates the strengths of Native Americans before Columbus's arrival in the New World. Native Americans had advanced cultures with strong family structures, devout religious beliefs, representative and elective governments, respect for elders, sophisticated medicine, and an ecologically sound way of life (Worsnop 1992, 387). In recent years, a renewed interest in Indian art and spiritual values has surfaced. The values of native people have not really changed; they have merely been adapted to a changing lifestyle.

Educators and library professionals can learn much from outside sources about native culture in general. As they learn about the tribal groups with whom they work, recognizing that each community and group of students is different, they must determine which values are applicable to the Indian children they serve if they are to promote the positive aspects of American Indian culture. Variations among and between tribes can be gleaned through additional research and study. Metoyer (1978) advises those who select American Indian materials to develop an accurate, authentic, working knowledge of the history, cultures, and contemporary concerns of the American Indian.

Stone presents a fourteen-point list, "Ways to Help Pupils Improve Their Self-Image," which includes the suggestion that "school libraries should contain books in which Indian children and adults figure realistically and prominently. In the classroom, teachers may read or recommend such books" (Stone and DeNevi 1971, 367). Bataille concurs, providing a reason to study the American Indian through integrating the literature into the curriculum to reinforce the "values of this group which are a part of American society and to provide students with the knowledge and materials which will enable them to make decisions in a pluralistic society" (Bataille 1979, 7).

A very strong stand is taken by Roessel (1979) on the importance of those involved in education understanding the value system of the American Indian people. He believes, as does Metoyer (1978), that there are certain values and beliefs held in common by most Indian tribes. Values are a cultural component. Because culture is the total way of life of a people, Roessel determines that there are at least two extreme positions in regard to values one could take. The first is cultural ethnocentrism, and the second is cultural relativism:

> Cultural ethnocentrism means that the values of one particular culture are superior to the values of other cultures and that therefore the superior values ought to supersede the values of the other culture. This philosophy prompted much of the conquest of America. The values of the white man were felt to be vastly superior to those of the "savages." Therefore, it was only fitting and proper that those values of the superior culture should be imposed on the inferior culture.
>
> Cultural relativism means the opposition of the above. In other words, the values of any culture are relative to the cultural background out of which they arose. There are no superior or inferior cultures or sets of values. Under this philosophy mankind is seen as being everywhere equal and the values of western "civilized" man are in no way superior to those of the most "primitive" Indian. The criteria would be only as to how successful each value was in meeting problems faced in each particular culture (Roessel 1979, 305).

Cultural ethnocentrism and cultural relativism are extreme views. The educator may wish to take a more moderate position. However, Roessel strongly admonishes that the fact remains that any person who teaches American Indian children and who fails to grasp or understand the Indians' set of values, who instead tries to impose the values of the dominant culture, is in for considerable difficulty. The pride of an Indian mother in her people and heritage is clearly expressed in an excerpt from a letter to teachers of Indian children:

> Too many teachers, unfortunately, seem to see their role as rescuer. My child does not need to be rescued; he does not consider being Indian a misfortune. He has a culture, probably older than yours; he has meaningful values and a rich and varied experiential background. However strange and incomprehensible it may seem to you, you have no right to do or say anything that implies to him that it is less than satisfactory (Gilliland and Reyhner 1988, 18).

For some Indian children and young adults, developing a better self-image may be primary. Non-Indian teachers and non-Indian students with whom they interact need to develop a better understanding of and greater appreciation for the American Indian value system. This is also true of school and public librarians, who have an opportunity to provide acceptable and positive reading materials in a nonthreatening environment.

Frequently, educators and librarians have little opportunity to learn about American Indian cultures, their diversity, and their importance to Indian people. Naomi Caldwell-Wood, President of the American Indian Librarian Association in 1992, is the school library media specialist at Nathan Bishop Middle School in Providence, Rhode Island. She suggests that librarians should learn more about Native American cultures and network with Indian groups in their areas. To gain a real sense of history from an Indian point of view, she recommends visiting reservations and museums. She explains why all children deserve to know about the real Native Americans, and to those librarians who may not recognize Indian students in their schools, she offers this advice.

> We are diverse sovereign nations each possessing unique traditions, customs, religion, and dress. While many Native Americans live on reservations, there are also those of us who live in cities, suburbs, towns, and villages. We may not choose to wear our traditional dress everyday. But we still exist. You may not be aware but perhaps there are Native Americans in your own neighborhood. If you are looking for buckskins, feathers, and beads, you might not see us (Caldwell-Wood 1992, 48).

Research suggests that an American Indian child's self-image may depend on the image held by white society. Prejudice can yield to education. Public and school library professionals can make a contribution by changing the stereotypical views many non-Indians have about American Indian people. By being provided with accurate American Indian reading materials of reference values that are devoid of stereotypes, American Indians and non-Indians can be exposed to positive concepts of cultural pluralism, the concept that people of all cultures are of equal dignity and worth.

Treatment of American Indians in the Literature

One cannot isolate the literature on the value system of the American Indian from the literature on the treatment of the American Indian. Three criteria—accuracy, authenticity, and objectivity—are vital concerns in selection of American Indian nonfiction materials. Bibliographers, educators, textbook evaluators, and others concerned with American Indian resources have discussed these three areas extensively.

Six bibliographers of American Indian resources—Slapin and Seale (1988, 1992), Wiget (1985), Stensland (1979), Bataille (1978), Lass-Woodfin (1978), and Revai (1972)—prepared American Indian bibliographies that included nonfiction for school-age children. Slapin and Seale (1988, 1992), Wiget (1985), Lass-Woodfin (1978), Stensland (1979), and Byler (1973) discuss specific titles to clarify areas of concern when selecting American Indian books. These authors also include evaluation criteria for each selection. Others, such as textbook evaluators of ethnic materials, provide detailed word lists and evaluation instruments. Historians, social critics, and educators all mention their concern with stereotypical myths in the literature of the American Indian.

Accuracy

The area of accuracy is determined to have four points: reliable sources, careful documentation, thorough research, and factual information. Because the treatment of the subject matter is extremely important, books of reference value on American Indians should be carefully checked for accuracy. Not only should the sources be reliable, but they should also be carefully documented and reflect thorough research procedures, ensuring authentic content and factual information (Shores and Krzys 1978, 146-47).

According to Metoyer (1978), numerous books focus on various American Indian tribes, with children as their principal audience. In the 1960s, public and school library professionals began to realize that much of the published material, both fiction and nonfiction, did not represent reality (Metoyer 1978, 13). Echoing this concern, Byler (1973) notes that many authors write sheer fantasy that contains little authenticity or value. Paxton (1976) reveals the inaccuracy of material depicting the American Indian so that the Indian does not become a projection of generalized stereotyping.

Accuracy and authenticity are considered by the Project Media (1975, 1978) staff to be one of the five general categories of evaluative criteria. In the annotations that accompany their bibliography entries, the staff members include a statement specifically detailing this concern. Project Media annotations appear to be one of the most helpful in determining the accuracy of nonfiction materials. Some other sources choose not to include poor materials.

Banks (1975) feels that school children who study American Indians most often learn myths and stereotypes rather than accurate information. Though there is a great deal of information on American Indians available, Bataille (1979) is disturbed that much of it depicts the American Indian in inaccurate or stereotypical ways. Readers are seldom exposed to contemporary Indian experiences or realistic interpretations of the past. Teachers then must counter inaccurate information that students read by presenting new reading materials to foster a more realistic understanding of American Indian culture (Bataille 1979, 5). Henry (1968) also expresses concern that textbooks do not adequately and accurately describe the life and situation of the American Indian in the world of today. A book by Hirschfelder (1982) contains essays for teachers and librarians about children's toys, books, and programs designed to convince adults to dispel offensive, inauthentic, and unreal images of American Indians and replace them with accurate, authentic, and real depictions.

Concerns for inaccuracies regarding Indian life and culture focuses on textbooks, histories, and historical fiction. To develop an appreciation for native culture and contributions and to accept Indian people as friends and equals, the non-native child must read books that are culturally and historically accurate, as well as realistic about the contemporary world. Gilliland expresses the need to assure historical accuracy:

> Materials ... need to present a balanced, honest portrayal of Native American history and society. Battles and strange (usually unexplained) customs should not be emphasized. Theories and educated guesses based on incomplete evidence should not be stated as simple facts. Native American traditional views and oral history should have a place in the curriculum along with archaeology, historical analysis, and other scientific/humanistic interpretations.
>
> Particular cultural practices of the past should be considered in comparison with contemporary practices in other parts of the world rather than with current practices. For example, writers have made scalping a significant aspect of Indian life and used this as an evidence of savagery. Usually they do not make clear that the Indians of the New

England and Southwest areas were encouraged to take scalps by the French, English and Spanish, who also took scalps and paid bounties to the Indian for scalps of their enemies. Similar "savage" customs in Europe were usually downplayed or ignored.

Native Americans also are portrayed as nomads who did not use the land when in fact many more Native Americans lived in villages growing corn and other crops that they had domesticated over the years than hunted buffalo on the plains (Gilliland and Reyhner 1988, 88-89).

The "Guidelines for the Evaluation of Indian Materials for Adults" adopted by the American Library Association contain only one statement on accuracy: "Does the material contain factual errors or misleading information?" (Metoyer 1978, 5). However, four sources for evaluating the role of the American Indian in textbooks put more stress on accuracy as an evaluative criterion. In *Stereotypes, Distortions, and Omissions in U.S. History Textbooks* a "Native American Textbook Checklist for Accuracy" is provided to check for accuracy, distortions, or omissions concerning events in which American Indians were involved (Council on Interracial Books for Children 1977, 84-85).

In the most extensive instrument located, Haley, Hustleby, and McCormick (1978) include some analysis of accuracy in "Ethnic Studies Materials Analysis Instrument for School Librarians." The questions on realism and accuracy evaluate accuracy of the historical facts presented and determine whether major omissions or overgeneralizations distort the accuracy of the materials (22-23). Similarly, Henry (1968) is concerned that the data contained in the text should accurately describe the special position of the American Indian in the history of the United States, socially, economically, and politically.

The trend in some small publishing companies is toward offering American Indian books by Indian authors. However, non-Indians continue to write most nonfiction American Indian books published by major firms. Writers of nonfiction books often rely on printed materials for facts. These documents are usually written records of Indian history, social life, and culture left by travelers, historians, and anthropologists. Rarely did writers learn the language of the tribal people. Occasionally they relied on native informants and translators. Often they recorded their impressions. Excerpts from letters and journals, also paintings and photographs, are additional sources for information on early American Indian life.

Printed materials may not always be termed "accurate" for several reasons. Any form of writing includes the viewpoint of the author and can be patronizing, prejudiced, or romanticized. Some informants and translators, to protect their people, may have told the writer what they felt outsiders wanted to hear. Artists and photographers frequently took liberties with their subject. Generally, Indian people prefer not to divulge their culture and religious ceremonies. Outsiders were not provided with complete information because native people felt they might be judged from a different set of beliefs. While some early writers were sensitive to the culture, others looked upon Native Americans as having a primitive culture with little to contribute to European civilization. Cultural information written by outsiders can lack an Indian point of view.

Accuracy is very important. Many books being written today lack even a basic bibliography of sources the author consulted. Frequently, books for elementary students only contain a list of books for further reading. Caldwell-Wood (1992, 48) notes, "Many writers of Native American material for young people have relied heavily on printed documents and have had little personal contact with the actual people they write about." Librarians and teachers should select only those books, even for young readers, that have been thoroughly researched and documented. Even this process does not guarantee authentic and objective writing.

Although ethnic and racial minorities share some common characteristics such as poverty, discrimination, and poor education, they are not entirely alike. The biggest difference between the American Indian people and other minorities in the United States is that this country has always been home to the American Indian people. Although they were dispossessed of most of their land, American Indians retain reservations and own the land as nations within the United States. They have retained the right to be labeled the "authentic" native people of this continent. Consequently, looking at the history of the American Indian as separate from the history of the nation creates further problems.

> A "them" and "us" approach reflects extreme insensitivity, as well as a misconception of historical facts. "They" are more truly "us" than anyone else. Native peoples are the original Americans and are the only indigenous Americans in the sense that all of their ancestors were born on this land. Everybody else in this country came from some other place originally (Heinrich 1986-87, 7).

Authenticity as an evaluative criterion is best illustrated through examples given by bibliographers of American Indian materials. Eight areas of concern are established:

1. *Is the American Indian culture evaluated from the perspective of Indian values and attitudes rather than those of another culture?* To answer this question, the definition of culture becomes important. Culture is the sum total of beliefs, accomplishments, and behavior patterns of a group of people, acquired by members of the group through social learning and transmitted from one generation to another. Banks recommends viewing American history from an American Indian point of view to understand America's social and political institutions. Students need to study the diverse and complex native cultures that had already developed in the Western Hemisphere when the Europeans arrived in the fifteenth century. The cultures should be viewed from a humanistic perspective that respects differences and regards all human cultures as valid. To evaluate them by imposing an ethnocentric conceptual framework, such as an Anglo-Saxon norm, would violate their integrity and do more harm than good (Banks 1975, 17-19).

In a doctoral dissertation, Clemmer (1979) studied the portrayal of the American Indian in Utah state-approved United States history books. She concluded that American high school students are recipients of traditional, erroneous, and limited information on American Indians.

Authors of American history seek to reenact the conflict between Native Americans and the first white settlers, who arrived in the early 1600s. The material draws on a one-sided view of history. "From contact with the first European settlers, the people writing the books were the Europeans," says Duane Hale of the American Indian Institute at the University of Oklahoma. "There were very few Indian writers giving an Indian account of the story. Down through the pages of history,

Indians became people without names and faces, people who are very stoic, and have no feelings" (Eskin 1989, 21).

2. *Does the literature discuss the contributions of American Indians to Western civilization?* Literature in the social sciences and history should include more than just politics and dates. The daily life, the ideas, and the values of each group of people studied, as well as their contributions, should be included. The fields of astronomy, genetics, mathematics, and architecture should not be ignored in history books, nor should political contributions. Vogel (1968) refers to the "disparagers" who minimize or deny the many contributions Indian people have made to Western culture. Refuting those who assert that the Indian has contributed little to civilization, he cites their medical and pharmaceutical skills; the advanced civilizations manifested by the Central and South American Indians; the Indian elements in Western drama, music, literature, agriculture, art, architecture, language, and military tactics; and finally the Indians "who have successfully participated as individuals in the 'rival culture' of the United States."

Stereotypes, Distortions, and Omissions in U.S. History Textbooks (Council on Interracial Books for Children 1977) states that Native American technology and knowledge are achievements in their own right. Most textbooks imply that Native Americans "gave" certain elements of their culture to the United States. A less ethnocentric view would result if the texts stated that Europeans adopted Native American technology and achievements for survival. Textbooks would not then read as does *The Pageant of American History*, published in 1975: "The Indian gave us the snowshoe, the canoe, and the moccasin" (quoted in Council on Interracial Books for Children 1977).

Southwestern motifs adorn decorative as well as household items, and stores sell books and posters of native art. These artistic designs have long been admired by non-Indian people. However, an appreciation of other contributions of the Native American is far more important:

> Native arts have long commanded worldwide interest and admiration. But far more important for human and ecological survival are Native American philosophies of life. Respect for the land; love of every form of life, human and non-human; harmony between humans and nature rather than conquest and destruction of nature—these are vital characteristics of Native ways of life. All peoples in the U.S. can and must learn to live in harmony with the natural world and with one another. That is one lesson Native peoples can teach the world, and that is one of the most significant lessons you should teach your students about "the Indians" (Heinrich 1986-87, 9).

3. *Does the author recognize the diversity among tribes, cultures, and life-styles?* Stensland (1979) notes that "whether students are Indian or white, the literature should recognize the diversity of Indian life styles and cultures." American Indians are not a homogenous society. Ewers reports on the emergence of the Plains Indian as the "symbol" of the North American Indian (Hirschfelder 1982, 16-32). Illustrations also convey a stereotypical picture of the Indian, according to Bataille (1979). If all Indian people shown in pictures are men carrying bows and arrows or living in tipis, readers find it difficult to recognize diversity among tribes

and, more important, may find it difficult to actually visualize contemporary Indian men and women.

Although the word *Indian* evokes a single stereotypical image in the popular mind, American Indian people are both physically and culturally diverse. Their skin colors range from dark to light. Height, hair texture, and facial features also vary greatly. Native people speak 2,200 different languages, which anthropologists have attempted with difficulty to categorize into six major language families. Subsistence patterns have varied from gathering food by hunting and fishing to sophisticated agriculture in sedentary communities and the complex cultures of the Southwest Indians. Political institutions were also as diverse as hunting methods, house types, clothing, tools, and religious ceremonies (Banks 1975, 139-78).

For both the educator and the library professional, Heinrich stresses that Native Americans must not be "lumped" together:

> There were no "Indians" before the Europeans came to America—that is, no people called themselves "Indians." They are Navajo or Seminole or Menominee, etc. The hundreds of Native groups scattered throughout the U.S. are separate people, separate nations. They have separate languages and cultures and names. Native Americans of one nation were and are as different from Native Americans of another nation as Italians are from Swedes, Hungarians from Irish or the English from the Spanish. When referring to and teaching about Native Americans, use the word "Indian"—or even "Native American"—as little as possible. Don't study the Indians. Study the Hopi, the Sioux, the Nisqually, or the Apache (Heinrich 1986-87, 7).

Writers of American Indian literature must recognize the diversity among tribes, cultures, and lifestyles, especially in historical materials. In recent years, a cross-tribal cohesion has emerged, and Native Americans are pressing their demands as a distinct people. "For most, tribal identifications remain at least as strong and usually stronger," Harvard University sociologist Stephen Cornell wrote in *The Return of the Native*. "But increasingly for large numbers of Indians, Indian identity—as distinct from tribal identity—has become a conscious and important basis of action and thought in its own right." Ironically, the introduction of off-reservation boarding schools that required students speak only English provided young Indian students from different tribes with a common language. The multitribal experience yielded significant results. "It was at these schools," says Cornell, "that an Indian journalism—as opposed to tribal or community journalism—got its start. Lasting friendships and even marriages were made across distant tribal boundaries. Such relationship helped to break down traditional barriers to a common Indian consciousness" (quoted in Worsnop 1992, 391).

4. *Are Indians portrayed accurately as individuals and not groups?* Indians, like non-Indians, are individuals, not groups. Indians are not all short, tall, or artistic. They are unique human beings with different talents and vocations, of great diversity and complexity, and with loves, hates, and yearnings. Stensland advises: "It is not the Indian the whites created whom we need to know and understand, it is the real, complex Indian" (Stensland 1979, 19). She urges teachers, librarians, and readers to make this distinction.

Suzan Shown Harjo, President and Executive Editor of the Morning Star Foundation, explains that a priority of Native Americans today is on rediscovering Indian national and personal names, and on substituting traditional tribal names for those imposed by missionaries and government officials. In his 1976 memoir *The Names,* Pulitzer Prize winning author N. Scott Momaday, a Kiowa, addresses the individuals in their own language, using their traditional names. Written "in devotion to those whose names I bear and to those who bear my name," the opening words are, "My name is Tsoai-talee. I am, therefore, Tsoai-talee; therefore I am. The storyteller Podh-lohk gave me the name Tsoai-talee. He believed that a man's life proceeds from his name, in the way that a river proceeds from its source" (quoted in Harjo 1993, xli-xliii). Harjo counsels readers and travelers to simply ask Indians how they would like to be addressed and referred to, and to respect their responses.

Another aspect of individuality appears in the literature in the form of the question: Does the text deal with average persons or is it hero-dominated? Some authors tend to view the American Indian either as a "superman" or a "primitive man." Indian persons should be viewed as acting in response to their own natures and their own times. Biographers should show American Indians as people of religion and peace who fought to save their lands. As stated in Fire Thunder's list of values, responsibility is undertaken without pay as a commitment to the community (Metoyer 1978). However, Deloria (1970) reminds readers that the early literature has a tendency to classify all Indian warriors as renegades. Later, the literature glamorizes the "patriot chiefs." The patriot chief interpretation conveniently overlooks the fact that every significant leader of the previous century had been eventually "done in" by his own people in one way or another. The example Deloria cites is Sitting Bull, who was killed by Indian police working for the U.S. government.

Focusing on the historical origin of Indian stereotypes, Iglitzin emphasizes the collective psychological nature:

> The dominant white society justified its violent campaigns against the Indians by first vilifying them because of their race, then claiming the whole race to be inferior, and finally, to be less than human. Once the Indian was conceived of as a stereotype (shiftless, a hunter, incapable of rational thought, childlike, and so on) instead of an individual, the dehumanization process was complete and violence against him was made acceptable to respectable people (Shaughnessy 1978, 21).

5. *Does the literature recognize the American Indian people as an enduring race, not vanishing or assimilated?*

> Books and filmstrips often have titles like "How the Indians Lived," as though there aren't any living today. The fact is that about 800,000 Native Americans live in what is now the United States, many on reservations and many in cities and towns. They are in all kinds of neighborhoods and schools and are in all walks of life.... If the people who write books and filmstrips mean "How (particular groups of) Native Americans Lived Long Ago," they should say so (Heinrich 1986-87, 7).

Statements such as "Indians must be civilized or eliminated" should be a warning signal to the reader. Ethnologists of the past and present have worried that the Indians' culture is disappearing. Missionaries and humanitarians traditionally have wanted to "civilize" and "Christianize" the Indian (Stensland 1979, 16-17). Much of the literature gives this impression.

Is the Indian vanishing? No one knows how many Indians were in North American when Columbus arrived. Some estimates suggest there may have been 1.5 million people. Deven A. Mihesuah, Ford Foundation dissertation fellow and professor of Native American history, asserts in the Spring 1991 issue of *Phi Kappa Phi Journal* that there were 5 million. Warfare, confinement on reservations, disease, poverty, and alcoholism had devastating effects on the population. By 1910 there were only 220,000 survivors (Waters 1992, 2). Many believed the "Vanishing Red Man," his traditions, and culture would disappear by the end of the century.

Although the numbers have increased to 2 million in 1990, Native Americans are still socially and educationally disadvantaged. The school dropout rate is three times that of whites. They are faced with prejudice, injustice, the lowest poverty level in the country, and substandard health, education, and living conditions. The average age of those living on reservations is twenty-one and the average life span is only forty-three years (Waters 1992, 2). American Indian people have not disappeared. They are an integral part of the national commonwealth. The statistics emphasize the importance of education and the recognition of native people. At least half of the 300 Indian languages spoken in the area north of Mexico in the fifteenth century are still in use. Indian kinship systems still function, and there has been a resurgence of Indian values, religion, and ceremonies (*Education Week* 1989, 2).

6. *Are Indian languages and dialects respectfully portrayed?* A cartoon by Freeman (1971), a Sioux and Mission Indian, shows a chief saying, "Let me make 'um one thing perfectly clear." Shaughnessy (1978, 21) reports: "Many think of the American Indian as inarticulate. Language communicated in English takes on artificial dialects. This makes the reader think that even in his native tongue, the Indian was halting and awkward."

Deloria (1970) explains that perhaps the first aspect of stereotyping is the tendency to exclude people on the basis of their inability to handle the English language. Other minority groups have their language ridiculed, but they are better off than the Indians because the Indian is frequently portrayed as devoid of any English-language skills whatsoever. Indians are only allowed to speak when an important message has to be transmitted, or they are limited to "ugh." Deloria blames this stereotype on the motion picture industry (33-45).

An author of Native American books for young adults and professor of native studies at Dartmouth College, Michael A. Dorris, of Modoc ancestry, emphasizes that " 'I' is not for Indian":

"I" isn't for Indian, it is often for Ignorance. In the Never-Never land of glib stereotypes and caricature, the rich histories, cultures, and the contemporary complexities of the indigenous, diverse peoples of the Western Hemisphere are obscured, misrepresented and rendered trivial. Native Americans appear not as human beings but as whooping, silly, one-dimensional cartoons. On occasion they are presented as marauding, blood-thirsty savages, bogeys from the nightmares of "Pioneers" who invaded their lands and feared for the consequences. At other times they seem preconcupiscent angels, pure of heart, mindlessly ecological, brave and true. And worst of all, they are often merely cute, the special property of small children.

It's hard to take seriously, to empathize with, a group of people portrayed as speaking ungrammatical language, as dressing in Halloween costumes, as acting "wild," as being undependable in their promises or gifts. Frozen in a kind of pejorative past tense, these make-believe Indians are not allowed to change or in any other way be like real people. They are denied the dignity and dynamism of their history, the validity of their myriad and major contributions to modern society, the distinctiveness of their multiple ethnicities (Slapin and Seale 1992, 24).

The concern for authenticity of language is unique to *Stereotypes, Distortions, and Omissions in U.S. Textbooks* (Council on Interracial Books for Children 1977). The introduction stresses the use of the actual names of Native American individuals, rather than the names applied to them by Europeans. "King Philip" and "Sitting Bull" may sound exotic and certainly are easier to pronounce, but authentic names such as Metacom and Tatanka Lotanka are recommended. The dignity of the name should not be challenged by attempting English translations.

7. *Does the literature give a realistic description of Indian life?* Unfortunately, the American Indian is still being romantically portrayed as uncorrupted by civilization. Deloria is very adamant about this topic in his books. He believes that the reason the Indian has not been heard from until recently is that Indians were completely misrepresented by motion pictures. He also decries the covering up of weak points in the minority group's history by a sweetness-and-light interpretation based on what the minority group would like to think happened rather than what did happen. The consequences will be decades of further racial strife. History should try to present a balanced story (Deloria 1970, 39).

Not only have Indians been portrayed as silent savages, they are sometimes written about as "the noble red man," a peace-loving naturalist. This image springs from the writings of sixteenth-century European philosophers who believed Indians lived in perfect harmony with God, nature, and one another. Authors sometimes use this material for research and documentation. The romantic notion was popular in American culture of the 1960s and 1970s. "The noble savage translates into modern times as the naturalist, the ecologist," says Robert Thomas of the University of Arizona. "Indians became thought of as people who are spiritual, who know how to live in communities and with nature." Both stereotypes hold an element of truth. Indians and whites fought. Indians did not damage the environment very much. Most Native Americans, though, reject both the "savage" and the "noble" labels. Positive and negative stereotypes are not based on reality and can lead to unrealistic expectations (Eskin 1989, 22).

8. *Does the literature portray realistic roles for American Indian women?* Lass-Woodfin states that "in the genre nonfiction the treatment of Indian women is inadequate. Most authors do not realize women participated in hunting and war. Women's lives are usually portrayed as unexciting" (Lass-Woodfin 1978, 13-14).

Stensland (1979) agrees that there is a slanted portrayal of women who helped the white man.

Another stereotype of Indian women deals with the beautiful Indian maiden. In *Custer Died for Your Sins* (1969), Deloria tells of people wanting to have Indian ancestry through an Indian grandmother. While Indian males are considered cruel and savage, a beautiful Indian princess is an attractive addition to a male's ancestry. Common stereotypes grew out of the Pocahontas legend. Although beauty, loyalty, and nobility are good qualities, more realistic, well-developed pictures of Indian women can be found in some good biographies (Stensland 1979).

According to an article excerpted from *The Graywolf Annual Five: Multicultural Literacy*, women were of central importance in much of Native American society. A female-dominated system of government, gynarchy, was common in tribal societies that honored individual autonomy, cooperation, human dignity, freedom, and egalitarian distribution of goods, status, and services. American feminists and other human liberation movements around the world have incorporated these beliefs, attitudes, and laws into their visions. Feminists frequently forget that American Indian women experienced a society based on women's empowerment (Allen 1989, 108-9).

Women in Native American society have always taken a major role. This is predicated on the fact that most tribal groups are matriarchal. Lineage and ownership of property have always been transmitted through matriarchal lines. Today, women continue to play a major role. An outstanding woman, Wilma Mankiller, the first woman elected to the office of Principal Chief of the Cherokee Nation, oversees the largest tribal group in the United States. Women are contributing in the fields of government, arts, medicine, and literature. They remain a vital force in tribal life. Educators should evaluate the role of women when evaluating resources to assure that they are not assigned to a subservient or romanticized role.

Objectivity

Bibliographers of material about American Indian life also express considerable concern about objectivity. Those bibliographers who appear to have included scholarship, purpose, and careful selection in their bibliographies allow extensive space for discussing the objectivity of the American Indian materials included in their entries. *The Encyclopedia of Library and Information Science* refers to objectivity as lack of bias in controversial issues (Shores and Krzys 1978, 147). In American Indian literature, this bias results in the perpetuation of stereotypical myths. The negative stereotypes fostered by textbooks are sustained and elaborated by communications media, the primary culprits being television programs, movies, and novels:

> Many Hollywood film makers still hold the same decades-old stereotypic views of Indians "wearing war bonnets and riding pinto ponies," ...
>
> "Film makers are still more comfortable seeing Indians in buckskins and feathers," said Bob Nicks, executive director of the American Indian Registry for the Performing Arts (*Farmington Daily Times* 1988a, B4).

Less noticed as a purveyor of stereotypes is the cartoonist, whose work also plays a significant role in shaping the images held about minority persons (Bahr, Chadwick, and Day 1972).

The literature identifies six areas for evaluation of objectivity:

1. *Is the material unbiased, devoid of obvious or subtle prejudice?* American Indian materials should be carefully scrutinized for obvious or subtle bias. The bias can be in terms of word choice, sarcasm, ridicule, exaggeration, irony based on white viewpoints, and clichés, creating a tone that distorts the events the author describes (Indian Education Advisory Committee n.d., 53).

Another subtle method used by authors, termed the "obliterative" technique by Vogel (1968), creates or perpetuates false impressions of aboriginal Americans. The obliterative technique includes conscious falsification, selective reporting, or simply ignoring the Indian. The successful application by authors of this technique serves to make a "nondescript person" of the Native American.

Prejudice is an attitude, an adverse judgement or an opinion formed beforehand or without knowledge or examination of the facts (Querry 1992, 1). In reference to American Indians, prejudice is based upon ethnic characteristics—race, religion, language, national origin, and cultural traditions. Prejudices are learned from parents, friends, and culture, and from books written for children and young adults.

> Positive nonfiction information about Americans of European descent is abundant. Books about Native Americans are abundant too; however, many of the historical works contain distortions and omissions. When Indian children look for positive role models, they may be presented with several mixed messages that suggest that their people are somehow inferior to their white counterparts (Caldwell-Wood 1992, 47).

Other causes of prejudice include intergroup rivalry and economic factors. When different ethnic groups compete for resources, they may feel threatened by each other and form attitudes of suspicion and prejudice. The majority of nonfiction books documenting the period after the early European settlements present negative images of Indians. Native people taught Europeans basic survival skills and contributed to their economic structure. Often European countries disputed over which would take the Native Americans' lands. History books for young people extol the new nation dedicated to democracy and religious freedom. However, little mention is made of the fact that the new nation was modeled on the democratic principles practiced by the Iroquois Confederation for generations. The helpful natives, who were essential to the survival of the first Europeans in America, were somehow transformed into savages who deterred white settlers in search of new lands to claim, lands belonging to Indian tribes. Statistics of broken treaties that promised Indians lands are not included in textbooks. As Indian people go to court asking for the return of their ancestral lands, their demands provoke intense opposition as they clash with the prejudicial interests of other population groups.

The manner in which certain groups are portrayed in the popular media is another way young people can learn prejudice. As early as 1950, sociologists noticed that audiences of motion pictures and television tend to accept as true that part of a movie or television story that is beyond their experience (Querry 1992, 2). Books, motion pictures, and television are often the only medium through which people learn about American Indian culture. Educators have an obligation to assure that materials they provide are unbiased and without obvious or subtle prejudice.

2. *Does the author avoid using stereotypes?* Most sources reviewed contain references to the use of stereotypes. Stensland (1979) lists some stereotypes used by authors to refer to Indians: noble red men, heathen savages, murderous thieves, idlers, and drunkards. The effects of the repetition of negative words used to stereotype American Indians on both Indian youth and non-Indian youth concern Stensland (1979, 12-15). Because of these effects, Byler (1974) advocates not using works by non-Indian authors. She views the large body of literature about the American Indian by non-Indian authors as presenting a broad range of stereotypes about American Indians. She reasons that the stereotypes are manipulated by non-Indians to fulfill some illusory public or personal need.

Still another challenge faces American Indian people. Frank Mclemore, a Cherokee and program manager for the federal government, reported for tribal representatives at the Tribal American Networks tenth annual conference that "American Indians need to be educated in their own history and languages before they can work to end discrimination and derogatory stereotypes." Because Indian children attended English-speaking schools and were forbidden to speak their own language, many parents and children do not know enough about their own language and culture. At that same conference, John Blindo, a Navajo-Kiowa and executive director of the Dallas American Indian Chamber of Commerce, emphasized that American Indians "must use education to combat stereotypes in textbooks, films and television commercials that depict Indians as savages and drunkards. We have to re-educate ourselves and then educate the community" (*Farmington Daily Times* 1988b, B6).

Native American leaders are denouncing the use of Indian names and terms for professional and school sports teams. They feel that eliminating Indian team names will help erase ethnic stereotypes. Many fans profess bafflement over Native American claims that Indian team names are demeaning. Some even believe the names flatter Indians by linking them to skilled athletes. However, appropriating Indian names and paraphernalia for sports use is offensive and sometimes blatantly racist. The feathered headdress often worn by fans and mascots is particularly distasteful, as Indians regard feathers as sacred symbols that must be earned before they can be worn. "It's analogous to somebody dressing up as the pope, going out on the field, waving a cross, and performing a mock communion," says Andrea Nott, a community activist in Naperville, Illinois (Worsnop 1992, 388). Harjo adds that Indian names for sports teams can lower the self-esteem of Native American teenagers and contribute to their high suicide rate. Possibly as damaging, she adds, is the stereotype of the drunken Indian passed out in the gutter, an image that may have especially dire consequences for young Indians. Realizing they have little chance of becoming professional athletes, youths may emulate the other role model (Worsnop 1992, 388).

No longer does the Washington Redskins' marching band strut to the beat of tom-toms, cheerleaders wear squaw wigs with feathered headbands, and fight song include the words "Scalp 'em, swamp 'em ... we want heap more." Yet in the 1991 World Series, fans for the Cincinnati Braves still bellowed an Indian "war chant" and gave the "tomahawk chop." Indian demands were first dismissed, but are winning converts among sports writers, fans, and players. Journalists have a great influence on young adult readers. The question of sports team with Indian names underlies many concerns. Eliminating Indian team names will help erase ethnic stereotypes and make it easier for Americans to see Indians as individuals, insists Harjo (Worsnop 1992, 389-90).

Accurate American Indian literature that is free of stereotypical images can reflect a different view of the Indian. Bataille (1979) produced a set of slides with accompanying audiotape entitled *Inside the Cigar Store*, which gives examples of the efforts of advertisers, writers, and film producers to create an image of the Indian that is a twentieth-century anachronism. The slide program is helpful in promoting awareness for teachers and students. A selected bibliography is included, which provides general resources in American Indian studies, elementary level books, junior high level books, senior high and college level books, general references on American Indian literature, and resources on stereotyping and misrepresentation. The entries are annotated briefly.

3. *Does the material contain positive values, clear of negative influence?* Quality American Indian books can help Indian children and youth gain a sense of self-worth and positive values. The section in the review of literature on the values of the American Indian as an evaluative criterion looks at this criterion from the viewpoint of educators.

Pride in one's heritage can also exert a positive influence. Deloria states:

> Pride that can be built into children and youth by acknowledgment of the validity of their groups cannot be built by simply transferring symbols and interpretations arising in white cultural history into an Indian setting. The result will be to make the minority groups bear the white man's burden by using his symbols and stereotypes as if they were their own (Deloria 1970, 42).

He refers to the desire of contemporary church leaders to make Christianity relevant to minority groups by transposing the entire Christian tradition and archetypes into Indian terms. An illustration is the Christmas card that portrays the Holy Family as living in a hogan in Monument Valley on the Navajo reservation. While shepherds sing and tend flocks, little groups of Navajo angels announce the birth of the Christ child. Deloria's advice for each group is to understand its own uniqueness and examine the experiences relevant to the group (Deloria 1970, 39-45).

Of special concern are the books presented to children who are beginning readers. The literature should not just show Indians of the past. School-age Native American children will find it difficult to connect the feathered warriors of the plains in the history books with the Indian adults in their neighborhoods. They will also read about the "ideal" family and neighborhood in the basic readers. Reading materials about Indian culture or history allows Indian students to identify with and feel proud of their heritage, fosters a positive image of present-date Indian people, and encourages them to achieve (Gilliland and Reyhner 1988, 96). Native American children need interesting, true-to-life nonfiction about Native Americans that includes stories set in the present. These relative materials can reinforce a positive self-concept, motivate reading, and develop reading comprehension skills (Reyhner 1988, 143).

4. *Does the literature contain sensitive language, free from loaded or offensive words?* Vogel (1968) refers to loaded or offensive language as the "defamation" technique. The defamation technique consists merely of calling attention to the Indians' faults, real or imagined, and ignoring anything that might be said in their favor. The defamers depict Indians who are always on the warpath, bloodthirsty, debauched, idle, rootless, and barbaric. Such words as *squaws, bucks, drunken, lazy,* or *savages* can create stereotypes in the minds of readers of American Indian literature.

Byler (Slapin and Seale 1992, 91-97) refers to the "frequency with which non-Indian authors mention scalping, and the relish with which they indulge the bloody descriptions" as indicative that the authors, rather than Indians, are preoccupied with scalps. Words such as *savage, buck, squaw,* and *papoose* bring to the reader's mind different images than do the words *man, boy, woman,* and *baby.* Byler calls this "a more direct assault ... upon the humanity of American Indians by the use of key words and phrases which trigger negative and derogatory images."

Suzan Shown Harjo discusses the term "Indian" as the legacy of the lost European sailors in 1492. "American" was also derived from the first name of a European. She notes that Native peoples could have been called "Vespuccinders" as easily as American Indians or Native Americans, the most commonly used misnomers these days. With North-American-born descendants of immigrants referring to themselves as "natives," the issue becomes further clouded. "Indian" is the term that is used in United States and Canadian treaties, statutes, caselaw, governance documents, and modern English and French parlance. "Indian" replaced loaded and offensive words such as "savage," "redskin," or "L'Indian Rouge," which are considered fighting words. To Harjo, the words "American Indian," "Canadian Native," "Native American," "Indian," and "native" are inexact and silly, rather than offensive. While she recognizes that most native peoples in North America use the imprecise and awkward terms interchangeably when referring to the whole race, she places more emphasis on tribal names (Harjo 1993, xlii).

5. *Are human strengths and weaknesses included in writing about American Indian people and their life?* When selecting biographies of Indian people, the portrayal of human strengths as well as weaknesses is especially important. Research conducted by the American Indian Historical Society is reported in a pamphlet entitled "Common Misconceptions of American Indians" (Shaughnessy 1978, 23). It includes a stereotypical statement with which Indians are often labeled: "Lo, the poor Indian! The noble Indian! The true American who has been so long oppressed and mistreated! Pity the poor Indian!" This attitude is distasteful to Indian people. Some may be poor, some are not. The Indian may be a noble race, but the individual may not be noble. There are shirkers, drunkards, and ignoramuses among all groups. The Indian is not necessarily noble, poor, nor angelic. "He is an individual who is to be respected for his individual attainments, and criticized for his individual errors" (Shaughnessy 1978, 23).

Writers may use the words of Native Americans out of context and often even invent words they feel Indians might have said. With sincerity, they attribute these words to individuals they admire. The words of Chief Seattle, a nineteenth-century Suquamish Indian who lived on the Puget Sound, have been distorted by environmentalists. According to historians, Seattle was a skilled diplomat and a great orator. But he never spoke the words canonized by the ecology movement. Screenwriter Ted Perry penned the words after being inspired by some writings unwittingly attributed to Chief Seattle (Marsa 1992, 15-18). The sad part of this story is that the book *Brother Eagle, Sister Sky: A Message from Chief Seattle* for children is on the shelves of almost every school and public library. Children will unwittingly believe in the greatness and foresight of Chief Seattle testimony's on environmental problems, when he should instead be admired for words he actually said.

Library professionals and educators should look for real native people in the literature, not the Indian frequently portrayed in the movies. Real Native Americans come from different nations; their physical features, body structure, and skin colors vary a great deal; and none has red skin. Native and non-Native Americans have intermarried, and they do not all act and look alike, no more than all Europeans act and look alike (Heinrich 1986-87, 8). They are individuals.

6. *Does the material present both sides of an event, issue, or problem?* Byler (1973) discusses this issue in terms of the conquest of Indian lands and the practice of scalping. Settlers were threatened by and afraid of Indians. However, Indians were also threatened by the settlers and had much more to lose. Native Americans were fighting to defend their homes, families, and land. Contrary to what many people have been led to believe, scalping was not a widespread practice among American Indian tribes. Spread of the scalping practice over a great part of the central and western United States was a direct result of scalp bounties offered by the colonial governments (Byler 1973, 8-9). The literature rarely mentions that non-Indians also scalped people.

The literature on the history of the American Indian can be very biased as it reviews the battles through which land was appropriated by the government. Readers may easily get the impression that a few "brave" Europeans defeated millions of "Indian savages" in battle:

> How could a few Europeans take away the land of Native Americans and kill millions of them? This did not all happen in battle. Historians tell us that considering the number of people involved in the "Indian" wars, the number actually killed on both sides was small. What really defeated Native Americans were the diseases brought to this continent by the Europeans.... It was germs and disease, not Europeans' "superior" brains and bravery, that defeated the Native peoples (Heinrich 1986-87, 8).

Summary

The literature reviewed provides a frame of reference for those concerned with selecting the best American Indian literature for young people. Four major areas of concern emerge as evaluation criteria for selecting books of reference value: (1) the authorship of entries, (2) the recommendation of entries by Indians, (3) the value system of the American Indian, and (4) the treatment of American Indian life in the literature. Most sources cite accuracy, authenticity, and objectivity as predominant areas of concern in effectively judging literature on American Indian life.

Educators, including school and public library professionals, recognize that children believe the material they read or that is read to them. Therefore, the literature available in school and public libraries should be reliable and interesting. Cultural and historical resources can stimulate interest in reading, develop pride in heritage, and increase knowledge of the fascinating world of present and past Indian life among readers of all ages.

3

Using the Evaluative Checklist for American Indian Materials of Reference Value

The evaluative checklist at the end of this chapter is a tool designed to be used with a minimum of effort and time by school and public library professionals in selecting American Indian printed materials of reference value. The authorship of American Indian books, the American Indians' recommendations of books, and the value system and educational needs of students establish an understanding of the concepts that are considered fundamental to the understanding of American Indian life.

The first part of the "Evaluative Checklist for American Indian Materials of Reference Value" provides room for complete bibliographic information. Included in this section is space for the address of the publisher. Frequently, addresses of publishers of Indian materials are difficult to locate, and consequently they should be noted. (A directory of publishers for all the books in the annotated bibliography is included in the appendix.) Following the bibliographic information, the media specialist can note the reading level and subject areas.

The evaluation criteria, items I-VIII, are based on authority of author, recommendation of the entry, scope of the subject matter, and treatment of the content in determining quality American Indian literature. Item I covers authority. Although some bibliographers and writers of American Indian literature feel that only American Indians can write realistically about American Indians, the recommendation is that the treatment of American Indian subjects in the literature is more important than the ethnicity of the author. The evaluation criteria should be used to determine the selection of nonfiction materials. Indian and non-Indian authors' works that satisfy the evaluative criteria should be included. The rest of the form, items II through VIII, can be completed by checking the appropriate box or inserting comments.

Scope (item II) includes concern with (1) the extent to which the statement of purpose in the preface is fulfilled in the text, (2) the range of subject matter and its limitations, (3) recency of the material, and (4) the extent to which the bibliographies include scholarship and direct the reader to additional information. The areas of presentation and format, items III and IV, are the same as those that library professionals would apply when selecting any printed materials.

Evaluating the topics under treatment of the text, item V, requires understanding the evaluation criteria for American Indian literature discussed in chapter 2. The material on stereotypes in the area of American Indian life should be studied carefully. The treatment of the literature is divided into three broad subdivisions: accuracy, authenticity, and objectivity. These are the most critical evaluation criteria for American Indian printed materials. Bias and stereotypical myths may be difficult to detect because of subtle language, omission of words, distortion of events, loaded language, or presentation of only one side of an issue or event.

Illustrations, item VI, are evaluated according to the same criteria as text. The drawings should authentically depict Indians of the time and location:

> Books as well as motion pictures sometimes depict Indians of the Southwest wearing Plains Indian headdresses, New England Woodland Indians living in teepees, or Navajos living among Saguaro cactus. These errors do not necessarily reflect upon the knowledge of the writer, as the author does not always see the illustrations that the publisher will use, but it does indicate that all of the content needs to be checked for accuracy. The illustrations themselves can teach misinformation regarding the history and culture of the people depicted (Gilliland and Reyhner 1988, 97).

Special features of each bibliography entry should be noted. Finally, the book is evaluated as being of (1) significant value as a reference book, (2) marginal value as a reference book, or (3) no value as a reference. By noting the checkmarks on the form and scanning the comments, the library professional should be able to determine whether the purchase of a specific book is advisable.

Unfortunately, some books dealing with American Indian life are selected because they are the only source available on the subject, not because they are quality books. The evaluative criteria checklist, designed to provide specific items by which American Indian printed materials can be determined to be of significant reference value, demands careful analysis of authority, scope, presentation, format, treatment, illustrations, and special features.

School and public library professionals, as well as all educators of school-age children, are encouraged to use this basic tool to select American Indian materials for inclusion in their collections. The evaluative criteria provide a method of selecting books that are meaningful, realistic, and representative of American Indian people and their culture. By using an effective evaluation tool for selection of American Indian printed materials, library professionals and educators can develop an awareness of poor materials and avoid their purchase and use.

EVALUATIVE CHECKLIST
FOR AMERICAN INDIAN MATERIALS
OF REFERENCE VALUE

Editor, Compiler, or Author: Subject Areas:

_____

       last name   first name

Title _____

Publisher's Name _____

      Address _____   Fry Reading

Pages _____   Level (FRL)

Illustrator _____

I.   Authority:

      1.   Authorship qualification: experience, education, credibility, previous work, ethnic affiliation _____

      2.   Reputation of publisher or sponsoring agency _____

      3.   Edition: new, revised, supplement, based on other work (supply title)

INSTRUCTIONS: Check and/or comment on items II through V using this scale: E = excellent; F = fair; P = poor; N/A = not applicable

II.   Scope:

	E	F	P	N/A
1. Purpose fulfilled				
2. Inclusion, range of subject matter				
3. Recency, up-to-date				
4. Bibliography, scholarship				

Comments: _____

III.   Presentation:

	E	F	P	N/A
1. Creative				
2. Sincere				
3. Original				
4. Readable				

Comments: _____

(Evaluative Checklist continues on page 38.)

IV. Format: E F P N/A
- 1. Physical make-up
  - a. Readable type
  - b. Sturdy binding
  - c. Good graphics
  - d. Quality paper
- 2. Arrangement:
  - a. Preface
  - b. Table of contents
  - c. Accessible footnotes
  - d. Index
  - e. Appendixes

Comments: (description of arrangement) _____

V. Treatment: E F P N/A
- 1. Accuracy
  - a. Reliable sources
  - b. Careful documentation
  - c. Thoroughly researched
  - d. Factual information
- 2. Authenticity
  - a. Culture evaluated by Indian values and attitudes
  - b. Contributions of American Indian to Western civilization
  - c. Recognition of diversity among tribes, culture, lifestyles
  - d. Accurate portrayal of Indians as individuals, not groups
  - e. Recognition as enduring race, not vanishing or assimilated
  - f. Respectful portrayal of Indian language and dialects
  - g. Realistic description of Indian life, past or present
  - h. Realistic portrayal of role of American Indian women

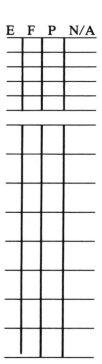

From *American Indian Reference and Resource Books for Children and Young Adults,* Second Edition. © 1995. Libraries Unlimited. (800) 237-6124.

3. Objectivity | E F P N/A
   a. Unbiased, devoid of obvious or subtle prejudice
   b. Avoidance of stereotypes
   c. Positive values, clear of negative inference
   d. Sensitive language, free from loaded or offensive words
   e. Portrayal of human strengths and weaknesses
   f. Presentation of both sides of event, issue,
   problem
   Comments: _____

VI. Illustrations: | E F P N/A
   1. Authentic depiction of Indian way of life, past
   or present
   2. Creative
   3. Quality workmanship
   4. Captions compatible with text
   Comments: (include type of illustrations) _____

VII. Special features:
   1. Does the book have distinctive features? If so, identify:

   _____

   2. Has the publication been recommended by a person or group
   knowledgeable about American Indians? If so, identify:

   _____

VIII. Conclusion (check one)
   _____ 1. Significant value as a reference book
   _____ 2. Marginal value as a reference book
   _____ 3. No value as a reference book

4

Publishing American Indian Books

Most educational leaders recognize the importance of providing materials on the American Indian for all young people at every grade level that are accurate, authentic, and objective. Equally imperative is the critical need to provide American Indian school-age children with quality literature on their heritage and contemporary Indian affairs. Because Indian students may view themselves as others see them in print, carefully selected literature can play a major role in improving the Indian student's self-concept, and consequently the student's achievement in school. Well-selected literature may have a positive impact on the long-term quality of life of the young Indian reader. Unfortunately, poorly selected materials may negatively influence the reader's life. Thus, the library professional must be knowledgeable in selecting accurate and stimulating books if the potential of the young Indian reader is to be fulfilled.

In attaining the major goal of cultural pluralism, that is, mutual respect among all ethnic groups, the publishing world plays an important role in providing adequate resources for all readers. Those responsible for publishing the best American Indian literature available face the challenge of selecting materials that pertain specifically to the interests and reading needs of young people. This is not an easy task and rarely takes precedence with editors.

The greatest problem in selecting books to publish is that few editors have developed an awareness of the problems in the American Indian books that are purchased by libraries, schools, and the public. According to J. R. Cook, executive directory of UNITY, the United National Indian Tribal Youth, Inc., "Over half of this country's Native American population is under the age of 22" (*Farmington Daily Times* 1988c, B2). To have a positive effect on Indian youth who are in a high-risk category, library professionals and educators are constantly searching for materials to build their collections. Publishers can help fill this need.

In the field of children's books, children's authors "are expected, and rightly so, to keep their work free of racism, sexism, and religious bias" (Babbitt 1990, 150). This stipulation can be especially meaningful as publishers of American Indian materials review materials for school-age children.

Indian people are becoming increasingly aware of research and publishing on American Indian topics by non-Indian scholars. The recommendation of the American Indian professionals and tribal members for the National Dialogue Project in December 1988 was that tribal people safeguard their cultural domains against research and publishing incursions:

> Community-based research in Indian communities needs to be conducted in conjunction with the endorsement by tribal authorities for the purpose of ensuring that the finished product has value to Indian people and is educationally beneficial....
>
> Scholarly research on Indian history and culture must take into account Indian perspectives. Published and unpublished manuscripts germane to Indians, as well as tribal history projects, could provide writers with a wealth of untapped information and historical and cultural processes not found in primary and secondary source materials. This methodology will help scholars avoid perpetuating stereotypes of Indians based on mythology, misconceptions, and romanticism. American Indian scholars need to become involved in producing research rather than serving as subjects and consumers. Measures such as these will ultimately introduce more accurate depictions of Indian experiences and lifestyles into the classroom (American Indian Science & Engineering Society 1989, 6-7).

Historically, publishers of both fiction and nonfiction have varied in their interest in promoting American Indian topics. During the 1960s, public consciousness of the educational needs of American Indian children surfaced. This period also saw the emergence of American Indian writers: "Momaday, Welch, Silko, and Ortiz at first, were recognized as outside the great tradition of Western literature" (Lincoln 1983, 7). In the 1970s, national attention was focused on the Indian movement, and federal money was available for writing and publishing Indian educational resources. The publishing industry also was affected, and many books were published, some excellent and others poorly written, containing inaccurate and stereotypical material. Paula Gunn Allen, American Indian ethnic studies professor at the University of California, Berkeley, reports that, in 1977, the Modern Language Association sponsored a national conference to promote Native American literature. "Since then, new critical studies and scholarly journals have appeared, lost or forgotten works have come back into print, and many new works of poetry and fiction and collections of traditional oral narratives have found their way into publication. By the early 1980s, Allen said, 'What we had on our hands was a literary revolution, a Native American renaissance'" (Coughlin 1990, A7, A12). During the 1980s and 1990s, the focus has included other ethnic groups who have become the dominant minorities in the classrooms of America. Consequently, publishers have published more fiction and poetry by members of minority groups.

Publishing and Purchasing

"America's appetite for books is keener than ever ..." (Brophy 1990, 41). Both large and small bookstores are vying to sell books to the public. However, the large suppliers are interested in the more popular titles, which sell in large volume. Many small booksellers have cashed in on markets ignored by the giants. About 50,000 new titles are published each year, and 860,000 books are continuously in print, so there is plenty of room for specialization. In the smaller bookstores, special sections are frequently devoted to Western Americana nonfiction, and sometimes an entire section will be devoted to American Indian nonfiction. In addition, children's bookstores are increasing in number, from a dozen outlets a decade ago to more than 300 today. Small bookstores, working in specialized areas, are willing to stock small sellers, find readers for them, and build a loyal clientele. Library professionals can locate small bookstores that will supply a continuous selection of both current and recognized quality books on American Indian topics. Many stores supply catalog and ordering services, eliminating the need to order from a number of small publishers directly and increasing the availability of specialized titles. Still, the major sources of American Indian materials for school-age children, especially Indian youth, are school and public libraries. Both new and used bookstores should not be overlooked by those educators and library professionals searching for quality American Indian titles.

Most national monuments and parks have gifts shops that frequently stock American Indian titles, usually including a few that are appropriate for school-age children. The library professional or educator should look carefully at the materials to be sure that the readability and vocabulary levels are appropriate for the intended readers.

Other excellent sources are university presses, especially the University of Oklahoma and University of Nebraska, which publish excellent, well-researched volumes for young adults. Some reprint houses publish American Indian materials. Flea markets and trading posts also may be sources for locating out-of-print books.

Publishers of Indian Books
and Materials

Educators and librarians who serve children are concerned about the publication of American Indian books. Byler declares:

> Down through the years the publishing industry has produced thousands of books about American Indians—a subject that fascinates many. Fact and fiction—it is not always possible to tell which is which—have rolled off the presses since "frontier" days. But American Indians in literature, today as in the past, are merely images projected by non-Indian writers.
>
> Most minority groups in this country have been, and are still, largely ignored by the nation's major publishing houses—particularly in the field of children's books. American Indians, on the other hand, contend with a mass of material about themselves. If anything, there are too many children's books about American Indians.

> There are too many books featuring painted, whooping, befeathered Indians closing in on too many forts maliciously attacking "peaceful" settlers or simply leering menacingly from the background; too many books in which white benevolence is the only thing that saves the day for the incompetent, childlike Indian; too many stories setting forth what is "best" for American Indians (Slapin and Seale 1992, 81).

It is hoped that some changes are being made in the publishing world and that editors now more carefully scrutinize the American Indian reading materials they publish. They have become cognizant of misleading and derogatory references about any minority group. The lack of reliable and accurate information about American Indian culture and history, however, still results in false or biased literature being printed. Therefore, the publication date of a book is not a guarantee of its reliability as an American Indian book of reference value. In the past, some excellent materials were published. Gilliland reports that, while facts are not distorted as much in current materials, omission of facts remains a serious problem:

> The treatment the Indian received is usually omitted from children's literature, as are Indian contributions to agriculture, medicine, architecture, biological science, and other aspects of modern life.
>
> Writers seem unaware of the Indian's philosophical thought, close family ties, emphasis on cooperation and sharing with others, respect for the land and all of nature, hospitality and generosity, and the relation of all of these to the Indian's spiritual life (Gilliland and Reyhner 1988, 94-95).

Sharron L. McElmeel, the library media specialist in the Cedar Rapids, Iowa Community Schools, sends a message to librarians about the need for publishers to show the real faces of America's children (McElmeel 1993, 50). Because of the lack of good multiethnic children's books, elementary school librarians find it difficult to develop a collection representing a variety of cultural backgrounds. Locating well-written titles that represent a variety of cultural backgrounds is a challenge. One of the points made in the article is the need for books that portray Native Americans and members of other minority groups as they are today. An informal poll conducted by McElmeel asked approximately 250 primary students how they could recognize an American Indian who walked into their classroom. The answers were usually responses like "they'd be wearing feathers," "they'd have war paint on," or "they'd be carrying a tomahawk." She noted that only one child suggested an Indian child would be similar to other children—wearing jeans, a T-shirt and tennis shoes. Many books published for children are legends, contain outdated information, and promote historical images of the past. Newly published books on Native American ceremonials are replete with pictures of children in feathered headdress and traditional clothing. Librarians should urge publishers to include an image of present-day Native Americans who go to school in a modern setting. McElmeel states, "Children growing up in this diverse environment should not think of Indians as warmongers wearing feathers and face paint.... The most celebrated inventors, the most prominent politicians, the 'forefathers' we read about ... all seem to be Caucasian. Children should not grow up thinking that only the predominant culture has helped to shape and improve our society."

The other important point made in the article is that the vision of cultural awareness should not become too narrow. When children are exposed to cultural diversity and heritages, "they grow, become tolerant of differences and learn to respect others and their ideas." McElmeel urges library media specialists to "write to every publishing house they buy books from and explain the need for books that show the faces of the real America—and include a photograph or two of the children we see every day."

A positive note is that publishers are actively seeking multicultural materials to meet the growing demand from teachers, librarians, and parents. Karen McWilliams became interested in multicultural children's books as an elementary school teacher with the Department of Defense Overseas Schools. She asserts, "Long before Europeans, Latin Americans and Asians immigrated to this country, the United States was 'multicultural.' Hundreds of Native-American tribes with unique languages, religions, and customs lived throughout the Americas. Today, with the continuing arrival of immigrants from around the world, most schools have many students from a variety of cultures" (McWilliams 1993, 22). The mainstream presses McWilliams queried stated that 10 to 20 percent of their titles are multicultural. They would publish more if well-written manuscripts were submitted. Small presses have experienced a growth in multicultural and bilingual books during the last decade. Editors are looking specifically for books about a particular culture written by an author belonging to that culture. They will also consider well-written and researched manuscripts by authors not of that culture. Manuscripts submitted about a particular ethnic group should show what the culture of the book has in common with other cultures and what makes the culture unique.

The publication of American Indian folklore books deserves special consideration. In selecting books of reference value for part 2 of this guide, "Annotated Bibliography of American Indian Books of Reference Value for Children and Young Adults," great discrepancies were noted in citing references for retold folklore. Books without references were not included, although they may have been excellent choices otherwise.

Betsy Hearne is the editor of *The Bulletin of the Center for Children's Book* and faculty member of the Graduate School of Library and Information Science at the University of Illinois-Champaign. She addresses the issue of respect for folklore:

> Folktales belong to all of us, but we do not own them. Like the air we breathe, and the earth we stand on, they are ours to take care of for a short while. The more we give to them, the more we find in them. In recreating a folktale for children in picture-book form, we are borrowing an old story, adding to it, and returning it to the world renewed. That is the ideal scenario, but sometimes more is subtracted from a story than is added.
>
> Achieving a balance between old and new depends on equal respect for both old and new, ... for the 'original' source of a story (i.e., where we heard or read it) and for the possibilities of recreating it. If for no other reason, we should respect a story's past because we shall soon become part of it (Hearne 1993b, 33).

Hearne equates respect with identifying the specific culture and source from which the story has been taken.

What defines an authority for librarians evaluating picture-book folklore? An authority could be a well-read expert or a member of the ethnic group raised in the culture of the story. Graciela Italiano (Hearne 1993b, 34) delivered a paper at the 1992 Allerton Institute that said knowing a cultural tradition from both experience and study can be more valuable than the formal qualifications of being a registered member of the culture. Another conference presenter, Hazel Rochman, refutes the misconception that only Indians can judge books about Indians, and only members of other minorities can judge resources about their own culture. These attitudes are, she says, "locking us into smaller and tighter boxes." Hearne offers the example of a noted author of children's Sioux folklore books, Paul Goble. An Englishman, he lived with the Sioux, was adopted by them, and has retold their lore respectfully, carefully citing his sources and explaining the cultural significance of his stories.

Other elements that separate folklore of reference value are accuracy in graphic translation and fidelity of tone. Navajo author Shonto Begay works traditional graphic motifs into the retelling of the stories of his people. Markedly different is Goble's detailed and often humorous art that incorporates Sioux culture into the illustrations. Both artists provide background appropriate to the tales. Illustrations are a vital part of picture-book folklore. Unfortunately, publishers are producing books with stilted, simplistic drawings, mistakenly believing that these are of "elementary" level and of appeal to children.

Folktales are part of the oral culture of American Indians. The stories are well known to the native people and are adapted over a long period. Anthropologists recorded this folklore, but today copyright laws no longer apply. Any writer can receive credit for a story with no responsibility to cite the source. Perhaps this is why some authors who do try to verify retold stories with tribal elders are refused an audience. Hearne offers the criteria for a well-made source note:

> The truly exemplary source note cites the specific source(s), adds a description for cultural context, and describes changes the author has made in the retelling, with some explanation of why. This delivers all the essential information to harried lay readers and leaves room for scholars to verify its accuracy or make a study of picture-book adaptations of folklore if they're burning to do so (1993a, 25).

Publishers of all folklore, including American Indian stories, should require writers to include this information.

The writer who retells the folktale, the illustrator who provides background for the story, and the publisher who accepts their work bear the initial responsibility for quality folklore children's books. Hearne (1993b) recommends that librarians check for source citations and critical reviews, compare adaptations to their printed sources, and determine what context illustrations provide the story so that they may make more informed selections. These factors should weigh heavily in the decision to purchase folklore books of any culture.

Some educators and librarians may naively view the publishing industry as having high ideals and standards. The actual situation may be very different. The publishing world is about as "genteel" as the steel or electronics industry. It is a fiercely competitive, global business in which sheer size means strength. A handful of multinationals now control nearly 50 percent of the market, shelling out huge premiums to swallow up smaller competitors (Powell 1988, 41). Slapin, concerned about the quality of American Indian literature being published, states that "books about the People are still being written by, published by, and promoted by, outsiders" (Slapin and Seale 1988, 4). She further writes, "On the other hand, fewer and fewer Native writers and artists, talented people with unique perspectives to offer, are being published by mainstream presses, a fact which is also true of other writers of color" (Slapin and Seale 1988, 5).

Publishers have responded to the complaints of parents, educators, and booksellers and are publishing more multicultural titles for children. Stephen Roxburgh, publisher of Farrar, Straus & Giroux's Books for Young Readers, credits the revolution in children's books to the relationship that exists between children's publishing and educators. The libraries and schools are dealing with a culture that is increasingly diverse, and publishing has reacted accordingly (Jones 1991, 64).

Still, multicultural titles account for only 10 percent of the books published for children, although many of the new titles are superior to those previously published. Harriet Rohmer, founder of Children's Book Press in San Francisco, is the one person who is largely responsible for these higher standards. Every book she publishes is multicultural and told (often bilingually) by an author who shares the story's culture (Jones 1991, 65). When Rohmer began publishing, her insistence on ethnic storytellers was unique. Now it is more generally accepted. Multiculturalism has become well established in children's literature. Children from ethnic groups enjoy reading about someone who looks like them. Not only are the books popular among minorities, they provide all children with the experience of reading about children of different cultures.

Ironically, *The Education of Little Tree*, a book that became a best-seller, was accepted by publishers, educators, and many Indians as having been written by a Native American. Proclaimed as a self-taught writer and a cowboy by trade, Forrest Carter died of a heart attack in 1979, leaving behind the "true" story of his Depression-era childhood with his Cherokee grandparents in the Tennessee mountains. The couple share the mysteries of their people with the young boy (McWhorter 1991, 119-20). *The Education of Little Tree* became a beloved and best-selling biography for children and adults.

But when the book topped the New York Times best-seller list, Emory University historian Dan T. Carter exposed Forrest Carter's identity as Asa Carter, a violent white supremacist. "If I were a Native American," said Dan T. Carter, "I would be appalled that someone assumed my cultural voice, wrote out of my experience—and pain—and then peddled it deceitfully" (McWhorter 1991, 119). Forrest Carter presented himself as a self-taught Cherokee author and a spokesman for American Indians. Dan T. Carter reported that Asa Carter was a Ku Klux Klan terrorist between 1946 and 1973 and a speech writer for George Wallace (Reid 1991, 16). Originally published in 1979, the book quietly went out of print in 1984. Reprinted by the University of New Mexico Press in 1986, the book's jacket proclaims that the book is "a true story." According to Leland (1991, 62), strong word-of-mouth and New Age credulousness parlayed it into the top spot on the New York Times paperback best-seller list. Asa Carter's widow has received twenty-seven film offers. The book has fooled at least two Indian historians and has been used in education classes on college campuses.

Geneva Jackson, a member of the Cherokee Eastern Band in North Carolina, says the book distorts the tribe's legends and language. She refers to *Little Tree* as "the closest thing to a farce that has been published in the Cherokee name"

(McWhorter 1991, 119-20). In the promotion copy, Forrest Carter is described as a "storyteller-in-council" to the Cherokee Nation. No such position exists. Forrest Carter also claimed he was making a donation to the Cherokee from his book royalties. The tribe has no evidence of any such donations. Even so, Rennard Strickland, a Cherokee professor of Indian law at the University of Oklahoma who wrote the introduction to the latest edition of *Little Tree*, responds, "If Forrest Carter was in fact a member of the Klan, it gives us hope that a cure of the soul is possible even late in life."

The controversy has involved literary critics, librarians, and the general public in a lively debate over how to separate authentic ethnic literature from counterfeit. The UNM Press continues to sell the *The Education of Little Tree*. Cataloged in some bookstores and libraries as a biography, the book awaits unsuspecting readers who are unaware of the book's questionable origin.

Despite the commercialism of the large publishing houses, an increasing number of small, independent book publishers with limited capital and low overhead are promoting middle-level books that typically have print runs of 5,000 or fewer copies. Hundreds of these small presses, including those that publish exclusively American Indian materials, have sprung up in America during the last decade. As the giant publishers are merging, the little publishers are reaping profits in the neglected areas. According to *Publishers Weekly*, America has up to 20,000 independent presses. Most publish a mere dozen titles each year. Yet their cultural clout outweighs the size of their press runs. The small concerns often spot regional talents overlooked by the giants. They can wait years for books to sell, counting on the continual sale of popular backlist titles. They target tiny, but lucrative, niches. As these publishers develop stocks of quality books, well-written American Indian books may become more available. Even in a mass society there is always an audience for good literature: "There is something about the way people light up when they read or hear about a good book. It's a unique personal experience, and nothing is going to change that," says Erwin Bilkes, president and publisher of the Free Press (Sanoff 1984, 65).

Small presses have always been interested in the children's book market. More high-quality children's books are being published by small presses. Frequently, these books offer information not usually found in children's books from mainstream publishers. Many small presses are carving out a niche by publishing books that are regionally based. A few publishers are presenting titles on Native American subjects, particularly folklore. Through direct-mail catalogs, small presses are targeting consumers (Metts 1991). Catalogs are one of the tools librarians can use to search for American Indian materials.

New opportunities for smaller publishers have opened in chains of book superstores. In the past, books from small and independent publishers, many of which publish American Indian titles, were rarely found in major chain stores. In the 1990s, these books have become a staple of large-inventory bookstores. Tom Simon, vice-president of merchandising for Waldenbooks, reports that the chain's superstores will have more books from smaller presses than are carried in the Waldenbooks mall stores. This development means small presses need a larger inventory and a marketing philosophy to access the market. Very small presses may find that they are not helped by the trend if they are lacking in marketing and sales distribution staff (Barbato 1992).

There are also a few small presses (see appendix) that specialize in American Indian titles and, specifically, in tribal life. Library professionals should receive their catalogs on a regular basis. Nonfiction books from small presses, including American Indian presses and locally developed materials, should be carefully evaluated using the same standards as for other books.

Local Publishers of Tribal Culture

Many excellent books are available from major publishers of books on Indian life and culture. However, there is a prevalent and growing need for Indian children to have reading materials on their own people, material that is about their real world. Some materials have been developed locally by tribal educators, and a few by commercial publishers. To meet the educational needs of their students for accurate information about culture, Native American and other educators are continually developing and publishing resources for school children. Many of the educational centers of the larger tribes have published materials that deal specifically with the history, mythology, and biographies of their people. The materials are used to support the curriculum with culture-based learning resources.

Drawing on the oral knowledge of people in the community and on written sources that they feel are truthful, educators strive to provide information that will enrich the lives of Indian children. These resources are still scarce, and many more need to be written and published. When they are written, it is often as a result of the dedicated efforts of classroom teachers. Most materials published by large publishers, and those recommended in this bibliography, deal with the American Indian people as a whole. The literature dealing with the specific tribes that school and public libraries serve, if available, forms a valuable addition to the basic collections of these libraries.

Building Blocks for Success

The education of minority students has become one of the greatest challenges of our time. Helping school-age children become academically successful is a task that cannot be taken lightly. Education must make a major commitment to provide equitable resources for all students. Too often, the needs of American Indian students are forgotten because they are not considered immigrants or "new" minorities.

Public and school library professionals can play a major role in changing the traditional materials used in education. Their stance should include (1) unity of purpose—setting evaluative standards for minority literature that will ensure obtaining quality materials to which American Indian students can relate; (2) building on strength—developing and continually upgrading a collection of adequate, culturally sensitive American Indian learning resources that meet the educational needs of all school-age children; and (3) implementation of resources—assuming the responsibility for ensuring the use of quality American Indian books of reference value rather than blaming the authors, publishers, or educational system for failing to supply these materials.

As public and school library professionals build well-balanced and accurate collections of reference books on American Indian culture and contemporary issues, a major step in providing equitable education for American Indian students will be achieved. As noted by educators, reading is one of the major keys to academic success for these students. The library professional must take a leading role, along with teachers and parents, in motivating young American Indian students to read and to fulfill their academic potential.

5

Incorporating American Indian Resource Materials into the Curriculum

Making education relevant to Indian school-age young people can be possible if quality American Indian materials are available for instructional assignments and are incorporated by teachers into subject areas. This approach can be implemented in two major ways: (1) by providing school library media centers with an adequate number of quality fiction and nonfiction resource materials by and about American Indians, and (2) by encouraging schools to create classroom settings in which Indian students can speak, read, and write about their own cultural experiences. The following subjects are suggested to library professionals and educators as an introduction to the many areas in which American Indian books can be incorporated into the educational experience of all children and young adults.

Social Sciences

Social studies classes and assignments are prime areas in which Indian culture may be ignored, stereotyped, or debased. Textbooks do not always include accurate and objective material on American Indian history and, in many cases, omit the Indian influence. In other cases, texts present romantic or negative images of the Indian people, perpetuating the stereotype that the Indian represents savagery and presenting the Anglo culture as superior. Textbooks also may pay little attention to contemporary Indian affairs, which leaves many students with the idea that tribal life and culture are a thing of the past.

Carefully selected American Indian resource materials, especially those written by Indian people about their own history, can supplement textbooks for providing information on the American Indian's social, economic, and political contributions. Through resource materials that are carefully evaluated, students can gain a knowledge of the Indian perspective and philosophy on government, history, and contemporary affairs. Students should be provided with resources to read and do research on current tribal issues such as economic development, land tenure, fishing rights, and self-determination.

American Indian Languages

The survival of respective tribal languages is important to Indian people. Schools can reverse the decline of native languages if they are offered as part of a bilingual/bicultural education. Other students who have an interest in learning a second language may choose to learn an American Indian language. Quality cultural materials written in a native language are very helpful in supplementing this type of curriculum. Tribal presses have prepared many excellent materials in both English and native languages.

Mathematics

Mathematics is an academic area that many schools are slighting for their American Indian young people. This critical discipline should include practical applications to "real world" situations. To help young people realize that Indian people have a broad historical dimension to contribute to this field, teachers and students can read of the ancient uses of mathematics in Indian cultures. Contributions to math, such as the medicine wheel and the Aztec calendar, can be incorporated into the curriculum or assigned for outside reading. Geometric figures used in pottery and rock art, as well as the mathematical principles incorporated into the architecture of dwellings, can provide projects in math and science for Indian youth in which they can blend modern knowledge with ancient contributions.

Computer Literacy

Computer literacy, a lifeline to the modern world of technology, can be linked to the area of American Indian symbolic images for communication. As the use of computers in educational settings continues to expand, libraries serving Indian students will be called on to supply teachers with high-quality computer materials in all subject areas. The Indian student's learning style, which is generally recognized to be visual and tactile, will combine effectively with the use of computers in classrooms and media centers.

Science

Very few books of reference value have been written about American Indian contributions to science. Those that were located for this review are more helpful for elementary and middle school students. This poses a greater challenge in making biology, chemistry, physics, and other science courses relevant for tribal youth. The Indian concepts of natural phenomena, astronomy, medicine, and mythology, such as the legends of the moon and of the seasons, can be integrated into the curriculum and assigned for outside reading. Concerns with ecology, the greenhouse effect, the ozone layer, and waste disposal, as well as air and water pollution, can give cross-cultural significance to the Indian message of harmony with nature.

Fine Arts

Many excellent books of reference value on American Indian fine arts, including visual and performing arts, provide a perspective on Indian life that allows individuals to express themselves in many media. Students can use American Indian reference sources and their own creativity in art, music, and dance. Materials on historical and contemporary Indian culture also have applications in drama.

Physical Education and Health

A primary focus in traditional Indian culture is the belief in physical and intellectual development. There are many excellent sources for integrating Indian recreational activities into the curriculum and teaching health in accord with tribal values. American Indian games are discussed in many books. Many activities already used by elementary teachers have their roots in Indian culture. Sports played by middle and high school students also are part of American Indian history. By integrating the history of games and sports into the curriculum, all school-age children and young adults can recognize that the values and skills native people needed for survival are perpetuated through games and sports. Health topics can address relevant problems facing Indian populations.

Home Economics

Books containing recipes for American Indian foods can teach students how to prepare traditional foods in wholesome and nutritional ways. The authors of many of these books incorporate stories, legends, and material about plants and animals into the text, making the information culturally as well as scientifically valuable. Students in vocational classes can be encouraged to use library resource materials to make and learn about traditional clothing and continue working in traditional crafts, such as pottery, basketry, and silversmithing.

English and Language Arts

To promote competence in English, teachers of American Indian students can encourage them to use Indian resource materials to speak, read, and write about their own cultural experiences or heritage. Books about American Indian mythology, legends, and poetry are effective tools for building an appreciation of reading and literature. Anthologies and books by American Indian authors and poets are excellent for developing literacy as well as providing role models.

Poetry, an important form of expression for native people, allows students to understand how they use words and gain an understanding of their feelings. Oral Native American literature is a way of teaching children about behavior and moral values. Through good Indian stories and legends, school children can learn proper behavior and values, at the same time building a good self-concept. Written versions of stories children have heard at home bridge the gap between oral and written communication and promote reading. Biographies of notable Indian people, especially contemporary role models, can shape character. The written literature by and about American Indian people can inspire creative writing in young adults.

Teachers and librarians are strongly encouraged to read and learn from tribal people about the place and proper time and use of American Indian stories.

Technology

The future of young Native Americans rests in keeping abreast of the modern technological advances. Schools can use technology to preserve and teach native languages, tribal histories, and local cultures as well as the traditional curriculum. Improved communication through satellite and inter-school computer linkage can introduce reservation schools to the information superhighway and help alleviate the isolation of Native American communities. Television, film, and video production classes offer Indian students opportunities to create their own visions of Native American reality. Camcorders can be used in collecting oral histories. Desktop publishing programs provide an excellent opportunity for students to provide their own perspectives on historical and current issues. As students prepare for these creative activities, public and school libraries can provide them with materials of reference value.

Reference Sources

Allen, Paula Gunn. 1983. *Studies in American Indian Literature: Critical Essays and Course Designs.* New York: Modern Language Association.

———. 1989. America's Founding Mothers: Our Native American Roots. *Utne Reader* (March/April): 108-9.

The American Heritage Dictionary of the English Language. 1978. New York: Houghton Mifflin.

American Indian Science & Engineering Society. 1989. *Our Voices, Our Vision: American Indians Speak Out for Educational Excellence.* New York: College Entrance Examination Board.

Babbitt, Natalie. 1990. The Purpose of Literature: Who Cares? *School Library Journal* 36 (March): 150-52.

Bahr, Howard M., Bruce A. Chadwick, and Robert E. Day, eds. 1972. *Native Americans Today: Sociological Perspectives.* New York: Harper & Row.

Banks, James A. 1975. *Teaching Strategies for Ethnic Studies.* Belmont, Calif.: Allyn & Bacon.

———. 1981. *Education in the 80's: Multiethnic Education.* Washington, D.C.: National Education Association.

Barbato, Joseph. 1992. Chain Superstores: Good Business for Small Presses. *Publishers Weekly* 239 (9 November): 50-52.

Bataille, Gretchen Mueller. 1978. *American Indian Literature: A Selected Bibliography for Iowa Schools.* ED 170 100. Bethesda, Md.: ERIC Document Reproduction Service.

———. 1979. *Inside the Cigar Store: Images of the American Indian.* Ames: Iowa State University Research Foundation.

Berry, Brewton. 1968. *The Education of the American Indian: A Survey of the Literature.* Washington, D.C.: Government Printing Office.

Broadus, Robert N. 1981. *Selecting Materials for Libraries*. New York: H. W. Wilson.

Brophy, Beth. 1990. America's New Bestsellers. *U.S. News & World Report* 102 (16 April): 41-43.

Byler, Mary Gloyne. 1973. *American Indian Authors for Young Readers: A Selected Bibliography*. New York: Association on American Indian Affairs.

———. 1974. The Image of American Indians Projected by Non-Indian Writers. *Library Journal* 99 (15 February): 546-49.

Caldwell-Wood, Naomi. 1992. Native American Images in Children's Books. *School Library Journal* 38 (May): 47-48.

Chiago, R. K. 1980. Making Education Work for the American Indian. *Theory into Practice* 20 (Winter): 20-25.

Clemmer, Janice White. 1979. A Portrayal of the American Indian in Utah State Approved United States History Textbooks. Ph.D. diss., University of Utah.

Coughlin, Ellen K. 1990. Despite Successes, Scholars Express Ambivalence About Place of Minority Literature in Academe. *Chronicles of Higher Education* 10 (January): A7, A12-13.

Council on Interracial Books for Children. 1977. *Stereotypes, Distortions, and Omissions in U.S. History Textbooks*. New York: Council on Interracial Books for Children.

Deloria, Vine, Jr. 1969. *Custer Died for Your Sins*. New York: Avon.

———. 1970. *We Talk, You Listen*. New York: Dell.

———. 1978. The Indian Student Amid American Inconsistencies. In *The Schooling of Native America*, edited by Thomas Thompson. Washington, D.C.: American Association of Colleges for Teacher Education.

Donahue, Deirdre. 1992. Satisfying a Hunger for Ethnic Variety. *USA Today* (18 March): D1-2.

Education Week. 1989. A Special Report on the Education of Native Americans. 2 (August): 1-16.

Eskin, Leah. 1989. The Tonto Syndrome. *Scholastic Update (Teachers' Edition)* 121 (26 May): 21-22.

Farmington (New Mexico) Daily Times. 1988a. American Indians' Images in Movies Haven't Changed (21 September): B4.

———. 1988b. Network Fighting Indian Stereotypes. (19 September): B6.

———. 1988c. Indian Values Still Important. (2 October): B2.

Freeman, Robert. 1971. *For Indians Only*. San Marcos, Calif.: Palomar Press.

Gilliland, Hap, and Jon Reyhner. 1988. *Teaching the Native American*. Dubuque, Iowa: Kendall/Hunt.

Haley, Francis, Susan Hustleby, and Regina McCormick. 1978. *Ethnic Studies Handbook for School Librarians*. Boulder, Colo.: Social Science Education Consortium.

Harjo, Suzan Shown. 1993. A Native American Guide to Indian Country. In *North American Indian Landmarks*, by George Cantor. Detroit: Visible Ink Press.

Hearne, Betsy. 1993a. Cite the Source: Reducing Cultural Chaos in Picture Books, Part One. *School Library Journal* 39 (July): 22-27.

———. 1993b. Respect the Source: Reducing Cultural Chaos in Picture Books, Part Two. *School Library Journal* 39 (August): 33-37.

Heinrich, June Sark. 1986-87. Native Americans: What Not to Teach. In *Fremont Unified School District Native American Studies Program*. Fremont, Calif.: Fremont Unified School District.

Henry, Jeanette. 1968. Textbook Distortion of the Indian. *Civil Rights Digest* 1 (Summer): 4-8.

Hill, Howard D. 1989. *Effective Strategies for Teaching Minority Students*. Bloomington, Ind.: National Educational Service.

Hillyer, Mildred. 1969. *Bibliography of Spanish and Southwestern Indian Culture Library Books*. ED 047 846. Bethesda, Md.: ERIC Document Reproduction Service.

Hirschfelder, Arlene B. 1973. *American Indian and Eskimo Authors: A Comprehensive Bibliography*. New York: Interbook.

———. 1982. *American Indian Stereotypes in the World of Children: A Reader and Bibliography*. Metuchen, N.J.: Scarecrow Press.

Idaho State Department of Education. 1970. *Indian Education: Books About Indians and Reference Materials*. Boise: Idaho State Department of Education.

Indian Education Advisory Committee. n.d. *American Indians of Utah: A Guide for Teachers*. Salt Lake City: Utah State Board of Education.

Jones, Malcolm, Jr. 1991. It's a Not So Small World. *Newsweek* 118 (9 September): 64-65.

———. 1993. Kid Lit's Growing Pains. *Newsweek* 122 (22 November): 54-58.

Jones, Malcolm, Jr., and Ray Sawhill. 1992. Just Too Good to Be True. *Newsweek* 118 (4 May): 68.

Klein, Barry T., ed. 1986. *Reference Encyclopedia of the American Indian*. 4th ed. New York: Todd Publications.

————. 1990. *Reference Encyclopedia of the American Indian*. 5th ed. New York: Todd Publications.

Klein, Bernard, and Daniel Icolari, eds. 1973. *Reference Encyclopedia of the American Indian*. New York: B. Klein.

Kluckhohn, Clyde, and Katherine Spencer. 1972. *A Bibliography of the Navajo Indians*. New York: J. J. Augustine.

Lass-Woodfin, Mary Jo, ed. 1978. *Books on American Indians and Eskimos: A Selection Guide for Children and Young Adults*. Chicago: American Library Association.

Lehman, David. 1985. In Praise of the Independent. *Newsweek* (25 July): 71-72.

Leland, John, and Marc Peyser. 1991. New Age Fable from an Old School Bigot? *Newsweek* 112 (14 October): 62.

Lincoln, Kenneth. 1983. *Native American Renaissance*. Berkeley: University of California Press.

Marken, Jack Walter. 1973. *The Indians and Eskimos of North America: A Bibliography of Books in Print Through 1972*. Vermillion, S. Dak.: Dakota Press.

Marker, Michael. 1992. The Education of Little Tree: What It Reveals About the Public Schools. *Phi Delta Kappan* 74 (November): 226-27.

Marsa, Linda. 1992. Talk Is Chief: When Seattle Spoke, Were Environmentalists Listening? *Omni* 15 (December): 15-18.

McElmeel, Sharron L. 1993. Towards a Real Multiculturalism. *School Library Journal* 39 (November): 50.

McWhorter, Diane. 1991. Little Tree, Big Lies. *People Weekly* 36 (28 October): 119-21.

McWilliams, Karen. 1993. Multicultural Books for Children. *The Writer* 106 (November): 22-25.

Metoyer, Cheryl A. 1978. American Indian People and Children's Resources. In *Cultural Pluralism and Children's Media*, compiled by Esther R. Dyer. Chicago: American Library Association.

Metts, W., Roback D., et al. 1991. Carving out a Niche. *Publishers Weekly* 238 (15 November): 36-38.

Nafziger, Alyce J. 1970. *American Indian Education: A Selected Bibliography*. ED 030 780. Bethesda, Md.: ERIC Document Reproduction Service.

National Advisory Council on Indian Education. 1976. *Third Annual Report to Congress of the United States.* Washington, D.C.: Government Printing Office.

National Commission on Excellence in Education. 1983. *A Nation at Risk: The Imperative for Educational Reform.* Washington, D.C.: Government Printing Office.

Paxton, S. Gabe. 1976. The Native American Indian. In *Ethnic American Minorities: A Guide to Media and Materials*, edited by Harry A. Johnson. New York: R. R. Bowker.

Pialorski, Frank, ed. 1974. *Teaching the Bilingual: New Methods and Old Traditions.* Tucson: University of Arizona Press.

Pomice, Eva. 1989. Small Has Never Looked So Beautiful. *U.S. News & World Report* (9 January): 49, 52.

Powell, Bill. 1988. Buying a Crown for Random House. *Newsweek* (2 August): 41.

Project Media. 1975. *Index to Bibliographic and Resource Materials.* Minneapolis, Minn.: National Indian Education Association.

———. 1978. *Media Evaluations and Disseminations by Indian Americans.* 2d ed. Minneapolis, Minn.: National Indian Education Association.

Querry, Ronald B. 1992. *Native Americans Struggle for Equality.* Vero Beach: Fl.: Rourke.

Reid C. 1991. Widow of "Little Tree" Author Admits He Changed Identity. *Publishers Weekly* 25 (October): 16-20.

Revai, Loretta Z. 1972. *An Annotated Bibliography of Selected Books About American Indians for Elementary Through High School Students.* ED 065 642. Bethesda, Md.: ERIC Document Reproduction Service.

Reyhner, Jon, ed. 1988. *Teaching the Indian Child: A Bilingual/Multicultural Approach.* Billings: Eastern Montana College.

Robinson, Antony Meredith. 1979. *Systematic Bibliography: A Practical Guide to the Work of Compilation.* 4th ed. with an additional chapter by Margaret Lodder. London: Clive Bingley.

Roessel, Robert A. 1979. *Navajo Education, 1948-1978: Its Progress and Its Problems.* Rough Rock, Ariz.: Navajo Curriculum Center.

Sanoff, Alvin P. 1984. Book Publishers Turn to a Happier Chapter. *U.S. News & World Report* 18 (June): 64-65.

School Library Journal. 1990. Kids Need Libraries: School and Public Libraries Preparing the Youth of Today for the World of Tomorrow. 36 (April): 33-37.

Shaughnessy, Tim. 1978. White Stereotypes of Indians. *Journal of American Indian Education* 17 (January): 20-24.

Shores, Louis, and Richard Krzys. 1978. Reference Books. In *Encyclopedia of Library and Information Science*. New York: Marcel Dekker.

Slapin, Beverly, and Doris Seale. 1988. *Books Without Bias: Through Indian Eyes*. Berkeley, Calif.: Oyate.

———. 1992. *Through Indian Eyes: The Native Experience in Books for Children*. Philadelphia, Pa.: New Society.

Smith, June. 1971. Guidelines for Evaluation of Indian Materials for Adults. *American Libraries* 2 (June): 610-11.

Stensland, Anna Lee. 1979. *Literature by and About the American Indian: An Annotated Bibliography*. 2d ed. Urbana, Ill.: National Council of Teachers of English.

Stone, James C., and Donald P. DeNevi. 1971. *Teaching Multi-Cultural Populations: Five Heritages*. New York: D. Van Nostrand.

United States Department of the Interior. 1972. *Indian Bibliography: Professional Library Collection*. Washington, D.C.: National Indian Training Center.

United States Senate. Special Subcommittee on Indian Education. 1969. *Indian Education: A National Tragedy—A National Challenge*. Washington, D.C.: Government Printing Office.

Vogel, Virgil J. 1968. The Indian in American History Textbooks. *Integrated Education* 6 (May/June): 16-32.

Waters, Frank. 1992. *Brave Are My People: Indian Heroes Not Forgotten*. Sante Fe, N. Mex.: Clear Light.

Wiget, Andrew. 1985. *Native American Literature*. Boston: Twayne.

Worsnop, Richard L. 1992. Native Americans. *CQ Researcher* 2 (8 May): 385-408.

Wynar, Bohdan S. 1967. *Introduction to Bibliography and Reference Work*. 4th ed. Littleton, Colo.: Libraries Unlimited.

———, ed. 1981. *Recommended Reference Books for Small and Medium-sized Libraries and Media Centers*. Littleton, Colo.: Libraries Unlimited.

Wynar, Christine Gehrt. 1981. *Guide to Reference Books for School Media Centers*. 2d ed. Littleton, Colo.: Libraries Unlimited.

Selected
American Indian
Bibliographies

Allen, Paula Gunn. *Studies in American Indian Literature: Critical Essays and Course Designs.* New York: Modern Language Association, 1983.

Antell, Will, and Lee Antell. *American Indians: An Annotated Bibliography of Selected Library Resources.* ED 040 004. Bethesda, Md.: ERIC Document Reproduction Service, 1970.

Bataille, Gretchen Mueller. *American Indian Literature: A Selected Bibliography for Iowa Schools.* ED 170 100. Bethesda, Md.: ERIC Document Reproduction Service, 1978.

————. *Inside the Cigar Store: Images of the American Indian.* Ames: Iowa State University Research Foundation, 1979.

Books About Indians. Carson City, Nev.: Department of Education, 1972.

Books About Indians. New York: Museum of the American Indian, Heye Foundation, 1977.

Bureau of Indian Affairs. *An Annotated Bibliography of Young People's Books on American Indians.* Washington, D.C.: Bureau of Indian Affairs, 1973.

Byler, Mary Gloyne. *American Indian Authors for Young Readers: A Selected Bibliography.* New York: Association on American Indian Affairs, 1973.

Byler, Mary Gloyne; Michael Dorris; and Arlene Hirschfelder. *A Source Bibliography in Native American Studies.* Chicago: American Library Association, 1979.

Caduto, Michael J., and Bruchac, Joseph. *Keepers of the Earth: Native American Stories and Environmental Activities for Children.* Golden, Colo.: Fulcrum, 1988.

Center for Indian Education. *North American Indians: An Annotated Resource Guide for the Elementary Teacher.* Tempe, Ariz.: Center for Indian Education, 1972.

61

Derman-Sparks, Louise, and the ABC Task Force. *Anti-Bias Curriculum: Tools for Empowering Young Children*. Washington, D.C.: National Association for the Education of Young Children, 1989.

Evans, Edward. *Bibliography of Language Arts Materials for Native North Americans, 1965-1977*. Los Angeles: University of California, 1977.

Fox, Sandra J. *An Annotated Bibliography of Young Peoples' Books on American Indians*. Washington, D.C.: Bureau of Indian Affairs, 1973.

Fremont Unified School District. *Ohoyo Ikhana: A Bibliography of American Indian–Alaska Native Curriculum Materials*. Fremont, Calif.: Fremont Unified School District, 1982.

Gallup McKinley County Schools. *Navajo and Zuni: A Bibliography of Selected Materials*. Gallup, N. Mex.: Gallup McKinley County Schools, 1975.

Gilliland, Hap. *Indian Children's Books*. Billings, Mont.: Council for Indian Education, 1980.

Hillyer, Mildred. *Bibliography of Spanish and Southwestern Indian Culture Library Books*. ED 047 846. Bethesda, Md.: ERIC Document Reproduction Service, 1969.

Hirschfelder, Arlene B. *American Indian Authors: A Representative Bibliography*. New York: Association on American Indian Affairs, 1970.

———. *American Indian and Eskimo Authors: A Comprehensive Bibliography*. New York: Interbook, 1973.

———. *American Indian Stereotypes in the World of Children: A Reader & Bibliography*. Metuchen, N.J.: Scarecrow Press, 1982.

Horne, Gerald, ed. *Thinking and Rethinking U.S. History*. New York: Council on Interracial Books for Children, 1988.

Hoyt, Anna K. *Indians of North America—For Young Adults: A Selected List*. Stillwater: Oklahoma State University, n.d.

Idaho State Department of Education. *Indian Education: Books About Indians and Reference Materials*. Boise: Idaho State Department of Education, 1970.

Indian Education Advisory Committee. *American Indians of Utah: A Guide for Teachers*. Salt Lake City: Utah State Board of Education, n.d.

Klein, Barry T., ed. *Reference Encyclopedia of the American Indian*. New York: Todd Publications, 1986.

———. *Reference Encyclopedia of the American Indian*. 5th ed. New York: Todd Publications, 1990.

Klein, Bernard, and Daniel Icolari, eds. *Reference Encyclopedia of the American Indian*. New York: B. Klein, 1973.

Klesner, Peg. *Beyond Hiawatha: A Bibliography of Juvenile Literature with Native Themes and Content (K-12)*. Vancouver: University of British Columbia, 1988.

Lass-Woodfin, Mary Jo, ed. *Books on American Indians and Eskimos: A Selection Guide for Children and Young Adults*. Chicago: American Library Association, 1978.

Lincoln, Kenneth. *Native American Renaissance*. Berkeley: University of California Press, 1983.

Marken, Jack Walter. *The Indians and Eskimos of North America: A Bibliography of Books in Print Through 1972*. Vermillion, S. Dak.: Dakota Press, 1973.

Nafziger, Alyce J. *American Indian Education: A Selected Bibliography*. ED 030 780. Bethesda, Md.: ERIC Document Reproduction Service, 1970.

Pilger. Mary Anne. *Multicultural Projects Index: Things to Make and Do to Celebrate Festivals, Cultures, and Holidays Around the World*. Englewood, Colo.: Libraries Unlimited, 1992.

Project Media. *Index to Bibliographic and Resource Materials*. Minneapolis, Minn.: National Indian Education Association, 1975.

———. *Media Evaluations and Disseminations by Indian Americans*. 2d ed. Minneapolis, Minn.: National Indian Education Association, 1978.

Revai, Loretta Z. *An Annotated Bibliography of Selected Books About American Indians for Elementary Through High School Students*. ED 065 642. Bethesda, Md.: ERIC Document Reproduction Service, 1972.

Ruoff, A. LaVonne Brown. *American Indian Literatures: An Introduction, Bibliographic Review, and Selected Bibliography*. New York: Modern Language Association of America, 1990.

Schniedewind, Nancy, and Ellen Davidson. *Open Minds: A Sourcebook of Learning Activities to Promote Race, Sex, Class and Age Equity*. New York: Prentice Hall Press, 1983.

Slapin, Beverly, and Doris Seale, eds. *Books Without Bias: Through Indian Eyes*. Berkeley, Calif.: Oyate. 1988.

———. *Through Indian Eyes: The Native Experience in Books for Children*. Philadelphia, Pa.: New Society. 1992.

Slapin, Beverly, and Rosemary Gonzales. *How to Tell the Difference: A Checklist for Evaluating Native Children's Books*. Berkeley, Calif.: Oyate, 1992.

Stensland, Anna Lee. *Literature by and About the American Indian: An Annotated Bibliography.* 2d ed. Urbana, Ill.: National Council of Teachers of English, 1979.

Swindler, Luke. *Guide to Reference Sources Dealing with North American Indians.* Grand Forks: North Dakota University, 1979.

Verrall, Catherine, and Patricia McDowell. *Resource Reading List, 1990: Annotated Bibliography of Resources by and About Native People.* Toronto: Canadian Alliance in Solidarity with Native People, 1990.

Wiget, Andrew. *Native American Literature.* Boston: Twayne, 1985.

Part 2

Annotated Bibliography of American Indian Books of Reference Value for Children and Young Adults

Introduction: Preparation
of the
Bibliography

Rationale

Many bibliographies on American Indian life have been published. However, most of the bibliographies published were not developed specifically to meet the reference needs of school-age children and educators who use school and public libraries. In most, three major elements are missing. First, the materials have not been evaluated with the Indian student as the primary user. Second, the resources have not been selected for inclusion and use in the school curriculum. Third, the books have not been evaluated for both Indian and non-Indian users. In addition, most bibliographies do not mention the importance of providing a core collection of American Indian printed materials of reference value in public and school libraries that serve American Indian students.

The annotated bibliography of American Indian books of reference value that follows this section can be useful to (1) school and public library professionals interested in building collections of American Indian materials for children and young adults, (2) teachers wanting to include American Indian materials in their curricula or needing supplementary reading materials pertinent to the study of the American Indian, and (3) Indian and non-Indian students seeking access to quality materials on American Indians.

In an American Library Association publication, Metoyer (1978, 13-25) states that American Indian students in public, private, and government schools are the major consumers of materials focusing on North American tribes. In many cases, the selection of materials for those patrons has not been based specifically on evaluation criteria for accurate and authentic materials, nor has the bibliography of sources been based on the reading abilities, interests, and curriculum needs of American Indian young people. Therefore, this annotated bibliography of American Indian books of reference value was created with an emphasis on understanding the educational needs and values of American Indian people and using evaluation criteria that incorporate an awareness of stereotypical myths perpetuated by much of the literature. Use of the evaluative criteria checklist (see pp. 37-39) helps to identify materials to be included or rejected.

The core collection in the bibliography contains three components essential for usability as basic references in school and public library collections: (1) specific evaluation criteria for selection of Indian literature, (2) major Dewey Decimal classification areas, and (3) annotations emphasizing application to instructional needs. Following the bibliography are a directory of addresses of all publishers whose materials are listed here, an alphabetical index of titles and authors, and a

67

subject index. Each book selected can be used for reference, consulted for specific information, and used for answers to specific questions.

The selected bibliography for a satellite collection on American Indians lists more than 200 titles that can serve as a basic collection. Additional titles can and should be added as need and financial resources dictate. Selected materials are limited to those of reading levels appropriate for elementary, middle, and secondary school students. The bibliography is selective rather than comprehensive in order to disseminate American Indian literature that meets the needs of the users. The form of the materials is limited to printed materials, mainly books, either paperback or hardcover.

Development

Of the titles included in the "Selected American Indian Bibliographies," (pp. 61-64) eighteen bibliographies have direct application. Six of these were prepared by American Indians: Bataille 1978, 1979; Byler 1973; Lass-Woodfin 1978; and Seale in Slapin and Seale, 1988, 1992. Two titles were written by an American Indian organization whose staff and evaluators are Indians (Project Media 1975, 1978). Eight bibliographies were prepared by persons or organizations involved in the field of education (Bataille 1978, 1979; Hillyer 1969; Hirschfelder 1970, 1973, 1982; Indian Education Advisory Committee n. d.; Idaho State Department of Education 1970; Lass-Woodfin 1978; Revai 1972; Slapin and Seale 1988, 1992; and Stensland 1979).

Although none were developed specifically for secondary school students, nine include references to secondary students, either in special sections or as part of the designated audience. Seven bibliographies were prepared for general use, and therefore are more comprehensive than selective compilations: Hirschfelder 1973; Klein and Icolari 1973; Klein 1986, 1990; Marken 1973; and Project Media 1975, 1978. Fiction entries are combined with nonfiction entries in sixteen of the bibliographies.

Some excellent bibliographies that list American Indian books can be located in current references on multicultural literature (Pilger 1992; Derman-Sparks 1989; and Schniedewind and Davidson 1983). Bibliographies located in new additions to the selected bibliography are Caduto and Bruchac 1988; Horne 1988; Ruoff 1990; and Verrall and McDowell 1990. These sources provided recommendations for recent books.

The 7,203 books considered for possible inclusion in this bibliography were gleaned from the "Selected American Indian Bibliographies" at the end of part 1, and included 2,529 titles found in other sources. From the entries, approximately 3,500 were selected as suitable for further evaluation. New entries were included as they were located or published. A tabulation of the entries found in the bibliographies shows that approximately one out of every twenty was recommended more than once. However, of those entries that had more than one recommendation, only (approximately) one out of every ten had three or more titles from those entries found in the "Selected American Indian Bibliographies." The bibliographers do not appear to be in agreement on their choices; this probably reflects the bibliographers varying rationales for their lists.

Approximately one of every three titles in the researched bibliographies is fiction. Many authors include as many fiction entries as nonfiction entries. Fiction titles are not separated from nonfiction titles. If users of the bibliography are not familiar with a title, they might have difficulty identifying it as fiction or nonfiction. Only when the bibliographer includes the words *fiction* or *novel* in the annotation can the title be clearly differentiated from nonfiction.

Bibliographers vary in their annotations. Most include a brief annotation, but few mention the curricular use of the material. Most annotations contain little information about authority, scope, presentation, or format—the four items listed as important by *The Encyclopedia of Library and Information Science* (Shores and Krzys 1978).

A review of the located bibliographies reveals that some bibliographers merely assembled their entries without the application of any criteria, while others selected entries on the basis of certain specifications. The background of the bibliographers usually influences the type of bibliography developed and the standards imposed. Although these bibliographies may provide a valuable source of information for library patrons looking for books on American Indian subjects, the bibliographies do not fulfill the need for students and teachers seeking books of reference value that adequately meet the proposed curriculum and reference criteria.

Those entries that had been listed in two or more bibliographies were examined if they could be located. The first step in the evaluation process was the application of the Fry reading level, which established whether a book was suitable for school-age children, grades one through twelve, in terms of reading difficulty. To expedite the evaluation, the MECC School Utilities Readability computer program (volume 2, version 1.0) was used to determine readability. Three to five sample passages of 100 or more words were copied from the beginning, middle, and end of the book for evaluation. After the selections were edited for corrections, the program provided six readability tests to analyze the sample passages: Spache, Dale-Chall, Fry, Raygor, Gunning-Fog, and Flesch. The Fry test was used to determine the readability level for books included in the annotated bibliography. The results of this test provide the readability level as well as additional information. The test records the number of times each word is included in a passage. The following items are also analyzed: number of sentences, number of words, number of syllables, words of six or more letters, words with three or more syllables, percentage of words with three or more syllables, average sentence length, average letters per word, and average syllables per word. The Fry test can be compared with other readability tests in the same computer program. The use of a similar program is recommended as the media specialist or teacher reviews other materials for a collection of American Indian resources.

Determining the reading level will assist the library professional in purchasing materials. However, appropriate readability is very difficult to determine, because it includes sentence length and difficulty of vocabulary. Gilliland is also concerned with "how well the sentence construction, vocabulary, and means of expression match that of the reader, and how the content fits the student's background, and his desire to read" (Gilliland and Reyhner 1988, 97). Although a reading formula provides the librarian with an indication of the age level for which the materials may be suitable and will assist in eliminating materials that are inappropriate, the reading level will not indicate how the material will be received by Indian students.

Approximately four out of every five books were eliminated because the material presented was inaccurate or too difficult for the reading level of the intended age level of the students. Other books were eliminated because the style of writing was too elementary, detailed, uninteresting, or sophisticated for the clientele. For example, the material in books by ethnologists often held little interest for the secondary school students and often had limited application in the curriculum. Some books were also eliminated because of the lack of illustrative material, which is very important in determining immediate interest for the reader with second-language skills.

If the reading level was judged to be suitable for school-age children, the annotations provided in the bibliographies were studied and a review of the book by an Indian author or Indian organization was read, if available. If the book still met the criteria for inclusion, the work was read and thoroughly examined. The evaluation form on pages 37-39 was filled out and the results noted. If the work was judged to be of reference value, an annotation was written. Many books, approximately four out of every five examined, were found to be inappropriate in some area of the evaluation criteria.

Books selected for inclusion had to be located in either the current *Books in Print*, a publisher's catalog, or public and school libraries. (Because some of the publishing houses are small and specialized, their books are not always included in *Books in Print.*)

Entries in the bibliography for each book include author, title, place of publication, publisher, date, and number of pages. In addition, the Fry reading level, Sears subject headings for content of the text, and Dewey Decimal classification area are provided. All entries are alphabetized by the author's last name within the broad Dewey Decimal classification area. Prices are not included because they frequently change. However, purchasers can check *Books in Print* or consult publishers' catalogs.

School and public library professionals who wish to select the most appropriate reference books on American Indian literature will be able to use the annotated bibliography to develop a basic satellite collection. The reference books are selected on the basis of authority of the author, scope of the subject matter, and treatment in the writing of American Indian life. The lengthy annotations provide information for the reader to accurately judge the book as well as determine its use in the school curriculum.

References

Bataille, Gretchen Mueller. 1978. *American Indian Literature: A Selected Bibliography for Iowa Schools*. ED 170 100. Bethesda, Md.: ERIC Document Reproduction Service.

―――. 1979. *Inside the Cigar Store: Images of the American Indian*. Ames: Iowa State University Research Foundation.

Byler, Mary Gloyne. 1973. *American Indian Authors for Young Readers: A Selected Bibliography in Native American Studies*. Chicago: American Library Association.

Caduto, Michael J., and Joseph Bruchac. 1988. *Keepers of the Earth: Native American Stories and Environmental Activities for Children*. Golden, Colo.: Fulcrum.

Derman-Sparks, Louise, and the ABC Task Force. 1989. *Anti-Bias Curriculum: Tools for Empowering Young Children*. Washington, D.C.: National Association for the Education of Young Children.

Gilliland, Hap, and Jon Reyhner. 1988. *Teaching the Native American*. Dubuque, Iowa: Kendall/Hunt.

Hillyer, Mildred. 1969. *Bibliography of Spanish and Southwestern Indian Culture Library Books*. ED 047 846. Bethesda, Md.: ERIC Document Reproduction Service.

Hirschfelder, Arlene B. 1970. *American Indian Authors: A Representative Bibliography*. New York: Association on American Indian Affairs.

————. 1973. *American Indian and Eskimo Authors: A Comprehensive Bibliography*. New York: Interbook.

————. 1982. *American Indian Stereotypes in the World of Children: A Reader and Bibliography*. Metuchen, N.J.: Scarecrow Press.

Horne, Gerald, ed. 1988. *Thinking and Rethinking U.S. History*. New York: Council on Interracial Books for Children.

Idaho State Department of Education. 1970. *Indian Education: Books About Indians and Reference Materials*. Boise: Idaho State Department of Education.

Indian Education Advisory Committee. n.d. *American Indians of Utah: A Guide for Teachers*. Salt Lake City: Utah State Board of Education.

Kent, Allen, et al. 1978. *Encyclopedia of Library and Information Science (ELIS)*. New York: Dekker.

Klein, Barry T., ed. 1986. *Reference Encyclopedia of the American Indian*. 4th ed. New York: Todd Publications.

————. 1990. *Reference Encyclopedia of the American Indian*. 5th ed. New York: Todd Publications.

Klein, Bernard, and Daniel Icolari, eds. 1973. *Reference Encyclopedia of the American Indian*. New York: B. Klein.

Lass-Woodfin, Mary Jo, ed. 1978. *Books on American Indians and Eskimos: A Selection Guide for Children and Young Adults*. Chicago: American Library Association.

Marken, Jack Walter. 1973. *American Indian Education: A Selected Bibliography*. ED 030 780. Bethesda, Md.: ERIC Document Reproduction Service.

Metoyer, Cheryl A. 1978. American Indian People and Children's Resources. In *Cultural Pluralism and Children's Media,* compiled by Esther R. Dyer. Chicago: American Library Association.

Pilger, Mary Anne. 1992. *Multicultural Projects Index: Things to Make and Do to Celebrate Festivals, Cultures, and Holidays Around the World.* Englewood, Colo.: Libraries Unlimited.

Project Media. 1975. *Index to Bibliographic and Resource Materials.* Minneapolis, Minn.: National Indian Education Association.

———. 1978. *Media Evaluations and Disseminations by Indian Americans.* 2d ed. Minneapolis, Minn.: National Indian Education Association.

Revai, Loretta Z. 1972. *An Annotated Bibliography of Selected Books About American Indians for Elementary Through High School Students.* ED 065 642. Bethesda, Md.: ERIC Document Reproduction Service.

Ruoff, A. LaVonne Brown. 1990. *American Indian Literatures: An Introduction, Bibliographic Review, and Selected Bibliography.* New York: Modern Language Association of America.

Schniedewind, Nancy, and Ellen Davidson. 1983. *Open Minds: A Sourcebook of Learning Activities to Promote Race, Sex, Class and Age Equity.* New York: Prentice Hall Press.

Shores, Louis, and Richard Krzys. 1978. "Reference Books" in *Encyclopedia of Library and Information Science.* New York: Marcel Dekker.

Slapin, Beverly, and Doris Seale. 1988. *Books Without Bias: Through Indian Eyes.* Berkeley, Calif.: Oyate.

———. 1992. *Through Indian Eyes: The Native Experience in Books for Children.* Philadelphia, Pa.: New Society.

Slapin, Beverly, and Rosemary Gonzales. 1992. *How to Tell the Difference: A Checklist for Evaluating Native Children's Books.* Berkeley, Calif.: Oyate.

Stensland, Anna Lee. 1979. *Literature by and About the American Indian: An Annotated Bibliography.* 2d ed. Urbana, Ill.: National Council of Teachers of English.

Verrall, Catherine, and Patricia McDowell. 1990. *Resource Reading List, 1990: Annotated Bibliography of Resources by and About Native People.* Toronto: Canadian Alliance in Solidarity with Native People.

Selected, Annotated Bibliography of American Indian Books of Reference Value for School-Age Children

Books selected for inclusion in this bibliography are listed alphabetically by the author's last name under the major Dewey Decimal classification areas. The Fry readability test was used to determine reading level. This level (FRL) merely *suggests* the grade level. Library professionals will recognize that a book may be appropriate for younger and/or older readers, depending on their reading ability and interest level. Subject headings included for the annotated bibliographies were selected from H. W. Wilson's *Sears List of Subject Headings* (14th ed., 1991). The main subject heading "Indians of North America" should be assumed.

000-099 General Works

1. Furtaw, Julia C. **Native Americans Information Directory.** Detroit: Gale Research, 1993. 371p. FRL: 9. Subject: Directories.
   School and public libraries will find the first edition of the *Native Americans Information Directory* a valuable source for those seeking addresses relating to American Indian topics. Included are more than 4,500 resources: organizations, agencies, institutions, programs, services, and publications. They steer the reader to information on Native American culture, heritage, education, social concerns, politics, and employment. The directory covers North American Indians, Native Alaskans, and Native Hawaiians.
   Organized into five sections titled "Descriptive Listings," information resources are targeted specifically to groups of native peoples. The first four divisions include American Indians, Alaska Natives, Aboriginal Canadians, and Native Hawaiians. The fifth division, General Resources, addresses the needs and concerns of Indians, Eskimos, Metis, Inuits, and Native Hawaiians in general. Each section provides fifteen categories of information sources. The first six sections are alphabetic listings of (1) Tribal communities by state; (2) National organizations; (3) Regional, state/provincial, and local organizations; (4) Federal government agencies; (5) Federal Domestic Assistance Programs; and (6) State/provincial and local government agencies. The next three areas provide researchers with sources of (7) Library collections, (8) Museum collections, and (9) Research centers. Sections (10) Educational programs and services, (11) Studies Programs, and (12) Scholarships, fellowships, and loans are invaluable for native students seeking

educational opportunities. The last three listings, (13) Print and broadcast media, (14) Publishers, and (15) Videos, are the most difficult sources for educators to locate.

Entries include complete contact data: name, address, telephone number, and the name of a contact person. The Master Name and Keyword Index is helpful to the researcher and provides access to all entries. Former or alternate names and subjects that appear within the entry text are also indexed.

The Native American Information Directory has broad appeal in public and school libraries. Students can locate sources for specific tribes. Indian ancestry can be traced. Trips to Indian reservations can be planned. The comprehensive coverage eliminates the need to consult numerous and hard-to-find sources.

Although the book's primary value is for research purposes, school counselors will appreciate the listing of colleges and universities with Native American studies programs. Included are financial aid resources for all levels of postsecondary education. Schools and public libraries will find this book an invaluable aid to Native American sources of print and media materials that are difficult to locate.

2. Klein, Barry T., ed. **Reference Encyclopedia of the American Indian.** 5th ed. New York: Todd Publications, 1990. 1078p. FRL: 10. Subjects: Biography; Encyclopedias and dictionaries; Reservations; Politics and government; Museums; Education; Periodicals; Bibliography.

In the fifth edition of the *Reference Encyclopedia of the American Indian*, Klein condenses the previous two-volume work (published in 1986) into a massive single volume. Information has been added and updated in this standard reference on contemporary Indian affairs. The compilation of related source materials on the American Indian is organized by category, and listings are arranged either alphabetically or geographically. The directory lists organizations, persons, and print and nonprint materials about Native Americans in the United States and Canada.

Information is organized in four major sections by topic. Arranged alphabetically by state, section 1 provides names and addresses of reservations, tribal councils, government agencies, associations, craft centers, health facilities, Indian schools and colleges, and information centers. All colleges included offer courses in Native American history and culture. In section 2, the same type of directory information is furnished for Canada. The bibliography of in-print books in section 3 contains approximately 3,500 entries, arranged alphabetically by title and indexed by subject. The list is good, but not inclusive. Arranged by title, each entry includes ordering information and price. Books for children and young adults are marked with an asterisk. Although one cannot locate titles by author, there are indexes for publishers and broad subjects. These three sections comprised volume 1 of the fourth edition.

In section 4, which was volume 2 of the fourth edition, is a "Who's Who" with over 2,400 names of contemporary Indians and non-Indians active in Indian affairs. Biographies of American Indians focus on people in Indian affairs, business, arts, and professions. Individuals who are non-Indian are recognized in the fields of Indian affairs, history, art, anthropology, archaeology, and other areas. Each biography includes a brief outline of the person's professional life. The biographical data, compiled primarily from questionnaires, focuses on professional achievements.

All information is gathered from research questionnaires and may need to be supplemented with other reliable published sources. Many important books and well-known Native American facilities are omitted. Information data on some college course offerings is incomplete. The volume also has some typographical errors. Klein's reference will be useful for research if patrons are made aware of the content areas. Multiple subject listings will facilitate the use of this reference work. Biographical information on many of those included is difficult to locate, as is information in the other areas. School and public libraries that have the earlier edition may not need to purchase this one. If they do not hold the earlier edition, this volume provides a wealth of useful information.

3. Lass-Woodfin, Mary Jo. **Books on American Indians and Eskimos: A Selection Guide for Children and Young Adults.** Chicago: American Library Association, 1978. 237p. FRL: N/A. Subject: Bibliography.

This selection guide and annotated bibliography of 804 fiction and nonfiction books for children and young adults is unique in that the evaluations were prepared by Native Americans. Each title was read by at least two reviewers, and the lengthy annotations include a summary of the reviewers' thoughts, including differences of opinion. Brief information on the reviewers is included.

The materials by and about American Indians and Eskimos were selected from a variety of sources, including church publications and little-known publishers. Another unusual feature of the bibliography is the inclusion of materials that reflect diversity in attitudes toward the Indian people. Most bibliographers only include the best books they can locate for their stated purpose in their bibliographies. However, Lass-Woodfin includes a classification of "good," "adequate," or "poor" for the books included. Grade level for readability is also indicated.

The index, arranged alphabetically, provides access to entries by tribe, person, and events. Because the annotated selections emphasize information about and understanding of contemporary and historical cultures, this book can provide library professionals and teachers with guidelines and sources for selection of Native American and Eskimo books for young people.

4. Stensland, Anna Lee. **Literature by and About the American Indian: An Annotated Bibliography.** 2d ed. Urbana, Ill.: National Council of Teachers of English, 1979. 382p. FRL: N/A. Subjects: Bibliography; Stereotypes.

This annotated bibliography and excellent introduction to the literature by and about the American Indian should be considered essential in any school or public library serving American Indian youth. The bibliography includes over 775 titles on the American Indian in North American and Mexico. The selection emphasis was on the literature of the Native Americans: mythology, legends, poetry, fiction, and biography, including new titles on the Native American experience, historical studies, and oral literature of tribal times. Other areas, such as history and anthropology, are not neglected. Books are organized by type, such as fiction or biography. Material for all grade levels, from elementary through high school, is included. Over 200 books for elementary students, selected and annotated by Anne M. Fadan, will also be useful for the teacher who needs high-interest, low-reading-level materials for students with special needs.

The lengthy introduction should be required for all educators who plan to incorporate any material on the American Indian into the curriculum, and especially those who have American Indian students in their classrooms. Even if the educators do not teach American Indian students, they could benefit from reading this material because the American Indian is an essential part of American history and literature. Stensland's discussions of the important themes in Indian literature, Indian stereotypes in the literature, and recent trends in Indian literature provide a basis for careful selection of books.

The annotated bibliography can serve students looking for quality American Indian literature. Most of the titles have been published since 1973. A chapter for teachers provides a guide to curriculum planning, a basic library of Indian literature, and sources for additional material. Brief biographical sketches of fifty-four notable American Indian authors are also included. This book should be considered an essential selection tool for teachers and library professionals serving American Indian students.

5. Yenne, Bill. **The Encyclopedia of North American Indian Tribes: A Comprehensive Study of Tribes from the Abitibi to the Zuni.** New York: Arch Cape Press, 1986. 191p. FRL: 10. Subject: Encyclopedias and dictionaries.

North American Indian tribes existing since prehistoric times are alphabetically listed in encyclopedic format. Included are tribes that are extinct and those with fewer than fifty members, as well as those with more than 50,000 members that continue to flourish in this century. Concise information on (1) geographic region, (2) linguistic group, (3) principal dwelling type, and (4) principal subsistence type as practiced when the tribe first made contact with European civilization is provided for each entry. Emphasizing the diversity of the indigenous people, each article explores the group lifeway, the impact of white settlement and warfare, and changes in cultural identity. The 1985 statistics on tribal populations are especially valuable for research.

Condensed articles contain engaging facts that can be used by students from the fifth grade through high school. The oversized book is profusely illustrated with full-color and black-and-white photographs and art. All contain captions that complement and extend information found in the text. Because the tribes are listed alphabetically in the text, the index provides references to specific individuals, reservations, important events, and other terms not cataloged. The pictorial appeal and easily accessed specific information will make this beautiful volume popular with both browsers and researchers.

100-199 Philosophy and Related Disciplines

6. Amon, Aline. **The Earth Is Sore: Native Americans on Nature.** New York: Atheneum, 1981. 90p. FRL: 6. Subjects: Philosophy; Poetry; Nature in poetry.

Concerned with the ecological welfare of the earth, Aline Amon selects Native American songs, prayers, and statements whose eloquent and touching words express her feelings about nature. *The Earth Is Sore* focuses on the interrelationship between humans and their environment in areas of conservation of natural resources, reverence for living things, and rights of ownership. The differences that exist between Native American and non-Native American philosophies concerning the natural world are explored.

In the introduction the author shares her belief in the kinship of man and nature. If the land and air become polluted and the animals die, so will humans. She urges readers to heed the thoughts and ideas of the Native American people and become aware of abuse of the planet and its life. "The earth is sore," she states and pleads for healing.

The first part of the anthology celebrates the traditional Native American philosophy that the earth endures and provides. Living in harmony with nature, these people offer prayers and songs as they rejoice in intimate communion with nature, as demonstrated in the poem "Mouse Song" and in the Navajo testament concerning the return to their homeland, "We Loved It So."

With the coming of the white people came the concept of ownership, a view foreign to the native people, who looked on the world as belonging to everyone. The writings in the last part of the collection are laments for the abuse of "mother earth." The words ask thoughtful questions: "How can you sell the sky?" "What is a man without the beasts of the earth?" "Did you know that the trees can talk?" For those not familiar with the philosophy of Native Americans, each selection will provide a startling and fresh insight.

The author's notes at the bottom of each offering give the tribal origin and the cultural or historical significance. On the opposite page she illustrates the piece with delicate black-and-white collage prints using natural materials. For the reader's use, a table of contents and appended list of original sources are provided.

Classified as philosophy, this collection of Native American passages can be used individually or as a group for stimulating reading or discussion in many diverse subject areas, such as science, language arts, and social studies. The book is recommended for students with reading levels in grades five through twelve for three reasons: the vocabulary is fairly simple, the selections are different from those found in most Native American collections, and the words that express the philosophy are memorable. Although the thrust is highly personal, Aline Amon's concern is universal. Her carefully crafted plea, through the words of the Native American people, to preserve and respect the land and animals offers the reader an opportunity to reflect on nature from a different perspective.

7.   Bierhorst, John. **The Mythology of North America.** New York: William Morrow, 1985. 259p. FRL: 10. Subjects: Religion; Mythology.

This paperback guide to the study of Native American mythology presents an understanding of the vast plethora of Indian lore termed "old, sacred, or true" by its informants. The major themes and stories of gods and heroes of eleven major regions are outlined, from the Far North storytellers of the Arctic to the emergence tales of the Southwest, from the Western coastal ceremonies to the lost lore of the Eastern seaboard.

Many mythical stories are embedded in the cultural life of contemporary Indian people. The clever tricksters Coyote, Raven, Spider, and Hare; the gods and goddesses of nature and creation; and the little people and monsters inhabit the traditional literature. Bierhorst recognizes the similarity of some themes to the larger body of world culture but also emphasizes the uniqueness of specific tribal myths.

The discussion of the genre mythology and major stories for each geographic area is supported by Indian artwork throughout the text, from the traditional "Navajo Shooting Chant" ceremony sandpainting to the modern acrylic "When Coyote Leaves the Res." Tribal maps note key story locations. An index provides easy access to this excellent reference, and the author's notes on sources support the scholarship.

Not intended merely as a collection of myths, this volume offers a concise, organized summary of the most important and powerful myths of the native people of North America. Young adults and literature teachers will find the material captivating and gain understanding of the role of traditional mythology in the lives of American Indian and Eskimo people.

8. McLuhan, T. C. **Touch the Earth: A Self-Portrait of Indian Existence.** New York: Promontory Press, 1971. 185p. FRL: 8. Subjects: Philosophy; Ecology; Oratory.

T. C. McLuhan has collected artistic statements and writings by North American Indians from the sixteenth to the twentieth centuries. This outstanding and powerful collection of literature sheds light on the course of Indian history and the abiding values of Indian life. Arranged in four chronological sections, the historical and contemporary speeches range from the humorous to the eloquent, from the lyrical to the emotional. Even though the Indians relate the values that distinguish Indian life, their real message for all people today is the value of living in harmony with nature and regarding the land as a sacred creation. All passages speak of respect and courtesy for the land, animals, and objects, which are the Indian peoples' heritage. American Indians traditionally have not believed in people imposing their will on the environment. Consequently, many passages represent the Indians' hope that, through understanding their philosophy, the environment will be preserved. The author postulates that America's future lies in the adoption of the Indian philosophy of a harmonious relationship with the land and its resources to avoid destruction of nature and the consequent destruction of man.

Sepia-toned photographs by Edward S. Curtis from the early years of this century provide a record of North American Indian life. The pictures are identified only by tribe or name of the person. The book does not include an index of the contributors to the text, nor a list of illustrations. The author has included notes on some selections, sources for the text, and lists for further reading.

The collection is highly recommended for all middle and secondary school students because it presents a humanistic philosophy that will provide an understanding of the Native American's affinity and alliance with nature. Although Indian life is sometimes romanticized, the thought-provoking material should be useful in teaching literature, sociology, and speech classes as well as for personal enjoyment. This selection contains many excellent quotations and is a good source for developing appreciation of North American tribal culture and philosophy.

200-299 Religion

9. Bierhorst, John, ed. **Four Masterworks of American Indian Literature: Quetzalcoatl, the Ritual of Condolence, Cuceb, the Night Chant.** New York: Farrar, Straus & Giroux, 1974. 371p. FRL: 10. Subjects: Religion; Spiritualism.

John Bierhorst selected four major works of American Indian literature from noted translations as a step toward establishing outstanding examples of the cultures that produced them. In the commentaries and new or compiled translations,

Bierhorst presents an accurate account of four civilizations. Each selection has an excellent introduction and is followed by notes and a bibliography.

The first selection, about Quetzalcoatl, an Aztec deity, is a myth of death and revival. Bierhorst provides the first complete English translation of this hero myth. The next item, the Iroquois ritual of condolence, is composed of interlocking texts. This ritual is performed when a high chief dies so that his successor will inherit not only his position, but also his name. The third major work is the Cuceb, a Maya prophecy, whereby a priest seeks to deliver his people from an alien ruling class. The last major work, the Navajo night chant, was recorded by Washington Matthews in the late 1800s and is still performed today as a healing ceremony, an occasion for religious revival.

The literary works are explained in great detail, including information on their origin. The text is accurate and authentic and should be valuable to libraries and literature classes. The detailed index is excellent. Also included are text figures for the works and maps of the areas, with preference given to aboriginal place names.

10. Bierhorst, John, ed. **The Sacred Path: Spells, Prayers, and Power Songs of the American Indian.** New York: William Morrow, 1983. 192p. FRL: 9. Subjects: Poetry; Religion; Mythology.

People of the Native American cultures of North and South America believe that the power in words used in prayers, songs, and spells affects their lives. Language, when used at the proper time and in the proper way, connects the Indian people to the "sacred path" of their religious and cultural beliefs.

Bierhorst assembles ritual poetry in a thematic anthology that begins with birth as prayers are offered to protect the child and make it strong. As the child grows up, ritual ceremonies and initiations may be performed to prepare the boy for manhood and the girl for womanhood. During adult life, the individual may call on the power of the word for love songs and magic, to travel, against sickness and evil, for weather control, to plant and gather, and for hunting success. At the end of life, prayers are offered for the survivors and the dead.

To present the relationship between the life of an Indian person and the power of spoken words, Bierhorst selects poetry from more than fifty Indian tribes. Illustrations of American Indian fetishes and prayer sticks introduce each thematic subject. These objects were used to make prayers more effective and increase the power of the user.

This authoritative collection has a table of contents, scholarly notes, bibliographic references, and a glossary of tribes, culture, and languages. Young adult readers will gain an appreciation of traditional Indian poetry and an understanding of Native American life. Public and school librarians will find the book an important addition to the field of American literature.

11. Burland, Cottie. **North American Indian Mythology.** New York: Bedrick Books, 1985. 144p. FRL: 9. Subjects: Religion; Mythology.

To appreciate and understand the culture and history of any group of people, one must include their mythology. The interwoven tapestry of Native American mythology contains some common threads. However, this survey recognizes that the mythology also has distinctive motifs for each tribal group. Through search and study of the early records, the author guides the reader to the body of myths about the origin and history of eight major geographic groups, from the Eskimos of the North to the Mesa dwellers in the South. Each chapter introduces the influences of the environment on the people's lives and the development of their beliefs, including the principal deities and heroes, nature myths, and ceremonial life. The volume, first published in 1965 and revised in 1985 by Marion Wood, is not a collection of myths but a study of North American lore as a vital living force that affects all facets of tribal life.

More than 125 black-and-white and color photographs of American Indian artifacts (with captions) are incorporated into the text to show the intertwining of craftsmanship and mythology. The comprehensive text and index make this volume an excellent choice for public and school libraries to add to their American Indian collections.

12. Clark, Ella E. **Guardian Spirit Quest.** Billings, Mont.: Council for Indian Education, 1974. 36p. FRL: 4. Subject: Religion.

The quest for a guardian spirit for an Indian youth was considered very significant by tribal people. Most young Indian children were carefully prepared by their elders to seek a spirit in the proper way. The spirits took many forms and gave those to whom they appeared special powers, songs, and new names. The stories of the young seekers—of the great hunter and scout with the spirit of the wolf, of a warrior with power from the sun and moon, and of a healer with strength from the buffalo—are recalled. Some did not search for a guardian spirit. The spirit in the form of a large, blood-stained grizzly bear appeared to a young Nez Perce youth three times to give him protection from battle wounds. The tearful adventures of a young Salish girl's healing gifts from a grizzly and her cubs are recounted by her granddaughter.

This small, inexpensive paperback was selected and approved by an Indian editorial board for publication as an authentic, educational book for young readers. The simple, unadorned stories provide information about the cultural heritage of American Indian children. The retold narratives are illustrated by Alex Bull Tail.

13. Deloria, Vine, Jr. **God Is Red.** New York: Grosset & Dunlap, 1973. 376p. FRL: 12. Subject: Religion.

Vine Deloria, a controversial Indian spokesman, challenges the effectiveness of Christianity in the United States. Analyzing contemporary American theology and its effects on social issues, he contends that the church has failed and maintains that God should be sought on the North American continent and among its first inhabitants, the Indians. He places emphasis on the premise of land and God.

Filled with contemporary sources and issues, Deloria's book offers an alternative to Christianity through return to Indian beliefs and concepts. The thought-provoking ideas will stimulate perceptive eleventh- and twelfth-grade readers to consider critical issues. Although the material ranges from ancient to contemporary, primary modern sources and issues are stressed in the text and accompanying appendixes.

14. Highwater, Jamake. **Ritual of the Wind: North American Indian Ceremonies, Music, and Dance.** New York: Alfred Van Der Marck Editions, 1984. 199p. FRL: 12. Subjects: Religion; Rites and ceremonies; Anthropology; Songs and music.

Indian writer Jamake Highwater presents an intimate account of Indian ceremonies, as opposed to the detached version of myths written by many non-Indian writers. In the new and revised edition, a broad overview of traditional and modern Indian ceremonies of dance and music is accompanied by rare pictures of dances and rituals obtained from museums and historical societies. Detailed captions of each ceremony are combined with an informative philosophical text based on an Indian viewpoint.

The author's prelude, "On the Trail of the Wind," especially valuable to the non-Indian reader, defines the Indian concept of tribal as well as personal privacy. The reader is culturally initiated into the concept that Indian people do not need to "be the same" to be equal. He concludes that Indian people retain the right to a special relationship to their own world of reality through ritualistic dance, song, and music.

North American Indian music is distinctive for its use of drums, rattles, and flutes, and for its unique vocal quality. Personal and tribal songs relate life and death processes from the viewpoint of culture and are valued for their power.

Inserted throughout the text are sepia-toned illustrations of four different tribal ceremonies and transcriptions of oral texts. The purification ritual of the Navajo, the Night Chant or Yeibichai, continues as a contemporary ceremony of one of the largest tribes in the United States. The drama of the Tewa Rain-Power ceremony, held only in the ceremonial chambers, is restricted to tribal members. A ceremony whose original purpose was desire for offspring, the Pawnee Hako Ceremony, was later changed to insure peace and friendship between different clans or tribes. One of the most powerful ceremonies celebrating the drastic change in the lifestyle of the Plains Indians, the Sun Dance, is performed as a search for the renewal of communion with the earth, sun, and the supernatural.

The appendix provides valuable information for those wishing to attend Indian events. A calendar is provided with an introduction explaining acceptable manners for non-Indians wishing to attend Indian ceremonies and dances. The general geographic area, approximate time of year, location, and name of the event are listed. In addition to the selected bibliography and photography credits, librarians and readers should note the discography of American Indian music records, which includes the names and addresses of record companies. Because the photographs are such an important part of this book, the index includes page numbers referring to the extensive, informative text provided for each picture. Readers will gain insight into Native American ceremonial life both as the religious rites of the past and as a living presence in Indian life today.

15. Hirschfelder, Arlene, and Paulette Molin. **The Encyclopedia of Native American Religions: An Introduction.** New York: Facts on File, 1992. 367p. FRL: 10. Subjects: Religion and mythology—Encyclopedias; Rites and ceremonies—Encyclopedias.

Native American religious issues frequently make the news, but the public understands little about Native American religions. *The Encyclopedia of Native American Religions* addresses the spiritual traditions and religious practices of Native Americans in the United States and Canada. Hirschfelder and Molin accord these native traditions respect, carefully maintaining a balance between providing relevant information and avoiding specific descriptions that would offend native people.

In an encyclopedic format, the volume contains entries based on published information, but references to sources are not included. For more detailed information, a fifteen-page section on further reading, with topical divisions provides some leads. More than 1,200 entries, ranging in length from seventy-five words to several pages, are arranged alphabetically and cross-referenced for easy access, covering a broad view of Native American religion. The emphasis is on highlighting the interrelatedness of native cultures, religion, and the land. Biographies of Native American religious practitioners who chose to share their knowledge in published writings are included. Also included are biographies of Catholic and Protestant missionaries who influenced Native American religious traditions. Information on disease and native medicine is interjected because many illnesses are viewed as an imbalance of the mind, body, and spirit. Other entries discuss ceremonial races, games, and sacred clowns and their integral roles in Native American ceremonies. Information on student research topics includes court cases and legislation, prophets, repatriation, American Indian religious freedom, peyote religion, and burial desecration.

The authors chose to limit the entries. They exclude tribal cosmologies, myths, tales, and stories of deities and spirits. Texts of prayers, songs, and poetry that relate to spirits and deities are also omitted. A detailed subject index completes the volume.

The broad scope of this one-volume work offers secondary students and teachers an introduction to native traditions and to the people who continue to practice them. This work is a worthwhile addition to reference collections.

16. Marriott, Alice, and Carol K. Rachlin. **American Indian Mythology.** New York: Crowell, 1968. 211p. FRL: 9. Subjects: Mythology; Legends.

Anthropologists Marriott and Rachlin selected myths, legends, and contemporary folklore that represent more than twenty American Indian tribes for this comprehensive study. Included are creation myths, nature tales, moral stories, and afterlife mythology. The selected stories of the hero, the trickster, the trickster-hero, grandmother spider and her grandsons, and the twin war gods represent the universal qualities of wisdom, greed, femininity, and humanity in the lore of the American Indians. The authors' intent is to present the unwritten literature of a people whose ways and customs are steadily combining with white ways. Some selections are the original fieldwork of the compilers and others are drawn from the published works of other anthropologists.

The introduction traces the migration and development of Indian tribes and the subsequent government interaction on the North American continent. Emphasis on knowing the history of a given culture to determine fact from legend and myth is carefully explained. The myths tell the actions of supernatural beings, whereas legends, the humanized counterpart, recall the deeds of earthly heroes. The newer lore recalls stories that reveal tradition, religion, history, ethnic humor, and the effects of the white man's arrival.

The selections are written by anthropologists and lack the distinctness of Indian storytelling. Each story begins with a brief description of the culture, with mention of tribal names, linguistic stock, and cultural traits, so the myths can be read in the context of the societies in which they developed. A bibliography and black-and-white photographs are included. The collection should enhance any unit on mythology because the stories are easily and quickly read and provide new tales and old myths that show the development of Indian oral literature from long ago to the present. A paperback edition is available from New American Library.

17. Marriott, Alice, and Carol K. Rachlin. **Peyote.** New York: Crowell, 1971. 111p. FRL: 11. Subjects: Religion; Peyote; Native American Church.

Prepared by two distinguished anthropologists who have participated in peyote rituals, this book gives firsthand knowledge of the origin and growth of the peyote religion. To dispel the mysteries that have long surrounded the controversial philosophy of the American Indian, the authors explore the lifestyle and philosophy of the American Indian, including peyote's relationship to other facets of Indian culture.

From its religious origin by Comanche leader Quanah Parker to the organization of the Native American Church, the controversial peyote religion is scrutinized. Because peyote is a hallucinogen, believers have been persecuted by federal and state law, missionaries, and other Indians. Whether practiced covertly or openly, however, the religion's followers continue to increase. Young American Indians are interested in reading about the peyote religion. This easily read, compelling study has an excellent index.

18. Mooney, James. **The Ghost-Dance Religion and the Sioux Outbreak of 1890.** Chicago: University of Chicago Press, 1965. 359p. FRL: 9. Subjects: Ghost Dance Religion; Sioux Indians.

James Mooney's source material about the Ghost Dance Movement was written in 1892-93, when he was an ethnologist for the Bureau of American Ethnology. Anthony F. C. Wallace has now edited and abridged the report and added an introduction to the 1965 publication, still considered the most substantial and empathetic account of the Indian aspirations for a better, nativistically oriented way of life. Mooney's own life experience allowed him to prepare a report based on careful observation and intelligent interpretation. He understood the responses of a poor, oppressed minority to a religious cult that swept American Indian tribes west of the Mississippi. The Ghost Dance was a ceremony based on the revelations of two patriot prophets, Tavibo and Wovoka, who preached that the dead would soon return and, at the same time, that the white people and their culture would be destroyed by natural forces.

Although later research shows some errors in Mooney's report, the account is recognized as a classic study. Other books covering this topic should be included in a collection to offset the author's sentimental viewpoint. The extensive index makes the material easy to access. Native American youth will enjoy chapters on the ceremony of the dance and the songs used by the eight specific tribes. The book has sixty-seven illustrations with brief captions.

19. Underhill, Ruth M. **Red Man's Religion: Beliefs and Practices of the Indians.** Chicago: University of Chicago Press, 1963. 301p. FRL: 9. Subjects: Religion; Anthropology.

In this volume, written as a companion to her book *Red Man's America*, Underhill uses nontechnical language to describe and promote the understanding of the religious practices of Native Americans, past and present. The content is organized by categorizing the religious ceremonies of American Indians living north of the Rio Grande. The similarities and differences of the religious ceremonies and beliefs are presented by examining the diversity of the spiritual needs among tribes, cultures, and lifestyles. The last chapter discusses modern Indian religion, including the Ghost Dance and the peyote religion.

An anthropologist, writer, and worker in Indian affairs, Ruth Underhill has personal experience from which to illustrate her points. The work is scholarly, with footnotes and references for each chapter, and includes an extensive bibliography, a comprehensive index, and thirty-four captioned illustrations. Mature middle and secondary school readers will gain information on the religious practices and relate to the author's insight into the topics explained.

300-399 Social Sciences

20. Ashabranner, Brent. **Morning Star, Black Sun: The Northern Cheyenne Indians and America's Energy Crisis.** New York: Dodd, Mead, 1982. 154p. FRL: 9. Subjects: Cheyenne Indians—Government relations; Coal mines and mining—Montana; Conservation of natural resources—Montana.

Ashabranner and photographer Paul Conklin, in a brief account based on research and interviews, trace the history of the Northern Cheyenne's struggle to regain their traditional lands and maintain their tribal culture. This struggle is continued into current times as this small tribe of less than 4,000 confronts the United States government and some of the largest coal and energy corporations in America in an attempt to maintain control of their natural resources.

The text and photographs trace the history of the Cheyenne people as they were pushed from their original homeland in the area now called Minnesota to join with another tribe near the Missouri River, and finally onto the Great Plains. As the people hunted buffalo, they separated into the Southern and Northern Cheyenne. The message of their greatest teacher and prophet, Sweet Medicine, foretold the coming of the killers of the buffalo, the greed for gold, and the lust for the land. Retreating to eastern Montana after defeat in many battles, the Northern Cheyenne were forced to relocate in Oklahoma. After a daring escape, the Cheyenne returned to Montana while eluding the United States army. Sympathetic to their needs, General Miles eventually helped them secure a small piece of land in eastern Montana, where the Cheyenne learned to ranch and could retain their old ways. Again, the federal government created problems by mishandling their herds, leasing grasslands to white ranchers, pressuring them to allot land to individual tribal members, pushing relocation programs, and encouraging individual Cheyenne landowners to sell. The most recent crisis is the Cheyenne's legal fight to save the land from strip mining of coal and the air from pollution.

This excellent, compact book is well organized, and material is easily accessed through the index. The information provides research on a problem that confronts other Indian tribes as they face economic deprivation and must consider whether natural resources will help them maintain their tribal lands or threaten their way of life. This book also documents for all readers a sadly neglected era of American history—when Indian tribes were callously stripped of their homelands and human rights to benefit a materialistic American society.

21. Ashabranner, Brent. **To Live in Two Worlds: American Indian Youth Today.** New York: Dodd, Mead, 1984. 149p. FRL: 8. Subjects: Youth; Social conditions.

Many books on contemporary American Indian people dwell on the injustices of the past and the social problems of today. The uniqueness of this nonfiction book is the positive human-interest approach by Ashabranner and photographer Paul Conklin. Interviews with young American Indian men and women of high school, college, or beginning-career age communicate that, unlike many of their parents, who felt that the white way was the best way, they are developing confidence in their Indian heritage and have positive attitudes about maintaining their identity as American Indians. Many of those interviewed experienced extreme poverty, broken homes, alcoholism, inadequate education, language difficulties, and a record of repeated failure. Despite these adverse situations, these young Americans are coping with their fears through links to strong tribal culture.

As the collaborators visited the states with the largest Indian populations, they talked with young people who hoped they could live and find success in "two worlds." In Zuni pueblos and on reservations, where one feels the powerful and ever-present traditional world, the young people are searching for those things that will benefit all Zunis in the modern world. A young woman, who worries about losing her Indian identity while living in an urban environment far from the reservation, receives assurance from her extended family that she will always know she is a Navajo. Two brothers combine urban careers as rock musicians with major responsibilities in rural tribal affairs because they know that wherever they are, they are Miccosukee. Even a young Cheyenne with a prison record is developing pride in the culture and history of his people with the help of a chaplain. Confronting a school system with a history of failure for most students, a Tigua tells of his resolve to succeed in school and break the dropout pattern. A Cherokee overcomes the handicap of a poor self-image and dedicates his life to teaching Navajo children.

The personal experiences of these and other young Indian people convey the message that they can be successful in the two worlds that confront all American Indians. This outstanding nonfiction book, which would be valuable reading for all young adults, has a special message for minority young people. Readers will gain an understanding of the "two worlds" in which the American Indian young person lives.

22. Baylor, Byrd. **A God on Every Mountain Top: Stories of Southwest Indian Sacred Mountains.** New York: Charles Scribner's Sons, 1981. 64p. FRL: 4. Subject: Legends.

Baylor sets the stage for her poetic version of the myths, legends, and folktales of the Southwestern Indians as she describes the honor and esteem American Indian tribes accord to holy places. The magical stories explain the role of the sacred mountains in the culture of the Tewa, Mohave, Navajo, Taos, Apache, Papago, Maricopa, Yavapai, Yuma, Zuni, Yaqui, and Hopi tribes. The retold stories focus on the origin of the people, the power of the mountains, and the beings in the mountains.

The text is based on the oldest sources and best translations of early ethnologists and tribal publications selected by Baylor. A list of sources is included. The lack of an index makes it difficult to locate legends by tribal name and limits its use as a reference book.

The whimsical, black-and-white illustrations by Carol Brown portray the joy and affection that the people have for the stories of the sacred mountains. Children will delight in the characterizations, while some adults may view them as cartoons. The book is an excellent addition to the mythology section of any library for young readers. Indian children will relate to the legends as they learn the importance of keeping the ancient sacred sites from the hands of modern-day developers.

23. Begay, Shonto. **Ma'ii and Cousin Horned Toad: A Traditional Navajo Story.** New York: Scholastic, 1992. unpaged. FRL: 3. Subjects: Navajo Indians—Legends; Coyotes—Folklore; Horned toads—Folklore; Legends.

Shonto Begay, son of a Navajo medicine man, retells and illustrates a trickster myth of his people. Raised a traditional Navajo, Begay bases his retelling on the stories that he learned as a child. Among the Navajo, the mischief-maker Coyote is called Ma'ii. This particular "Coyote out walking story" is a teaching tale.

As usual, Ma'ii is hungry. He decides to visit his cousin Horned Toad, who is working in his cornfield. Being a kind fellow, Horned Road makes Ma'ii roast corn and squash stew. Ma'ii begs for more and finally Horned Toad scolds him and says he must work. Scheming a way to get his cousin's farm, the conniving coyote tricks the Horned Toad into his mouth and swallows him. The Horned Toad teaches the lazy coyote a lesson he never forgets. The Navajo believe the Horned Toad gives them strength of heart and mind.

This is a marvelous book to read aloud; the hero tale provides opportunities to discuss many things that are important for children's social development. The story would also serve as an introduction to a science unit on animals. Full-color illustrations reflect the beauty of the Southwest. The animal caricatures exude life. A short explanation of the Navajo myths about Coyote and Horned Toad and a glossary of Navajo words are appended. Young readers will delight in this excellent addition to folklore collections by a Native American.

24. Behrens, June. **Powwow.** Chicago: Childrens Press, 1983. 29p. FRL: 3. Subject: Rites and ceremonies.

The third book in the Festivals and Holidays Series, *Powwow* captures the spirit of a contemporary aspect of Indian life. Part of many Indian social gatherings, powwows provide opportunities for tribes and extended families to promote Native American traditions, pride, and fellowship. Combining the best aspects of the past and the present and permitting the elders to continue to instruct the young in the values and traditions of American Indian life, the book is written from a personal viewpoint as the information is shared by a young Sioux boy who takes his friends to a powwow, a celebration that includes traditional food, music, dancing, and crafts. Contests are held to find the best dancers and singers.

The author, educator June Behrens, skillfully blends the information on the culture and history of the American Indian people. Excellent full-color photographs compiled by Terry Behrens enliven the text. The powwow is an important part of Indian culture today. Although this volume lacks many components that would make it more valuable as a research tool, it fills a void on a subject of great interest to Indian young people.

25. Bernhard, Emery. **Spotted Eagle & Black Crow.** New York: Holiday House, 1993. unpaged. FRL: 3. Subjects: Dakota Indians—Legends; Legends.

Weaving the threads of a Lakota legend, Emery Bernhard and illustrator Durga Bernhard have produced a spirited book for young children. Longtime students of tribal art, they were inspired by the story of Spotted Eagle and Black Crow that Lakota storyteller Jenny Leading Cloud shared with storyteller Richard Erdoes. The legend is published in *American Indian Myths and Legends* by Erdoes and Alfonso Ortiz. Writer Emery Bernhard retells this narrative, magnifying the conflict by making the central characters brothers. This is the Bernhards' first Native American folktale for young readers.

Spotted Eagle and Black Crow lived "before the white man used his rifle to kill Wanblee, the eagle, before the white man stamped eagles on his silver coins...." They were brothers who loved the same woman, Red Bird. As Spotted Eagle played his flute for Red Bird in the Moon of the Grass Appearing, Black Crow plotted his brother's death. Only one of them returns to his tribe. Betrayed by Black Crow, Spotted Eagle is saved by the Great Spirit and the young eagles in whose nest he is left. At the end, Spotted Eagle is the only brother alive to give thanks to the Wanblee, the eagle brothers who saved him.

The artistry of Durga Bernhard celebrates Native American traditions as she incorporates Lakota designs into her childlike, detailed illustrations. The scenes tell the story without words. Children who have not learned to read will enjoy the tale as a picture book. The excitement and action of the story are evident in the brilliant colors of the illustrations.

Ideal for storytime, the book is sure to leave children with an appreciation of Native American culture. The tale provides both information and entertainment. Primary-school teachers and librarians will enjoy sharing the delightful story with children of all ages.

26. Bierhorst, John, ed. **The Fire Plume: Legends of the American Indians.** New York: Dial Press, 1969. 90p. FRL: 6. Subjects: Legends; Algonquin Indians—Legends.

John Bierhorst has edited a collection of legends from the great Algonquin family of tribes, which once occupied much of the northeastern United States and adjoining Canada. The tales, which were told on long winter evenings, were collected by Henry Rowe Schoolcraft over 100 years ago. An early explorer, he collected some tales from literate frontiersmen who were able to translate from the original languages, and others from his half-Chippewa wife and her family. As a recognized authority on Indian lore, Schoolcraft drew on his knowledge to complete the stories with details that make them more readily understandable to readers of English. The tales of adventure and romance include warriors, magicians, chiefs, princesses, and forest beasts.

The editor offers a young reader's edition in a highly romantic poetry story form. A glossary of Indian terms not sufficiently explained in the text is appended. Artist Alan E. Cober has accompanied the legends with striking black-and-white drawings. The tales are excellent sources of legends for language arts curriculum in the elementary, middle, and secondary schools and should stimulate all readers of Indian culture.

27. Bierhorst, John. **The Red Swan: Myths and Tales of the American Indian.** New York: Farrar, Straus & Giroux, 1976. 386p. FRL: 6. Subject: Legends.

From North, Central, and South American Indian tribes, Bierhorst carefully chose sixty-four myths and tales for serious scholars of legends as well as casual readers. Forty-four different tribes are represented, including the Navajo, the largest tribe in the United States; the Chinook, an extinct tribe of Southwestern Washington; the Maya, the native people of Yucatan; and the Micmac, the Algonkian people of Canada. Especially valuable is the editor's thirty-page introduction, an important essay on the nature, scope, and symbolism of myth.

The stories are organized in loose thematic groupings to allow the reader to make cross-cultural comparisons. Beginning with the theme of the creation and family relationships, tales of war, seasons, heroes, tricksters, ghosts, and white man follow. The final theme centers on the beliefs of death and afterlife. Bierhorst supplies a brief commentary on the theme of each section and includes historical engravings.

Many of the myths are considered classics; others are fascinating stories appearing in English for the first time. The stories vary in length from a few paragraphs to over twelve pages. The detailed critical notes explain the symbolic content of the more difficult myths, make cross-references, and examine sources. The glossary of tribes, culture, and languages, and the extensive bibliography, are useful for research purposes. This comprehensive volume is a welcome addition of readable American Indian myths and tales in varied styles, gathered into one source from a wide range of collections.

28. Bierhorst, John, ed. **The Whistling Skeleton: American Indian Tales of the Supernatural.** Collected by George Bird Grinnell. New York: Four Winds, 1982. 110p. FRL: 4. Subjects: Legends; Great Plains—Legends.

Considered by many to be the first modern collector of Native American folklore, George Bird Grinnell set high standards for recording Indian legends. In a straightforward and accurate manner, he gave the Indian storyteller "an authentic voice in English" by using tribal informants and their precise words. Termed by Grinnell as "mystery" stories, the tales were collected during the late nineteenth century from the Plains Indians he knew best. The stories reflected a broad range of subtopics dealing with the supernatural as well as with the real world of courtship, marriage, and war. The nine tales selected by Bierhorst in this volume include four from the Blackfeet of Montana and southern Saskatchewan; two from the Pawnee of Kansas and Nebraska; and three from the Cheyenne of Wyoming, Colorado, and western Nebraska.

The tales of animal spirits and ghosts will capture the interest of students of all ages as they read of "The Whistling Skeleton," "Wolf Man," "Deer Boy," and "The Stolen Girl." Other selections recount "Red Robe's Dream," "Sees in the Night," "The Death of Low Horn," "The Boy Who Was Sacrificed," and "Ghost Story." Bierhorst's foreword provides excellent reading for a clear understanding of the significance of Plains Indian life, the original storytellers, and the folklore of these colorful people.

The attractive volume features evocative and haunting black-and-white illustrations by Robert Andrew Parker for each tale. Helpful aids for readers are a guide to special terms and suggestions for further reading.

29. Bierhorst, John. **The Woman Who Fell from the Sky.** New York: William Morrow, 1993. unpaged. FRL: 3. Subjects: Iroquois Indians—Legends; Creation—Folklore.

Acclaimed author John Bierhorst offers his retelling of the Iroquois creation story. Creation stories are integral to the culture of American Indian people. He adapts the account from sources by anthropologists who recorded the creation stories of the six nations of the Iroquois—Mohawk, Oneida, Onondaga, Cayuga, Seneca, and Tuscarora. In the notes, the references on which the story was based are provided.

The sky people lived on a floating island in the air, their only light from the flowers of a tall tree. When a sky woman hears voices of children under her heart, her husband becomes angry and uproots the tree. She falls to earth, lands on turtle's back, and creates the earth, stars, and sun. Her twin sons, Sapling and Flint, are born. Sapling creates the plants and flowing rivers, birds, and animals, and makes humans. Flint makes life more difficult by causing rivers to flow one way, putting bones in fish, creating monsters, and making snow. Their work finished, they leave earth and travel the divided path of the Milky Way. Sky Woman also departs upward on the fire's smoke, reminding the people that their thoughts can also rise. The last page is the Iroquois people's prayer for the world created by Sky Woman and her sons.

The gouache and pen-and-ink art work in full color highlights every page. Illustrator Robert Andrew Parker uses soft watercolors to surround the drawings as the story unfolds. The depictions of the people and the creatures of the earth are sketches, rather than detailed drawings.

There are as many American Indian creation stories as there are tribes. Bierhorst's retelling of the Iroquois creation story explains the origin of the people from that tribe's world view. This book in its large format is excellent for sharing with children, who will enjoy the pictures. Older children can gain an understanding of another culture's understanding of creation.

30. Bruchac, Joseph. **Iroquois Stories: Heroes and Heroines, Monsters and Magic.** Trumansburg, N.Y.: Crossing Press, 1985. 198p. FRL: 5. Subjects: Legends; Iroquois Indians—Legends.

Although this collection of legends focuses on the stories of the Iroquois People of the Longhouse, the book is also valuable as an example of the breadth of lore that is handed down by generations of storytellers in all tribes. The anthology is unusual because the author heard the stories, researched the written versions until he felt he had internalized them, and then retold the stories aloud. His aim was "to rediscover the oral quality of each tale." After he had retold the material to an audience many times, he wrote his own version for this collection.

The introductory material by Bruchac explains his process of "Telling the Story," the history of the "People of the Longhouse," and the continuing endurance of Native American stories through "The Storyteller." The selections begin with how the stories came into the world ("Coming of the Legends"). The next selections in poetic verse explain "The Creation" and the coming of the Good Mind and the Evil Mind to earth in "The Two Brothers." The thirty-two legends include animal and hero tales, legends with important morals for young readers, and stories of how things came to be.

This anthology is a rich resource for storytellers and will appeal to readers of all ages. The material is fast-paced, and drama students will find that the words lend themselves to oral interpretation. To young children and reluctant readers, the animal stories and hero tales will have great appeal. The introductory section should be read by teachers who plan to use the legends in class.

The book has a table of contents, small glossary, five titles for further reading, and black-and-white line drawings by Daniel Burgevin for each selection. Legends play a continuing role in American Indian life as they entertain, empower, and teach important values.

31. Caduto, Michael J., and Joseph Bruchac.

31.1. **Keepers of the Animals: Native American Stories and Wildlife Activities for Children.** Golden, Colo.: Fulcrum, 1991. 266p. FRL: 5. Subjects: Legends; Animal ecology—Study and teaching (Elementary); Human ecology—Study and teaching (Elementary).

31.2. **Keepers of the Earth: Native American Stories and Environmental Activities for Children.** Golden, Colo.: Fulcrum, 1988. 209p. FRL: 5. Subjects: Legends; Religion and mythology; Nature—Study and teaching (Elementary).

Noted environmentalist Michael J. Caduto and storyteller Joseph Bruchac combine their talents in two books to become master teachers of teachers. Using selected stories of Native American tribes throughout the United States, the authors design creative lessons on nature that will enthrall students. *Keepers of the Earth*, as the title implies, uses stories to introduce activities designed to instill within the child love and respect for the wonders of nature. The sequel *Keepers of the Animals* contains an additional twenty-four Native American stories. The carefully designed activities awaken in the young child the appreciation for the important role that animals have in their lives.

Carefully crafted lessons use effective learning styles of children by appealing to listening, sensory, and visual skills. This holistic approach, used for centuries by storytelling elders of all tribes, is equally effective with the modern elementary student. Teachers will become more effective storytellers, a skill useful in all subject areas.

Both books provide an excellent index, a glossary, and pronunciation key. Black-and-white illustrations for each story are invaluable teaching aids. The authors have chosen to do their books in black and white, which keeps the cost reasonable and accessible to all elementary schools. Teacher's guides and audiocassettes are also available for each volume.

These books were written for two purposes: first, to help children understand the importance of preserving the environment; and second, to help the teacher effectively impart this critical knowledge. As an invaluable reference for understanding the earth and the animals, both volumes can be used by parents and teachers. The professional library of every school should have these books.

32. Cohen, Caron Lee. **The Mud Pony.** New York: Scholastic, 1988. unpaged. FRL: 3. Subjects: Pawnee Indians—Legends; Horses—Folklore.

This moving hero-story of the Skidi band of the Pawnee Indians is retold by Caron Lee Cohen in *The Mud Pony.* The Pawnee of the American Plains believe that one of low origin can become honorable through faith and courage. Cohen adapted this version from the words of Yellow Calf, recorded by George A. Dorsey from 1899-1902.

A poor boy in an Indian camp yearns for a pony of his own. He forms one of mud. When buffalo are spotted, the boy cannot be found and his family leaves him. Alone, he dreams that Mother Earth brings his mud pony to life. In the morning the pony is alive and the boy begins his quest. After becoming a powerful leader, he must release the pony back to Mother Earth and find his own strength.

The illustrations of Shonto Begay, son of a Navajo medicine man, portray the mystical qualities of the story. In muted colors, the visual images provide a surrealistic background for the legend. The sparse text and impressionistic drawings provide a sense of wonderment. For the many children who yearn for a pony of their own during childhood, this tale will strike a sympathetic chord.

33. Curtis, Edward S. **The Girl Who Married a Ghost and Other Tales from the North American Indian.** Edited by John Bierhorst. New York: Four Winds, 1978. 114p. FRL: 6. Subject: Legends.

The Indian tales and exceptional photographs of Indian people taken by Edward S. Curtis in the 1900s provide a rare source of authentic Indian traditional literature. Only 500 sets of the twenty-volume work *The North American Indian* were published. The twenty-three-year project was begun in 1907. Much of the material Curtis collected consisted of fictional narratives. He used interpreters to gather the tales, which were recorded by W. E. Myers in shorthand and later reworked by Curtis to provide a smooth English version. John Bierhorst gained access to the rare work not usually accessible to the public and selected nine tales for publication. To accompany the tales he chose photographs by Curtis from the original set to enhance the anthology selections. Bierhorst's purpose was to link the images in the photographs with the myths recorded.

Dividing the nine narratives into six geographic regions, Bierhorst features stories that are sometimes frightful, sometimes violent, and sometimes haunting, unlike many of the collections of Indian legends for children. Each section is introduced with comments about the culture of the tribal peoples of the geographic region and the stories.

From the Southwest tribes, Bierhorst selected the Navajo creation myth of the two brothers, Monster-Slayer and Child-of-the-Water. The romantic myth of "The Dirty Bride" recounts the story of one of the Hopi Indian holy places. An Eskimo tale of Alaska portrays a powerful old medicine woman with shamanistic powers who helps two lost boys return home. A spirit person, Gone-Down-to-the-Sea, provides a young man with unusual powers in a selection from the Wiyot of Northern California, a tribe now all but extinct. In the Apache trickster tale, the fox outwits the bear. One of the more unusual tales from the Northwoods, "The Woman Dressed Like a Man," includes romance, deception, and death. The story featured as the title of the volume, "The Girl Who Married a Ghost," really is a ghost story that also provides a cultural view of the lifeway of the Northwest-coast tribes. Each tale is unique, and readers will be caught up in the variety of selections.

This anthology is recommended for all collections. The tales will be prized by storytellers and teachers as action-filled and spellbinding. The beautifully reproduced, soft-toned photographs provide a realistic sense of the myths.

34. Curtis, Natalie. **The Indians' Book: An Offering by the American Indians of Indian Lore, Musical and Narrative, to Form a Record of the Songs and Legends.** New York: Dover, 1968. 584p. FRL: 7. Subjects: Mythology; Music; Art.

This durable paperbound book of American Indian songs, myths, and drawings was recorded as an unabridged replication of the revised second edition by Dover in 1968. Readers will find this treasury of material gathered from Indian oral tradition amazingly accurate. The myths were recorded directly from Indian storytellers. One hundred forty-nine songs from eighteen tribes have melodies and words in the original language as well as the English translation. The author's sentimentality and romanticization of the Indian are similar to those of other writers of the 1920s.

Curtis's work is an appeal for understanding and appreciation of the Indian people in a period of history when indigenous music, poetry, and legend were being neglected. In fact, Indian lore was being suppressed by government pressure to create "white" Indians. The author discusses the problems involved in locating and recording secret songs and the difficulty of obtaining information about Indian culture. She has produced a book that should give Indian youth a sense of worth in their race. This selection of songs and legends of the American Indians can be used with all school-age children.

35. Deloria, Vine, Jr. **We Talk, You Listen: New Tribes, New Turf.** New York: Dell, 1970. 227p. FRL: 13. Subjects: Minorities; Social conditions.

Deloria, a Standing Rock Sioux and minority spokesman, describes the problems that oppressed minorities face. He speaks in defense of tribal variables found in all minority cultures and attacks the corporate patterns of American life. The contract between the white cultural beliefs and values and the Indian, black, and Chicano ways of life provides unusual insight into the relationships that exist today. Deloria defines American minorities, discusses their future, and determines their needs in a white-dominated society. Topics such as cities, civil rights, ecological crisis, competitive nature, New Left, old liberals, black power, and politicians are covered.

This interesting and very readable book should serve as a valuable teaching tool in sociology classes. The chapter on stereotyping is especially valuable. The author demonstrates compassion for and understanding of the interaction among all American people.

36. Deloria, Vine, Jr., and Clifford M. Lytle. **American Indians, American Justice.** Austin: University of Texas Press, 1983. 262p. FRL: 12. Subjects: Government policy; Courts—U.S.

Focusing on the judicial function of government, political science professors Deloria and Lytle present an excellent overview of federal Indian law. This study of the federal, state, and tribal court systems contrasts the evolution of the American Indian historical and cultural perspective with that of the non-Indian judicial system. Actual cases and statutes are presented to clarify issues.

Tracing the history of the federal government's involvement in American Indian legal disputes from the first treaties to the present, the authors discuss the development of the present system of tribal courts. The concepts of tribal sovereignty and "Indian country" are presented to interpret this complex system for the average reader who has little training in law. Federal responsibility and control of Indian affairs are compared with the non-Indian system of justice. The evolution of tribal forms of government from traditional to the modern court system includes an adaptation of customs, values, and tribal forms of government to meet the needs of individual tribes. The discussion also defines the role of attorneys and legal-interest groups as well as the criminal and civil systems of justice under the modern Indian court system.

This complex topic is interpreted for the student and scholar of Indian affairs, social science teachers, and the tribal council person. The subject is timely because American Indians today are fighting battles in the courts for political and legal rights. As well as bibliographic references, the authors include an index of case law and topics. Available in both softbound and hardcover versions.

37. Deloria, Vine, Jr., and Clifford M. Lytle. **The Nations Within: The Past and Future of American Indian Sovereignty.** New York: Pantheon Books, 1984. 293p. FRL: 12. Subjects: Tribal government; Government relations—1934-1986; Civil rights.

Language, religion, and social customs are easily observed cultural traits that set the American Indian people apart from other Americans. An obscure difference is the concept of tribal lands as "nations," a uniqueness that many Americans find incomprehensible. Coauthors Deloria and Lytle explore the Indian "nations within" the United States, where native people practice a form of self-government. Both authors are attorneys who teach political science at the University of Arizona, Tucson, and are knowledgeable about the complexities of Indian government. The United States policy of Indian self-rule is a complex governmental system and continues to concern both the Indian nations and the federal government. Although many Indian tribes live on land designated as a nation, which should be free to determine its own fate, Indian nations are, in fact, allowed only limited self-government and authority over local decisions.

Self-government for the American Indian nations began with the organizations of reservations. The authors trace the continual reform movements and changes in policy, including the program of John Collier and the Indian Reorganization Act of 1934, the Indian Civil Rights Act, and the growth of Indian nationalism. The two concluding chapters look at recommendations for both self-government and self-determination as they affect the future of Indian nations. The small section on "cultural renewal" in the last chapter offers a new perspective for educators.

For everyone concerned with American Indian affairs today, this volume provides a scholarly examination of the status of American Indian nations and their complex relationship with the federal government. Social studies teachers and students who are looking for a reference to the unique position of Indian nations will find that this historical account provides the necessary background for better understanding. The book is recommended as a reference and includes an appendix, which compares the Wheeler-Howard Act and the original Collier Bill; notes; a bibliography; and an index.

38. De Wit, Dorothy. **The Talking Stone: An Anthology of Native American Tales and Legends.** New York: Greenwillow Books, 1979. 213p. FRL: 6. Subject: Legends.

Organized by geographic area and tribal affiliation, the twenty-seven selections of Native American folklore include creation stories, hero histories, and trickster tales. Selected by region of origin, the samples are from the Iroquois, Central and Northeast woodland, Southeast, Southwest, Plains, Plateau-California, Pacific Northwest, Far North, and Eskimo and Canada. Each regional section is introduced by the editor and contains general information on the culture and characteristics of the folklore of that region.

Based on forty-eight sources, the book provides a broad sample of Native American tales and legends that may be useful in reading programs. Some of the selections are retold by the author, and others are reprinted from other sources.

39. Dixon, Ann. **How Raven Brought Light to People.** New York: Margaret K. McElderry Books, 1992. unpaged. FRL: 3. Subjects: Tlingit Indians—Legends; Alaska—Legends.

Public librarian Ann Dixon, from Willow, Alaska, is a storyteller. In her first book for children, she draws on a legend told by the Tlingit Indians of southeastern Alaska. During long winter evenings, the Raven stories explain, inform, and entertain the people.

Raven, a trickster with magical powers, grows exceeding tired of darkness when the earth is new. He becomes mad when he learns that the great chief keeps the sun, moon, and the stars in three wooden boxes. Changing himself into a tiny spruce needle, he drops into the chief's daughter's hands as she scoops a drink from the river. Inside her, he turns himself into a baby and surprises everyone when he is born. The great chief loves the boy deeply. Raven tricks the chief into letting him play with the three boxes and releases light to the people.

Readers will relish this magical story. Dixon offers the daring legend of *How Raven Brought Light to People* for teachers and librarians to share with young children. The pace is fast and the language simple and direct. The sources from which Dixon drew her retelling are not provided. James Watts employs shaded watercolor and acrylic drawings, using Tlingit Indian detail and designs. Dixon draws on her knowledge as a librarian and presents an adaption of one Raven cycle tale in a delightful narrative that children of all ages can enjoy.

40. Downey, Fairfax, and Jacques Noel Jacobson. **The Red-Blue Coats.** Fort Collins, Colo.: Old Army Press, 1973. 204p. FRL: 10. Subject: Scouts.

Downey and Jacobson chronicle and pay tribute to the story of American Indian scouts. The most effective and dramatic service of scouts reached its pinnacle in post-Civil War hostilities. From the time of Sacajawea to World War II, Indian scouts were employed as allies by government forces. Without their services, the conflicts would have lasted longer and exacted a higher toll of lives.

This book paints a very different picture than that of the Indian scouts that most Indian and non-Indian youth see portrayed on film. Downey, a leading military historian, and Jacobson, an antique militaria dealer and consultant to the United States Army museums, have included a section of photographs and line drawings, with captions as well as a list of the awards of medals of honor given to Indian scouts.

41. Edmonds, Margot, and Ella E. Clark. **Voices of the Winds: Native American Legends.** New York: Facts on File, 1989. 368p. FRL: 7. Subject: Legends.

For ten years, Margot Edmonds and Ella E. Clark gathered a rich compendium of mythology, legends, and tales of Native Americans. Some were told to the authors by the elders of many tribes, the historians and storytellers. Others they carefully researched for this collection, and some they have retold in a style that strives to maintain the quality and rhythm of oral literature. Over 130 original North American Indian tales are organized by six regions: Northwest, Southwest, Great Plains, Central, Southeast, and Northeast.

Since the earliest times, North American Indian people have shared their beliefs through oral history. The rich and varied selections include creation myths, animal tales, and stories of human behavior. For each selection, an informative headnote discusses the history and culture of the specific tribal people and explains the origin or theme. A footnote provides the source of the story, and the reader can use the bibliography for a complete citation. This large volume also has a glossary and an index. The book is illustrated with line drawings of artifacts by Mollie Braun.

The vast array of material from most of the tribes of long-time North American Indian culture offers readers from upper-elementary grades to adults an outstanding and thoroughly enjoyable collection of oral literature, rich in Native American culture and life. This is an extensive and valuable anthology of oral literature from which readers can learn and understand more about North American Indian life.

42. Engel, Lorenz. **Among the Plains Indians.** Minneapolis, Minn.: Lerner Publications, 1981, c1970. 106p. FRL: 8. Subject: Great Plains—Social life and customs.

Most books on the North American Plains Indians emphasize text supported by drawings. In contrast, German author Lorenz Engel highlights the artistic renderings of Plains Indian life and accompanies the drawings with fictionalized accounts of the expeditions that produced the artwork. Selecting unique drawings and paintings from two unusual artists who recorded the world of the Plains Indians in the nineteenth century, the author presents a rare opportunity to gain knowledge of the lifeways of the early Indian world.

Illustrations from George Catlin's lithographs in the *North American Indian Portfolio*, published in 1844, and Karl Bodner's engravings in *Reise in das Innere Nord-Amerikas in den Fahren* (1839-1841), which accompanied the account of the expedition led by German Prince Maximilian, offer an exciting visual journey. To provide a text to accompany the excellent drawings, the author creates fictionalized accounts of two separate expeditions to the Plains Indian lands, one led by American artist George Catlin and the other by the German Prince of Wied. Both men visited Indians whom no other white people had previously documented in their villages and on their hunting grounds. The expeditions were unique because each explorer went to the Plains Indian region only to gain knowledge, not to conquer or to gain new lands. The text combines the information about the people and events gleaned from both men's accounts of their expeditions.

This unusual volume, first published in Germany in 1967 and later produced in the United States, is in its fourth printing. The book is highly recommended for young adults as an authentic view of Plains Indian life through story and picture.

The language families of the most important tribes are listed at the back, with a map locating each language group.

43. Erdos, Richard, and Alfonso Ortiz, eds. **Indian Myths and Legends.** New York: Pantheon Books, 1984. 527p. FRL: 9. Subjects: Legends; Religion.

One hundred sixty-six myths and legends from more than eighty Indian tribes of North America are gathered here in a single volume. Writer-artist Erdos and anthropologist Ortiz retell classic stories based on primary sources and accounts recorded from living storytellers. The abundance of folklore is organized in chapters showing common elements in stories, although selected from different tribal sources and distant geographic parts of the continent. Readers and storytellers will be entranced with tales of creation and tricksters, wars and warriors, love and lust, animals and ghosts, as well as the spirit world and visions. A brief introduction to each section details the thematic prototype, from the crafty coyote tales to the frightening monster stories.

The most unique feature of this anthology is that each myth or legend is introduced with a brief synopsis, and the original source is given at the end of the story. This feature is lacking in most compilations of myths and legends; usually the reference is provided only in the appendix. The dramatic world of mythology can be read for pleasure and education, but more important, legends have a place in literature as a link from the native people to their enduring beliefs and traditions. Another noteworthy feature is the appendix of tribes, including descriptive information, a bibliography of sources, and an index of tales by title. Black-and-white Indian-style motifs accompany the text.

44. Fichter, George S. **How the Plains Indians Lived.** New York: David McKay, 1980. 121p. FRL: 7. Subjects: Social life and customs; Great Plains.

This comprehensive description of the basic aspects of Plains Indian life prior to the coming of the white man serves as a quick reference for children to this colorful era in American history. More than twenty colorful tribes of North American followed the bison on the Great Plains: Arapaho, Arikara, Assiniboin, Blackfoot, Cheyenne, Comanche, Crow, Dakota, Gros Ventre, Iowa, Kansa, Kiowa, Mandan, Missouri, Osage, Oto, Pawnee, Quapaw, Santee, Wichita, and Yankton.

The detailed black-and-white illustrations by Alexander Farquharson and fascinating descriptions of lifeways by the author cover dwellings, clothing, agriculture, hunting, language, work, and the crafts of these nomadic people. Also described are beliefs and customs, tribal law and government, and games and sports. A brief summary of the traumatic change from a life of freedom to the confines of reservation life that these tribes experienced is included. Those seeking a text to enrich social studies units will find this volume valuable. Young readers searching for an account of Plains Indian life can easily access topics through the index. A bibliography of selected sources is included.

45. Gates, Frieda. **North American Indian Masks: Craft and Legend.** New York: Walker, 1982. 48p. FRL: 6. Subjects: Masks; Legends.

Frieda Gates, a part-Mohawk artist, writer, and teacher, combines an informative text with illustrations and instructions for making facsimiles of the masks used by natives of North America. For ritualistic ceremonies, almost all North American tribes created masks, which only certain members of the tribe were permitted to wear. Made from many types of native materials and in all sizes, from finger masks to larger-than-human size, the masks ranged from the elaborate to the primitive. They took myriad forms, such as humorous creatures, elaborately crafted or carved beaked birds, grotesquely distorted human faces, and animal shapes. Incorporating both the needs of the people and their spiritual beliefs, these fascinating legends of the Eastern Iroquois false faces, Southwest Kachina, Northwest Coast Indian, Alaska Eskimo, and seven other tribal groups are recounted by the author.

Following a brief description of the authentic picture masks, an illustration, materials list, and instructions are provided for making a copy of each mask. Although this book is primarily for children, the masks can be used as art objects or as craft projects. Art projects could be combined with the study of other aspects of American Indian culture to teach meaningful units on the culture of the native people of North America. For children who learn by doing, the informative text and accompanying crafts will be very meaningful.

46. Goble, Paul. **Buffalo Woman.** New York: Bradbury Press, 1984. unpaged. FRL: 3. Subjects: Legends; Buffalo—Fiction.

Few children can resist the bright splashes of color, the delicate and detailed North American motifs, and the distinct signature style of author-artist Paul Goble. His children's books feature North American Indian legends. For young readers, the imaginative legends are an excellent introduction to the mythology of the Plains Indians.

Buffalo Woman portrays the courage of a young hunter who faces death to rejoin his wife and son. When his relations reject his wife and son, they return to her people of the Buffalo Nation, where they assume the form of buffalo. The young hunter seeks and finds them and survives the buffalo chief's tests. He joins his family as a buffalo and becomes a link between the people and the buffalo. The fast-paced legend and Southwest scene will captivate the minds of the young.

47. Goble, Paul. **Crow Chief: A Plains Indian Story.** New York: Orchard Books, 1992. unpaged. FRL: 3. Subjects: Crows—Folklore; Plains Indians.

Before the coming of horses to the Great Plains, hunting buffalo was often difficult. Paul Goble dates the story *Crow Chief* from the times when buffalo was the main food of Indian people. Many Indian groups relate the triumphs of one known as "the savior," who goes by different names such as Stone Boy, Lodge Boy, or White Plum Boy. In Goble's tale, the person who rescues the Plains Indians is Falling Star. As in all the stories, Falling Star is brave, wise, kind, and generous. He never ages, and he travels unceasingly to help his people. In a prefatory note of special interest to storytellers, Goble suggests that Plains Indians tell a story like *Crow Chief* to explain the failure or success of the hunt.

Long, long ago before Plains Indian people had guns or horses, members of the Crow Nation (the birds, not the tribe) were white. Crow Chief was friends with the buffaloes. Whenever he saw the people leave camp with stone-headed spears and arrows, he would warn the buffalo "Caw-Caw-Caw! Hunters are coming! Save yourselves!" The people were very hungry because Crow Chief kept spoiling their hunts. Finally, their prayers are answered. The savior Falling Star comes to camp. He tricks the Crow Chief and teaches him that all must share and live together like relatives. As a reminder, the Crow People will always be black-feathered.

The illustrations by Goble are not as detailed as in some of his books. Very stylized and decorative, his signature paintings incorporate Plains Indian symbols and designs. Repetition, as of the buffalo and crow figures, emphasizes the importance of nature in the lives of the native people. The end page contains four old songs about the crow from the Lakota and Arapaho people. Goble's illustrated tale provides storytellers with another excellent book.

48. Goble, Paul. **The Gift of the Sacred Dog.** New York: Bradbury Press, 1980. unpaged. FRL: 3. Subjects: Legends; Horses—Fiction.

As the Plains Indians became owners of horses, their way of life and ability to hunt changed dramatically. Many legends are told of how they acquired the horse. In this tale, a young Indian boy journeys to a high mountain to seek the Great Spirit. His people are hungry and have not been able to find the buffalo. During his quest, the boy receives sacred dogs, a name the Indians used for horses, from heaven. The text concludes with Sioux Indian songs of horses and buffalo. The book is an excellent source to read aloud to younger children. The informative text and delightful drawings reflect an important part of Native American heritage.

49. Goble, Paul. **The Great Race of the Birds and Animals.** New York: Bradbury Press, 1985. unpaged. FRL: 5. Subjects: Cheyenne Indians— Legends; Dakota Indians—Legends.

This Cheyenne and Dakota Indian tale was based on five references and adapted by Goble as a captivating folktale of animals and birds. The Great Race was called by the Creator to determine whether the four-legged buffalo or the two-legged man should have power and become the Guardian of Creation.

50. Goble, Paul.

50.1. **Iktomi and the Berries.** New York: Orchard Books, 1989. unpaged.

50.2. **Iktomi and the Boulder.** New York: Orchard Books, 1988. unpaged.

50.3. **Iktomi and the Buffalo Skull.** New York: Orchard Books, 1990. unpaged.

50.4. **Iktomi and the Ducks.** New York: Orchard Books, 1990. unpaged.

FRL: 3. Subject: Great Plains—Legends.

Four entertaining tales of Iktomi, the Plains Indian trickster, by Caldecott Medalist Paul Goble will delight young readers. The folklore of Iktomi derives from amusing stories that often have moral lessons. Traditionally, the stories were only told after the sun had set. All North American tribes have trickster tales, most often portrayed by the wily coyote. In the stories Goble retells and illustrates, Iktomi is portrayed as a real person who has both bad and admirable traits.

Iktomi appears again after an unsuccessful hunt, seeing things that are not there. In *Iktomi and the Berries* he ties a rope around his neck and jumps into the river to gather some red berries so he can show off for his relatives. It was a day he did not wish to remember.

Iktomi and the Berries starts as do all the Iktomi trickster tales: "Iktomi was walking along ..." He was very boastful about his handsome appearance. As the sun grows hot, he generously gives his blanket to a boulder to keep the sun off. As thunderclouds gather, he decides the rain might spoil his appearance and takes it back. The boulder bounces and pins his legs. The result is that bats have flattened faces and rocks are scattered all over the Great Plains.

Iktomi (who, by the way, is married) proudly rides away to impress the girls. Thrown from his pony, he discovers the Mouse People having a powwow inside a buffalo skull. With his head stuck in the skull, Iktomi returns home to an angry wife. *Iktomi and the Buffalo Skull* reminds the reader that Plains Indians consider buffalo skulls to be sacred and respected.

Dressed in all his finery, Iktomi cannot find his horse to ride in the parade. Noticing some ducks (he's always hungry) he tricks them off the pond. His vision of roast duck is obscured by two trees and a wily coyote in the story *Iktomi and the Ducks*.

Adults and children will find themselves chuckling with delight at the Iktomi tales. Paul Goble uses a delightful device to encourage audience participation. Iktomi's thoughts are printed in small type as he boasts about himself. They do not need to be read with the story but can be read when looking at the pictures with children. The text printed in italics offers comments and rude remarks that listeners to the story might make. This literary device adds a dimension to the stories that is in keeping with traditional Iktomi storytelling. As in all of Goble's books, he provides the sources on which he bases his retelling of the Plains Indian stories.

Goble's detailed, stylized drawings are unique. Iktomi's spirit comes alive as the reader visualizes his feelings and actions. The tales do not need to be read in any order and will delight children of all ages. For sharing American Indian trickster tales in the traditional way, teachers, librarians, and parents can use the Iktomi stories and invite children to add their own words.

51. Goble, Paul. **The Lost Children.** New York: Bradbury Press, 1993. unpaged. FRL: 3. Subjects: Siksika Indians—Legends; Stars—Folklore; Legends.

Many Indian people of North America recount the origin of the Pleiades stars. According to a Blackfoot legend, the Pleiades were once children who went to the Sky World because their people did not look after them. Preserving the tone of the oldest versions recorded between 1890 and 1920, Paul Goble retells this sacred myth in simple language. The themes of American Indian myths pass from generation to generation. Storytellers are free to weave their own tales, preserving the essential truths.

The storyteller begins when the stars are brightly visible through the smoke-hole flap. Children are given to the people by the Great Spirit as a gift. This story is about what happened when people did not look after six little, orphaned children. No one cared for them and only the camp dogs were their friends. They were treated so unkindly that they no longer wanted to be people. They agreed to be stars because they would always be beautiful. When they reached the Sky World, Moon Woman and Sun Man greeted them. Sun Man punished the tribe, the Dog People, with drought. When the birds and animals suffered, he brought rain, and new life came to the thirsty earth. The lost children became the Pleiades, the Bunched Stars, and the camp dogs became the small stars that are nearby.

Outstanding illustrations have Goble's authentic designs and contemporary flair. The vivid colors and unique style lend beauty to the scenes of the Blackfoot painted tipis. The Bunched Stars, representing the lost children, are painted on the south smoke flap. A further explanation of tipi designs is included on the end page. References of the sources for the story are provided.

Besides its value as a storytelling tale, this book can be incorporated into lessons on astronomy. The simple message of the tale is that all children are gifts from God and should not be neglected.

52. Goble, Paul. **Star Boy.** New York: Bradbury Press, 1983. unpaged. FRL: 2. Subject: Siksika Indians—Legends.

A Caldecott Medal winner, this retold Blackfeet Indian legend of Star Child relates the story of a boy who is disfigured by the sun when he disobeys his mother. Called Scarface by his people, he is encouraged by the chief's daughter, whom he loves, to find his way to Sky World. Upon his arrival, he receives beauty, riches, and the secret of the sacred Sun Dance. The ceremony is a part of the tribe's culture today.

53. Harlan, Judith. **American Indians Today: Issues and Conflicts.** New York: Franklin Watts, 1987. 128p. FRL: 12. Subjects: Social conditions; Government relations.

Included in the series of Impact Book titles from Franklin Watts, Judith Harlan's brief overview of the societal problems facing the Indian people of the United States gives an informed and perceptive picture of these issues. The problems covered are those that are of major concern to young Indian people today. The conflicts between traditional and nontraditional culture affect the lives of American Indians who live both on and away from Indian lands.

The section on Indian nations begins with a historical treatment, from the arrival of the European settlers to present-day Indian policies and issues. The American Indian, unlike other citizens of the United States, is subject to federal and state government as well as tribal government. Indian people own over 90 million acres of land, and the battles over treaty rights to this land are in the courts today. As Indian tribes seek economic independence, they are faced with poverty and a lack of jobs. Even though they have made gains through utilizing natural resources and developing businesses on the reservations, the Indian tribes, in general, face major economic difficulties.

The second important section of the book deals with the major social problems of the people. In a sensitive manner, the author discusses cultural conflicts, health concerns, educational issues, and urban life. Throughout this section she includes information about beliefs, ceremonies, crafts, and Indian leaders.

By carefully considering the conflicts and the difficult decisions facing the Indian people from a sympathetic perspective, the author provides an understanding of the unusual circumstances facing the contemporary American Indian. The book should be read by teachers and others having contact with Indian young people to develop an understanding of their social conditions and cultural backgrounds. Listed as juvenile literature, the material will be valuable to students searching for research topics and current materials on the American Indian. Black-and-white photographs and an index are included.

54. Henry, Jeanette, and Robert Costo. **A Thousand Years of American Indian Storytelling.** San Francisco: Indian Historian Press, 1981. 125p. FRL: 5. Subjects: Legends; Short stories.

As an introduction to the vast body of American Indian literature, this collection of stories for children offers some history and some fiction in the form of myths, fables, and legends. Most of the forty-three stories were published in *The Weewish Tree*, a magazine of Indian America for young people. Some of the stories included are of ancient origin and others are modern tales, some even by children.

The selections span 1,000 years of storytelling and many have been translated into English. Five types of stories are included: stories of creation about the origin of the world and people; stories about celestial phenomena that explain the appearance of the moon, stars and planets, and constellations; storytelling in which children learned through listening; stories that are often funny and exciting and explain why and how certain things came to be; and favorites of the storyteller. Each section, and frequently each tale, has an introduction providing cultural information as well as an introduction to the storyteller. The stories are strong in spirit: "all of them have the flavor, the color, and the spirit of America's first people."

The broad variety of stories will appeal to readers of all ages. Many are extremely funny; two that have special appeal are "The Mare's Egg" and "Running Bear." Prolific illustrations by many different people accompany each tale, with styles ranging from the realistic to the humorous. This is an excellent book of delightful stories from many different tribes and nations that can provide knowledge on the heritage of the American Indian people for all readers.

55. Hirschfelder, Arlene. **Happily May I Walk: American Indians and Alaska Natives Today.** New York: Charles Scribner's Sons, 1986. 152p. FRL: 12. Subjects: Social problems; Social life and customs; Reservations; Education; Prejudices against Indians; Government relations; Economic conditions.

The thrust of this volume is stated by the author in her introduction: "This book, containing new information about the ways Native Americans live in the United States today, has been written to help you 'unlearn' Indian stereotypes." The scope of this informative text includes historical background, everyday life, and current efforts to maintain ancient culture.

In a readable style, the author details twenty-two separate topics. She discusses the uniqueness of the Native American in chapters on tribal government, reservations, language, religion, and sacred healers. Social problems that Indian and Alaska native people face are evident in the discussions of concern for the elderly, education of children, and life in the cities. These topics will be valuable to young people, especially Indian youth who are looking for contemporary research topics. The federal and state governments' role in regulating the lives of Indian people is considered in the deliberations on reservations' resources, treaty rights, termination and self-determination, and government relations. The historical background of these topics will provide a different view than that usually perpetuated in history textbooks. A welcome inclusion, rarely covered in most books on social life and customs, are the sections on professional Indian artists, performers, athletes, dancers, singers, writers, and journalists. American Indian and Alaska native youth need information on contemporary, successful role models in vocational fields.

The information on a wide range of vital current topics will fill a void in school and public library collections because most books on social problems are written for adults and do not always appeal to young people.

56. Hofsinde, Robert. **Indian Costumes.** New York: William Morrow, 1968. 94p. FRL: 5. Subject: Costumes.

Robert Hofsinde's book on Indian costume is a practical reference on the dress of ten different tribes: Apache, Blackfoot, Crow, Iroquois, Navajo, Northwest Coast, Ojibwa, Pueblo, Seminole, and Sioux. In readable text and detailed illustration, he captures the distinctive style of each Indian group. Ceremonial, warring, and everyday apparel are described in relationship to geographic location and availability of materials, customs and beliefs, and climate and seasons. When possible, Hofsinde includes information on how the costumes were made.

Hofsinde researched the material on costumes carefully and interspersed the text with valuable information on culture. This was published in 1968, and the last chapter of the book, "Indian Dress Today," needs revision. Most of today's Native Americans, except for a small number of traditional people, wear modern clothes. For ceremonial occasions, many Native Americans continue to don traditional dress. Black-and-white line drawings by the author provide excellent detail to accompany the text. Children of all ages can read and enjoy this excellent source.

57. Hofsinde, Robert. **Indians at Home.** New York: William Morrow, 1964. 96p. FRL: 5. Subjects: Housing; Social life and customs.

Although first published in 1964, Hofsinde's book on dwellings of the major North American Indian people is still in print and considered an excellent choice. Dispelling the commonly held belief that most Indians lived in tipis, the author-illustrator notes that Indian homes were made of different materials and in different shapes, depending on their geographic location and seasonal use.

Using major language families to determine the location of similar tribes, the author selects a typical tribal people and discusses how their homes were built. Information about the social life and customs of the group adds to the reader's understanding of the importance of the dwelling. The Ojibwa of the North Woods built four different homes, including the wigwam, as the seasons passed and they searched for food. The longhouse provided a large community dwelling in the villages of the Iroquois. A small group of the Seminole tribe fled to Florida and developed a new culture, which included building an open-wall house (a *chickee*) on stilts. Part of the Siouxan linguistic group, the Mandan, constructed villages of earth lodges. In the dry climate of the Southwest, tribes utilized natural resources to build adobe homes, and on the Northwest coast the people used native materials to build large plank houses.

The information on Native American dwellings is presented in a clear, simple style and will appeal to children. The text is compact and well illustrated with line drawings of homes and useful household objects. A map showing linguistic group location precedes the text, and a list of the tribes speaking a similar language is in the back of the book. The index also covers illustrations.

58. Hungry Wolf, Beverly. **The Ways of My Grandmothers.** New York: William Morrow, 1980. 256p. FRL: 10. Subjects: Siksika Indians—Women; Great Plains—Women.

While many books are written about the social life and culture of American Indian people, few are written about the ancestral lives of women. Beverly Hungry Wolf of the Blood people of the Blackfoot Nation writes of the ways of her grandmothers. The term *grandmothers*, following the tradition of her people, refers to her mother, grandmothers, and other older women in the tribe. From those to whom she is related or those who are good friends, she gathers teachings of the ancient ways, stories of their personal lives, and myths and legends about women. These people know and practice the ancestral ways of life.

Indian girls and young women will be inspired as they read of the author's personal life. As a child she was raised in a traditional home and spoke only her native language. She attended school, went to college, traveled, and returned home to teach. As she married and raised a family, she began her search for "lost" Indian ways as much for her children as for herself. She learned tribal history, culture, and traditional ways from her grandmothers.

The broad offerings make this book useful in many areas. Librarians can suggest the chapters on traditional household roles relating to children, clothing, food preparation, tanning, and crafts, which include everything from traditional recipes adapted to modern foods to home economics classes. The personal stories of the women are entertaining vignettes of oral history, while the myths and legends will appeal to children as well as young adults. They are very short and unusual in that women are the main characters as well as the narrators.

In a tribute to the women of her people, the author dispels the common misconception promoted in history that Indians often neglected women. Through the details of the lives of the grandmothers, the reader sees the respect and honor accorded these women as they continued their ancient rituals and domestic lives, from caring for the medicine pipe bundle to camping in a tipi.

Two black-and-white photograph inserts feature captioned pictures gathered from family albums, the National Museum of Canada, and the Glen-Bow-Alberta Foundation. The book also has an index for easy access to its variety of information.

59. Josephy, Alvin M., Jr. **Now That the Buffalo's Gone: A Study of Today's American Indians.** New York: Alfred A. Knopf, 1982. 300p. FRL: 12. Subject: Government policy.

Author of many prize-winning books on American Indians, Alvin M. Josephy, Jr. describes his book as a study of Native Americans in the United States today. He examines what Indians want, why Indians want it, and the source of these attitudes. Employing a method of historical narrative to link the past to the present, he traces case histories of current disputes between the Indians and the non-Indians. About 40 percent of the book concerns the histories of seven tribes or groups of Indians and the principal issues of their long and continuing dispute with whites.

Beginning with three case studies focusing on the inheritance of the American Indian, Josephy relates that, for five centuries, Indians of Florida (the Seminoles and the Miccosukees) have maintained their identity as Indians and their rights to aboriginal lands. The case history of the massacre of the Pequots by Massachusetts Pilgrims serves as an example of the roots of the racial stereotype that still influences white treatment of the Indians. By tenaciously protecting their sacred sites and resisting conversion to Christianity, the Taos Pueblo Indians have retained the spiritual basis of their life.

The middle section of the text concerns Indian life today. The Native American fight to maintain their land base stiffened when the Allegheny Senecas failed to stop confiscation of their lands for the Kinzua Dam. Indian tribes all over the country believe in their rights to water as guaranteed by treaties. However, the Paiutes of Nevada have still to solve the Pyramid Lake water conflict. Clashes over Native American hunting and fishing rights are numerous in the Northwest as the Washington state Puyallups, Misquallies, and Muckleshoots fight for their claims.

The final chapter traces a recent case in which the Sioux, accompanied by militant Indians of varied factions, tribes, and political groups, held Wounded Knee by cooperating in their quest to regain sovereignty and control of their affairs and resources. This is an example of the contemporary Indian quest for self-determination.

"For an informative, accurate and human understanding of the political and social relationships between Indian and White, this book clarifies the basic thrust of the modern Indian movement," states Vine Deloria, Jr. In social studies and history, the book should be required reading as a reference to urgent questions that are still unsettled in the area of contemporary Anglo-Indian relations. For Indians and non-Indians, the text is a well-balanced account of injustice and indifference by the United States governmental bureaucracy, which were supported by an uneducated public. A lengthy bibliography of primary and secondary sources and an extensive index are provided for scholarly use.

60. Katz, William Loren. **Black Indians: A Hidden Heritage.** New York: Atheneum, 1986. 198p. FRL: 9. Subjects: Blacks—Ethnic relations with Indians of North America; Intermarriage.

Author of twenty books on American blacks and other minorities, William Loren Katz chronicles the black Indian legacy in American history. Defining black Indians as people with dual ancestry or black people who lived with Native Americans for a period of time, he traces their quest for freedom from the earliest foreign landings in the Western hemisphere through the settlement of the West by whites. The relationship of the black people and the Native Americans developed in response to a common enemy, the Europeans who exploited both races. Runaway slaves found haven, acceptance, and family life among the Native American tribes. Readers will recognize the names of many famous Americans who can trace their family trees to Afro-American Indian ancestry, such as poet-laureate Langston Hughes, black advocate Frederick Douglass, cowboy and bulldogger Bill Pickett, and outlaw Cherokee Bill. Many black Indians were tribal leaders, soldiers, trappers, outlaws, explorers, and western scouts.

This excellent discussion of black Indians provides a new focus for student research. Very sensitive writing and black-and-white photographs and drawings support the author's focus on the special relationship between the two ethnic groups. The index provides access to both the text and illustrations, and the bibliography is annotated. Students and teachers of American history will find this account fascinating and thought-provoking.

61. Kessel, Joyce K. **Squanto and the First Thanksgiving.** Minneapolis, Minn.: Carolrhoda Books, 1983. 47p. FRL: 3. Subjects: Thanksgiving Day; Squanto; Pilgrims (New Plymouth Colony).

Thanksgiving, proclaimed an official holiday by President Lincoln in 1864, has its roots in the friendship between an American Indian and the Pilgrims who arrived in the New World on December 21, 1620. The first bountiful harvest of the Pilgrims resulted from a visit by the Paluxet Indian Squanto, who taught the colonists how to grow crops. The fascinating story of Squanto is related for children. Captured in the early 1600s by English explorers and sold in England as a slave, Squanto learned English. Upon being freed and returned to his native land, he was again seized and sold as a slave to the Spanish, where he learned of the Christian faith from Catholic monks. Finally freed, he returned to America to find that his people had all died from smallpox. In 1620, Squanto visited the Pilgrims, whose numbers had been reduced to only fifty-five after their first winter. He stayed to teach them how to survive during the winter and raise crops in the growing season. Their first harvest was recorded as the beginning of the Thanksgiving holiday, which the Pilgrims celebrated with Indian leader Massasoit and his braves.

The storyline of this children's book can be followed through the sepia-toned illustrations by Lisa Conze. For elementary-school students, the book can serve as a simple biography of the American Indian Squanto and the history of Thanksgiving Day. The afterword provides the subsequent historical background of the holiday. This is not the only material that should be used for Thanksgiving. Including in programs American Indian children who can talk about cultural contributions or stories of their tribal people as the original inhabitants of this country is just as effective, and perhaps more so. The traditional story of Squanto is usually romanticized and perpetuates the belief that Indians are valuable as people only if they "helped" the white man, because the only record available is in the history written by the colonists.

62. Lacapa, Michael.

    62.1. **Antelope Woman: An Apache Folktale.** Flagstaff, Ariz.: Northland, 1992. 41p.

    62.2. **The Flute Player: An Apache Folktale.** Flagstaff, Ariz: Northland, 1990. unpaged.

FRL: 3. Subjects: Apache Indians—Legends; Legends.

Many talented American Indian people are writing and illustrating their own legends, no longer relying on stories recorded by non-Indians. Michael Lacapa, award-winning author and illustrator, gains inspiration from traditional storytellers to retell a traditional Apache folktale. Drawing upon his Apache, Hopi, and Tewa cultural roots, he uses his artistic training to illustrate stories filled with designs and patterns of the Southwest. Bold-colored pen-and-ink drawings reinforce the storyline.

Honored as a "Best Book" by the Arizona State Library Association, *Antelope Woman* describes a mysterious young man who teaches the people to revere all things great and small. A young woman, intrigued by his teaching, watches him disappear through four sacred hoops and emerge as an antelope. He invites her to follow and she does. Young readers will learn why the Apache people never hunt or kill antelope. *The Flute Player* is another beautiful Apache story about two young people who become acquainted through what some say is the sound of wind blowing through the trees. The story reminds the reader that canyons are special places, and that love is a special way of feeling.

Lacapa heard these folktales told by the White Mountain Apache storytellers while he was growing up. Librarians and teachers will appreciate the simplicity and integrity of the words. These books present culturally relevant educational materials for children.

63. Martini, Teri. **Indians.** Chicago: Childrens Press, 1982. 45p. FRL: 5. Subject: Social life and customs.

The revised edition of *The True Book of Indians*, published in 1954 and written by Teri Martini, was edited by Margaret Frisky for publication as part of the New True Book Series by Childrens Press. Using a simple text that is printed in large, boldface letters, the lifestyles of the people Columbus called Indians are accurately portrayed. Readers are introduced to the way in which Indians lived before the arrival of the Europeans, a lifestyle that was deeply influenced by the environment. The Indians of the Northwest Coast, Plains, Southwest, Southeast, and Northeast woodlands used the resources of their natural environment and developed unique relationships with the land. The text will help students realize that, although Indians are referred to as a group, there are many differences among them because of the geographic areas in which they lived. Most pages contain either color or black-and-white pictures that usually relate to the text. Many have captions explaining their tribal relationship and importance to the Indian way of life.

Other Indian titles in the New True Book Series published in the 1980s provide information on specific tribes: *Apache, Aztec, Cherokee, Chippewa, Hopi, Inca, Maya, Navajo, Seminole,* and *Sioux.* These books are good additions to libraries where specific interest in different tribes warrant their purchase. They have a similar format and are excellent for younger readers. Two items make the Indian titles especially valuable as a reference for younger readers: the glossary of "words you should know" and the index.

64. Matson, Emerson N. **Legends of the Great Chiefs.** Nashville, Tenn.: Thomas Nelson, 1973. 125p. FRL: 7. Subjects: Legends; Nez Perce Indians; Nisqually Indians; Sioux Indians; Snohomish Indians; Makah Indians; Swinomish Indians.

Compiler Emerson N. Matson spent nearly three years researching and gathering material in an effort to preserve a few of the old legends and the history of these American Indian chiefs. Famous chiefs of the Nisqually, Nez Perce, Sioux, Snohomish, Makah, and Swinomish tribes maintained the culture of their people by telling and retelling tribal and family legends. The narratives centered around everyday routines of seven different American Indian tribes concerning cleanliness, explaining the creation of the people, and reminding children of the importance of community social life.

The author provides a brief history of the famous chiefs who told the lore. He recognizes that the legends are more meaningful in tribal language than when translated. The material is objective and authentic. A photograph of Chief Red Cloud and two maps showing the location of major reservations are the only visuals in the book. Intermediate, middle, and secondary school-age young people will enjoy the stories of the great chiefs. Language arts teachers should find the selections an asset when preparing units on folklore that include the American Indian.

65. Matthiessen, Peter. **Indian Country.** New York: Viking Press, 1984. 338p. FRL: 11. Subjects: Land tenure; Human ecology; Claims; Religion.

Land has always been sacred to Indian people. History reveals that the first white people on North American shores were intent on taking this land from the Indian inhabitants. In this decade the pattern is the same. Peter Matthiessen records in journal form his encounters with contemporary Indian people. As he traveled to their reservations and visited them in their homes, he noted their views as they struggle to survive in this century. He paints a disturbing and powerful portrait of the injustices inflicted on Indian people who are fighting to preserve their ancestral lands and their traditional way of life.

Drawing on historical background and perspective, his thrust is to document the continued interference of the United States government, beginning in the 1970s, in the affairs of ten Indian groups. His investigative reporting traces the ongoing struggles of Indian people who are involved in conflicts with the United States government and private industries to retain control of their ancestral lands. He journeys to the lands of the Miccosukee, Hopi, Cherokee, Mohawk, Yurok, and Kuruk of the Pacific Northwest; Lakota, Chumash, Paiute, Shoshone, and Ute of the Great Basin; and Navajo of Big Mountain. Indian people, who may be termed "traditionalists," are in many cases in conflict not only with the Bureau of Indian Affairs but also with some of their own people who are willing to allow ancestral land to be exploited for a price. The disputes involve strip mining, uranium mining, energy development, toxic waste dumps, pollution, water, roads, and logging; and also land appropriation, relocation, claims, disputes, roads, and treaty violations.

The reader will find a powerful message in Matthiessen's plea for public awareness of what is happening on Indian lands. He appeals to the reader to stop ignoring government policies that greatly disadvantage the Indian people. Each of the tribal conflicts presented can serve as a subject for unique and timely research. This book should be read by Indian youth and all young adults so that they can better understand the reasons for the continuing assault on the lands of the American Indian.

66. Mayo, Gretchen Will.

66.1. **Earthmaker's Tales: North American Indian Stories About Earth Happenings.** New York: Walker, 1969. 89p.

66.2. **More Earthmaker's Tales: North American Indian Stories About Earth Happenings.** New York: Walker, 1990. 89p. FRL: 6. Subjects: Legends; Weather—Folklore.

66.3. **More Star Tales: North American Indian Stories About the Stars.** New York: Walker, 1991. 96p. FRL: 6. Subjects: Legends; Stars—Folklore; Moon—Folklore.

66.4. **Star Tales: North American Indian Stories About the Stars.** New York: Walker, 1967. 96p.

Gretchen Will Mayo, a versatile writer and artist, delves into the rich treasury of Indian legends to provide readers with a rich treasury of Indian folklore. Stories about the earth and sky captivate children. The fascinating tales and beautiful illustrations intertwine Native American cultural history and environmental concerns in a unique way.

The two books on Earthmaker's tales center on natural phenomena that were mysteries to Native Americans. How did mountains come to be? Why did the great spirit make the waters like mirrors? How did thunder and lightning come? What causes tornadoes, ice storms, and floods? To explain why and how things happened, Indian people created stories that were told from one generation to the next. With wry humor and sensitive drawings, Mayo retells Indian stories about earth happenings. Each begins with an introduction that explains its origins.

Native American legends about the stars, moon, and night sky are retold in the two volumes of the Star tales. Indian storytellers often wove tales about the stars. In each book, representative legends are selected. Each story is introduced with an explanation of cultural beliefs. Young readers will find the Shoshoni tale of the antelope chase exciting, the trickster coyote tale about the constellations intriguing, and the Ojibwa animal story of the fierce and cunning fisher fascinating. The delightful text and evocative, realistic illustrations create a sense of wonder about the creation of the nighttime sky.

The legends in all four books were carefully researched, with original sources listed. For each tale, several realistic black-and-white illustrations incorporating Indian designs set the mood. A glossary of terms provides a tool for clearer understanding of Indian words, locations, and constellations or natural phenomena. The entertaining tales are easy to read and will be enjoyed by young readers. Science teachers will find the collection useful as a unique introduction to the study of astronomy or weather. The short, fast-moving tales are excellent material for oral reading. Libraries may consider buying the four-volume paperback set or individual hardback titles for circulation.

67. Mitchell, Wayne, and Marie Galletti. **Native American Substance Abuse: An Anthology of Student Writings.** Tempe: Arizona State University, 1982. 151p. FRL: 12. Subjects: Alcohol; Drugs; Inhalants.

One area of strong interest among young adults is that of drug and alcohol abuse. This volume, written by students in the School of Social Work at Arizona State University, provides some comprehensive research findings on substance abuse by Indians. The collection of papers reflects the student author's perspective on the problem and may present some conclusions that are controversial. Six student papers are presented on subjects mainly concerned with alcohol abuse, although inhalants and drug abuse are also discussed.

The papers explore the reasons for the high incidence of alcohol abuse on various reservations and provide some data on such areas as the effect of alcohol abuse on education and family life, a profile sketch of the problem drinker, and other information that should be considered in attacking the problem. Several of the papers provide only limited references, while others include some excellent resources for further research into this problem.

Inexpensively bound in a soft cover, this book will not last long on the average public or school library shelf. However, this type of information dates quickly, and it is hoped that it will be updated frequently. Teachers in social studies and health should be able to use this information readily in their classes. The papers provide a good resource for research on substance abuse.

68. New Mexico People and Energy Collective. **Red Ribbons for Emma.** Berkeley, Calif.: New Seed Press, 1981. 46p. FRL: 4. Subjects: Navajo Indians—Social conditions; Yazzie, Emma.

Emma Yazzie, a poor, Navajo Indian woman and grandmother, is an unlikely hero in our modern age. She lives a simple traditional life, herding sheep, living in a hogan, hauling water, and doing without any modern conveniences. The irony of her life is that she herds her sheep beneath the lines of a large power plant near her home during the day and at night she cleans the offices of a mining company that supplies coal to the power plant. Living on the Navajo reservation in the four corners area of Utah, New Mexico, Colorado, and Arizona, Emma's life is affected daily by the power plant that pollutes the air and water, destroys the fragile grass, kills the birds, and makes her life more difficult.

This book is unique. Rarely is a book written for children that details the life of an ordinary person struggling against a big company to maintain her lifestyle and land. Children who live on or near a reservation are familiar with similar or actual situations and may not realize that even one person can raise a voice and make a difference. For non-native children, this story can offer a way to make them socially conscious of how modern industries, such as electrical power plants, which they take for granted, can affect other people's lives. As Emma removes the survey stakes tied with red ribbons, burns the wood, and decorates her hogan with the ribbons, she represents a grassroots movement among her people.

The poignant story can provide a living example for young readers that tribal officials are not always cognizant of the impact of pollution and economic development on their people. For children of elementary and middle school ages, Emma is a hero, an ordinary person with a sense of humor and traditional values, who continues to live on the land where her mother and grandmother tended sheep.

The photographs provide a real sense of how this woman lives and the problems she faces. Her story will open doors for discussion on the many problems that economic development has caused on Indian lands. The book will be especially meaningful to American Indian children, who are reminded: "We still have plenty of chances to become heroes. We just need to think about becoming a different kind of hero."

69. Norman, Howard. **Who-Paddled-Backward-with-Trout.** Boston: Little, Brown, 1987. unpaged. FRL: 3. Subjects: Cree Indians—Legends; Names, Personal—Folklore.

Howard Norman lived with the Creek Indians, speaks their language, and has translated many of their stories into English. The source for this legend was George Wesukmin, an eighty-two-year-old man who lived in a Cree Indian village near Gods Lake in northern Manitoba, Canada. The tradition in the village was that if people were unhappy with the name given by their parents, they could try to earn a new name.

A young Cree Indian boy who is very clumsy receives the name Trout-with-Flattened-Nose from a dream of an elder in the village. Unhappy with his parent's choice, he leaves to earn a more flattering name. He attempts to become Who-Can-Sneak-Up-on-Owls, he practices to become Who-Can-Echo-Better-Than-a-Loon, and he works very hard to become Who-Paddles-a-Canoe-Better-Than-Anyone. The name he earns, given to him by the trout, is still not necessarily the one he wanted.

Children love stories that pique their curiosity, arouse their adventuresome nature, and tickle their sense of humor. Names also assume major importance and give them identity. Young readers and teachers will find the fascinating tale of the young Cree boy who searches for a name a high-interest story that is wonderful for reading aloud. The style is that of a storyteller, simple and descriptive. The black-on-white silhouettes by Ed Young amplify the text, giving a feeling of a journey into the unknown. This book is an excellent choice.

70. Pelton, Mary Helen, and Jacqueline DiGennaro. **Images of a People: Tlingit Myths and Legends.** Englewood, Colo.: Libraries Unlimited, 1992. 170p. FRL: 6. Subjects: Tlingit Indians—Social life and customs; Tlingit Indians—Legends.

Educators May Helen Pelton and Jacqueline DiGennaro present a book of Tlingit Indian folklore and culture. A native people of southeastern Alaska, the Tlingit pass their history, beliefs, traditions, and values from one generation to the next through oral tradition. This book includes both the lore and stories of the people.

Tlingit culture is based on kinship bonds, art forms, and spiritualism. The first part of the book traces the history and social structure of the people. A discussion of the Kushtaka (supernatural creatures who looked for human captives), shamanism, and witchcraft explain the spiritualism of the Tlingit traditions. Essays on the giant totems, spruce-root basketry, and bentwood boxes are included in the section on art and art forms.

The second part of the book contains the legends that the authors selected for retelling. All, except one, are based on John Swanton's *Tlingit Myths and Texts* (1909), collected for the Smithsonian Institute. An excellent discussion in the preface touches on the sources, their limitations, and comparative themes. Stories are arranged around five major themes: "The Creation and Why Things Came to Be," "The World of the Spirits," "The Animal Spirit Helper," "Stories That Teach the Values of the Culture," and "Kushtaka and Witches."

Images of a People is not intended as a picture book for young readers. The eight-page insert of color photographs and illustrations by Tlingit artist Jennifer Brad-Morales lends interest to the text for readers from grades four through twelve. A reference list and index make the book useful in research. Storytellers will find new additions to add to their repertoire.

This book is recommended as an excellent example of a folklore book. The delightful collection of twenty-two Tlingit legends is rich in images, drama, and spiritual content. Teachers and librarians will find that the stories carry the unusual message that all people are linked together by their ancient history.

71. Robinson, Gail. **Raven the Trickster: Legends of the North American Indians.** New York: Atheneum, 1981. 125p. FRL: 7. Subjects: Northwest coast of North America—Legends; Ravens—Legends.

Most Indian tribes have delightful traditional ancient stories of cunning animal gods, mythological beings who can assume either human or animal form. Among the Pacific Northwest Indians, the stories called "trickster" tales focus on the mischievous and clever Raven. A proud and boastful bird with a huge appetite, Raven frequently gets in trouble. However, as the creator of mankind, he helps those in danger and distress. As Douglas Hill points out in the introduction, Raven the trickster, like all human beings, can choose to be a hero or a buffoon.

Gail Robinson retells some of the stories she heard firsthand from the Pacific Northwest Indians. Each tale is illustrated in black-and-white ink drawings by artist Joanna Troughton. The collection of trickster tales is a welcome addition for storytellers of dramatic legends focusing on the theme of "courage conquers fear." These tales may be used as models for students to create their own "trickster tales."

72. Rosenstiel, Annette. **Red & White: Indian Views of the White Man, 1492-1982.** New York: Universe Books, 1983. 192p. FRL: 11. Subjects: Government relations—Sources; Oratory; History—Sources.

Collected for the first time, American Indian oratory selected from five centuries of historical accounts exposes Indian perceptions about the Europeans who invaded North and South America. Rosenstiel, professor of anthropology and sociology, shares American Indian words recorded in documents, letters, books, and speeches, many from obscure sources. The reactions to events that native people witnessed are from notable persons of historic and contemporary significance, including Pocahontas, Plenty Coups, Wovoka, Will Rogers, activist Russell Means, and prolific writer Jamake Highwater, as well as words of lesser-known people of both Americas. Each century is introduced with the author's synopsis of historical events that affected native people. Each quotation is preceded by introductory text and accompanied by a drawing, painting, or photograph of the period.

Faced with cultural extinction, Indian people used their long tradition of eloquent oratory to speak for themselves. The author's historical narrative provides the reader with an insightful perception of the history of North and South American by incorporating Indian voices. Notes and sources for each chapter, a reading list of additional sources, and an index support the scholarship. This book will be an excellent reference for young adults and teachers of Indian history and culture. The selective words offer an invaluable source for student speeches or research papers.

73. Steltzer, Ulli. **A Haida Potlatch.** Seattle: University of Washington Press, 1984. 80p. FRL: 10. Subjects: Haida Indians—Rites and ceremonies; Potlatch.

In ancestral times, the Haida potlatched and danced to celebrate a new house, to adopt or tattoo children, and to transfer names and crests. As the Haida people gradually abandoned art and ceremony under government pressure, the tribal tradition of the potlatch was discontinued. Robert Davidson, well known as a Haida artist, held a potlatch in 1969 to raise a totem pole in his village in Masset, Queen Charlotte Islands, Canada. Here he learned the proper ceremonial procedures from his people. In 1981, he held another potlatch at great personal expense and time and again solicited the help and knowledge of his family and the elders of his tribe. The ceremony was held to adopt a member of the Clayoquot band as his brother. He also encouraged the elders of his village to bestow Haida names on the young people at this ritualized feast.

Ulli Steltzer was invited to photograph and record the feast, dancing, speeching, gift receiving, and name giving on videotape. In interviews held later, she transcribed impressions of the participants and their concern about cultural revival. Her documentation of a modern potlatch in words and black-and-white photographs is an important record of Haida life. The book should help young Indian people to recognize that traditional ways continue to be a vital, living force today. As a photographic essay, this book will have great appeal to all readers.

74. Thorne, Ian. **Monster Tales of Native Americans.** Mankato, Minn.: Crestwood House, 1978. 47p. FRL: 4. Subjects: Legends; Monsters—Fiction.

Children of all ages love monsters. On winter nights beginning long ago, Native American children were entertained by their elders with monster tales. Some explained natural events. The Tuscarora Indian legend in this collection relates why the mosquitoes in New York and New Jersey are so large and so fierce. The voice of the mighty Niagara Falls reminds the Seneca people of the tale of Thunderer and the fever-monster. Other tales have spirit monsters who assume different forms. A beautiful maiden becomes a devilfish in the Haida legend, and a phantom elk is possessed by the demon Sayatkah in the Yakima story. The Cheyenne custom of offering gifts to the Mississippi River is based on the story of a young boy who turns into a snake and becomes the guardian of the water. From the owl monster tale of the Shahaptin people, naughty children learn a lesson. Other monster tales children will enjoy feature a horned lizard who is befriended by a kind Hopi, frog monsters who capture two Mohave Indian youth to ride as racing animals, and the Little People who steal the children of the Micmac tribe of Canada.

The author provides an introduction to the tales and concludes each selection with a brief note about the tribe that contributed the story. The sources the author used for reference are not listed. Also, the lack of a table of contents and an index to tribes makes the tales less effective as a reference source. The visually exciting black-and-white drawings accented with red by Barbara Howell Furan support the action-filled tales. Young readers and even reluctant readers will enjoy this book of monster tales.

75. Vizenor, Gerald. **Tribal Scenes and Ceremonies.** Minneapolis, Minn.: Nodin Press, 1976. 191p. FRL: 10. Subjects: Tribal consciousness; American Indian Movement; Reservations.

Historian, journalist, photographer, and poet Gerald Vizenor includes stories, editorials, and essays about tribal consciousness, the American Indian movement, reservation economic survival, radical revivals, sacred histories, profiles, and poetry images that he has written. An Ojibwa, Vizenor writes powerfully about many facets of Indian life in this anthology. The black-and-white photographs accompanying the text reveal a traditionally oriented people bound to contemporary society.

Much of this well-documented material was originally published in the *Minneapolis Tribune* and *Twin Citian Magazine*. The author gives his opinions on the differences in how the judicial system treats a person depending on his racial background. The book concludes with a brief bibliography. The table of contents is very detailed. The material should be useful to classes studying the role of society and the judicial system. Journalism students and teachers may also gain insight into reporting controversial issues.

76. Wheeler, M. J. **First Came the Indians.** New York: Atheneum, 1983. 27p.
    FRL: 3. Subject: Social life and customs.
    The delightful text by M. J. Wheeler and the appealing two-color illustrations
by James Houston will make this informational book a favorite with young readers.
Although the content is limited, the culture of six major North American Indian
tribes is described in simple language and sentences set in poetry form. Librarians
and teachers will want to add this title to their list of books that can be read aloud
to children.
    The book begins with a description of how Indian people came to the North
American continent and explains that each group developed a distinct culture.
Describing the environment and way of life, the author includes information on
religion, food, clothing, and shelter as well as beliefs. The tribes featured are the
Creek, Iroquois, and Ojibwa (Chippewa) of the Eastern woodlands; and the Sioux,
Makah, and Hopi of the West. The final section, which is valuable for all readers,
but especially to Indian children, explains in a positive manner that, today, Indian
people live like everyone else and have a valuable heritage that is important to all
Americans.

77. Whitney, Alex. **Stiff Ears: Animal Folktales of the North American
    Indian.** New York: Henry Z. Walck, 1974. 55p. FRL: 5. Subjects: Legends;
    Animals—Legends.
    Reminiscent of Aesop's fables, *Stiff Ears* is a group of fables that make a
cautionary point and employ animals that speak like human beings. The animal
legends are from many tribes, representing different geographical areas of the
United States. The author begins each tale with a brief and interesting essay on the
legends and storytelling customs of the Indian tribe in which the legend originated.
    Six delightful tales were researched, written, and illustrated by Alex Whit-
ney. In northeastern Arizona, the Hopi Indians' legend of an impatient rabbit called
Stiff Ears recalls the human foible of taking a shortcut instead of listening to
experience. The legend of a tiny mouse who won a war against the mighty buffalo
is told by the Pawnee of the Plains. "Never despair" is the lesson the rainbow trout
learns from the salmon in the Chinook tale from the Northeast. From the Midwest
woodlands, the Chippewa tell the story of the tortoise who is slow and wise and the
frog who thinks only one jump ahead. The porcupine in the Iroquois legend realizes
he cannot imitate other animals. The Cherokee folktale explains why only the
bravest can wear eagle feathers.
    This compilation of folktales reflects the wide variety of Indian heritage. The
author illustrates the text with three-color drawings. The text will serve as an
excellent model for children who are writing fables. Thoroughly researched, each
tale will teach a lesson for life as well as amuse readers of all ages.

78. Wood, Marion. **Spirits, Heroes, & Hunters from North American Mythol-
    ogy.** New York: Schocken Books, 1982, c1981. 132p. FRL: 7. Subject:
    Legends.
    Part of the World Mythology Series published in Great Britain, this collection
of American Indian and Eskimo myths and legends is retold by the author. The
settlement of North America and the skills and traditions of native groups as they
adapted to the natural environment and resources is briefly recounted. The varying
lifestyles account for the differing beliefs and myths as they reflect each group's

experience in the world. Many of the legends contain introductory material on the life of the people from whom the legend originates.

One of the fascinations of this book to young people will be the appealing, color artwork by John Sibbick, who specializes in accurate reconstructions of the past. This oversized volume contains double-spread pages of imaginative, vivid artistic drawings for each legend. In addition, other pages have numerous panels of black-and-white drawings, with some of the objects and symbols identified with the characters and events of the story. The symbols are explained in the appendixes and may be overlooked by the reader.

The value of the culture of the Indian and Eskimo people can be recognized by presenting these tales to young people. The author does not include the sources used for the legends. An index provides access to tribes and characters in the text. The book will be of value to collections where there is a demand for the mythology of North America.

400-499 Language

79. Amon, Aline. **Talking Hands: Indian Sign Language.** Garden City, N.Y.: Doubleday, 1968. 1985. 80p. FRL: 4. Subject: Sign language.

Using simple pictures and words, Aline Amon provides an instructional guide for young children who may wish to use authentic Indian sign language. The brief introduction explains that Indian tribes of the Western Plains who spoke different languages developed a language of gestures to communicate with each other. The instruction begins with the names of the fingers, demonstrates the basic position of hands, develops words into sentences, asks questions, tells stories, and concludes with conversations. Her clear and explicit line drawings feature an Indian boy demonstrating the signs. The manner of presentation also provides an opportunity to learn different forms of language.

The index includes more than 200 words that can be located in the text. This attractive book can be used by teachers and librarians as an educational tool to entertain children and teach them about nonverbal communication. The book is written for boys and excludes references to girls in both text and illustration.

Four other books provide slightly different approaches: George Fronval and Daniel Dubois's *Indian Signs and Signals* (Sterling, 1979) is a large-format book that uses photographs of members of a contemporary Kiowa family demonstrating sign language. *Indian Sign Language* by Robert Hofsinde (William Morrow, 1956) has a format similar to Amon's book but uses an Indian adult to demonstrate the sign language. *Indian Talk: Hand Signals of the North American Indian* by Iron Eyes Cody (Naturegraph, 1970) was also written for children and can be purchased in paperback as well as hardcover. A replication of the 1931 edition of *Indian Sign Language*, by William Tomkins, was printed as a practical working text for Boy Scouts. While Amon's book is probably the simplest, the other four books also provide illustrated instructions in this fascinating gesture language. All the books are written for children. Every library that serves young readers interested in American Indians should have at least one of these titles.

80. **Dictionary of Daily Life of Indians of the Americas.** Newport Beach, Calif.: American Indian Publishers, 1981. 1139p. FRL: 13. Subject: Encyclopedias and dictionaries.

This two-volume dictionary offers a scholarly approach to the study of American Indian culture. The entries are arranged alphabetically, and the descriptive material is encyclopedic in nature. Each entry begins with a general description for each major area of importance in the daily life of the New World culture. Further paragraphs provide specifics, such as tribal affiliation and archaeological findings. The entries cover the traditional culture in the subject areas of language, social organization and institutions, daily cultural characteristics, habitation and construction, technology, clothing, narcotics and stimulants, and myths and legends. Information covers the cultural periods before the arrival of Columbus, the changes during the period of European intervention in Indian lifeways, as well as the present status of Inuit and Indian people of the North American continent, including Latin America.

Scholarly in its approach, this set offers an excellent discourse on topics that cannot be located in a general encyclopedia. Secondary students and adults searching for details of specific American Indian cultures will find the source excellent as a reference. Although the dictionary is not "as attractively slick as many books with high quality paper and color," black-and-white illustrations of historical events add interest. An unusual feature for the dictionary format is the index of entries. The source for much of the material is the twenty-volume *Encyclopedia of Indians of the Americas* (Scholarly, 1974-1981).

81. Hofsinde, Robert. **Indian Picture Writing.** New York: William Morrow, 1959. 96p. FRL: 4. Subject: Cryptography.

As part of his sequence of books for children on the different areas of Indian culture, writer-illustrator Hofsinde presents Indian pictographs. Following a brief introduction on the use of picture writing by American Indians to record legends and important family and tribal history, he provides 248 symbols, with captions containing descriptive information about culture. Although most picture-writing symbols included are ancient, some are modern. The symbols are grouped by subject, such as family relationships and seasons. To locate a specific word, the book has a helpful alphabetized word index to the symbols and their key numbers.

A small section describes "exploit" markings, drawings that were painted on the body of the Indian and his horse before battle to symbolize past victories. Sample letters in picture writing show the reader how the symbols can be used. The book will appeal to boys and girls interested in coding as well as Indian history.

82. Patterson, Alex. **A Field Guide to Rock Art Symbols of the Greater Southwest.** Boulder, Colo.: Johnson Printing, 1992. 256p. FRL: 10. Subjects: Antiquities; Rock drawings, paintings, and engravings.

Upon completion of a successful business career, Alex Patterson studied and traveled to American Indian rock art sites in western North America. His extensive and systematic survey of rock art sites and literature in this vast region is published to benefit both the novice and professional. Patterson's objective is to either name or apply meaning to each depiction he located in the literature on the Southwest rock art illustrations. The introductory essay examines the meaning, dating, and style of rock art. Rock art site manners are explained and the use of the field guide on site is demonstrated.

The first section of this study, titled "Finders," aids the person who views a rock art site. Small boxed duplications of illustrations are organized as humanlike, animal-like, and abstract. Once the viewer has found the symbol, he turns to the second section, which lists ascribed meanings alphabetically along with a description of the symbol or feature. The final section is an alphabetical dictionary of rock art symbols with ascribed meanings from the original sources. Patterson collected rock art writings from archaeologists, anthropologists, researchers, Native American informants, and other writers, published during the last 125 years. From these he compiled more than 600 commentaries on specific symbols and illustrations, noting site location. Over 500 illustrations and photographs of symbols and rock sites provide keys to interpretation of American rock art.

The author carefully avoids giving personal interpretations of the subjects. Each site's general location is provided on a state map. Directions are given to eighteen rock art sites in national parks, state parks, and areas set aside for public viewing. A recommended reading list, organizations to join and events to attend, bibliography, and credits are provided.

As people view thousands of rock art sties in Utah, Arizona, California, New Mexico, Nevada and Colorado, they want to know what the pictures and symbols mean. Was there a message left by the ancients on the rocks long ago? Patterson does not claim to have found the real meaning of the rock art symbols cited in his paperback book. He has carefully collected and organized the meaning selected writers ascribe to the symbols. The field guide will enrich the experience of visitors to rock art sites as they study the symbols.

83. Patterson, Lotsee, and Mary Ellen Snodgrass. **Indian Terms of the Americas.** Englewood, Colo.: Libraries Unlimited, 1994. 275p. FRL: 5. Subjects: Encyclopedias and dictionaries; Biography.

The plethora of American Indian books published during the last ten years has created a need for a dictionary of American Indian terms suitable for children and young adults. *Indian Terms of the Americas* commendably fills the void. The compendium of Native American terminology was developed by Lotsee Patterson, University of Oklahoma School of Library and Information Studies Associate Professor and Comanche Tribal member, and Mary Ellen Snodgrass, freelance writer and former English Department chair at Hickory High School, North Carolina. The authors gleaned native terms from children's and adult literature. Dictionaries and encyclopedias inadequately answer questions about Native American terminology. This definitive reference work can aid readers in understanding American Indian vocabulary, places, people, and events in classical literature and nonfiction sources.

More than 850 terms describe a variety of activities, including names for objects, methods of doing things, and significant people, places, and events. Words from other languages naming or describing aspects of Indian culture that have become part of traditional terminology are included. Most of the terms are from the Indian tribes of North America, with some from Central and South American Indians.

Alphabetized entries provide pronunciation, based on the h-system found in children's books, which is easy to understand and requires no knowledge of diacritical markings. Alternate forms or spellings are noted. Boldface words guide the user to additional and related information. Definitions include dates or time periods and places to pinpoint the entry as fact, tradition or legend. A unique feature of the dictionary is the illustrative sentence for most terms. The entry appears in conversation, oration, printed material, oral traditions, or rituals of Native American life. The people incorporated in the sentences are either historical or current figures or characters from myth, film, or fiction. Two hundred black-and-white original and reprinted drawings, maps, diagrams, paintings, and photographs clarify the informative terms. An extensive bibliography lists a wide range of American sources on Indian subjects. A subject index and general index without page numbers are appended.

Schools and libraries should consider this reference work a basic volume in Native American collections. The encyclopedic dictionary format, designed for use by children and young adults, makes for fascinating reading. Entries offer wide coverage of tribal groups and stress home, family, and community interests. Unlike some sources on Indian life, notable women balance well-known men and connections between Indians, blacks, and Hispanics are noted. The use of nature for medicine, food, and ceremonies provides an understanding of a little-known side of Indian life. With the emphasis on understanding both the historical and present life of American Indian people, this quality reference book expands the multicultural horizons of young people.

84. Stoutenburgh, John L., Jr. **Dictionary of the American Indian.** New York: Crown, 1960. 459p. FRL: 8. Subject: Encyclopedias and dictionaries.

Containing thousands of words pertaining to American Indians, this dictionary is a very useful reference tool for those who need simple, brief definitions. Two definitions follow that demonstrate the format of this book:

Mohawk

The name Mohawk means "they eat live things," sometimes also known as "man eaters." This was the most easterly of the Iroquoian confederacy. The Dutch and the Mohawk Indians carried on a large amount of trade. They traded firearms, which made them very powerful against their neighbors, the Delawares and the Numsee. The main villages of the Mohawk were around Lake Mohawk in New York State.

American Horse

An Ogalala Sioux chief.... Fought with Sitting Bull in the Sioux war. He was killed at Slim Buttes in South Dakota on September 29, 1875. He was a signer of the treaty which was secured by the Crook commission.

Stoutenburgh's compilation should be valuable in all curriculum areas, especially for upper-elementary and middle school children. Because it was printed in 1960, an updated version would be even more helpful.

500-599 Pure Sciences

85. Freedman, Russell. **Buffalo Hunt.** New York: Holiday House, 1988. 52p.
     FRL: 4. Subjects: Buffalo; Great Plains; Hunting.
     Indian storytellers often spoke of the buffalo. Legends of buffalo giants and
ghosts, buffalo who ate Indians or magically became men, and buffalo who came
from gigantic caves or lakes were a few of the tales told by tribes such as the
Comanche and Blackfoot. To the Plains Indian, the buffalo, or American bison, was
the most important animal on earth. Russell Freedman in *Buffalo Hunt* examines
the significance of the buffalo in the day-to-day life of the Great Plains Indians.
     Over 150 years ago, countless millions of buffalo roamed the prairies and
plains. Native American hunters stalked the buffalo on foot for thousands of years
without guns or horses. In a factual account, Freedman examines the hunting
methods. Meat, hide, and bones provided the people with everything they needed.
The Great Plains Indians hunted in small tribal groups. Hunting involved the entire
community. Medicine men invoked visions and conducted dances and songs to lure
the buffalo. Scouts located the herd. Preparation of weapons and attack plans
preceded the men's hunt. When the animals were killed, women and children helped
with the skinning and butchering. Then the people celebrated.
     Later the Plains Indians became skilled horsemen, drastically increasing their
efficiency as buffalo hunters. For the most part, Indians hunted only when they
needed hides and meat. As white people came to the Plains and slaughtered the
buffalo, they also seized the land. Within a few years, the main source of food,
clothing, and shelter for the Indian tribes had vanished. The flourishing culture and
traditional way of life were gone. Only the storytellers kept the old tales alive.
     Freedman offers a pictorial record of two cultures in conflict. This portrait
of a vibrant people is well written and thought provoking. The distinctive feature
of this account is the reproduction of paintings and drawings that accompany the
text. Freedman selected the artwork of artist-adventurers George Catlin, Karl
Brodmer, and others who traveled the West during the time the Plains Indians
depended on the buffalo. The book has added value as an art portfolio.
     Although this is an excellent piece of nonfiction, references for the factual
content are not listed. The index contains only thirty-two main entries, sufficient
for children doing research. This well-written account will be welcomed by young
readers interested in the development of the West. Freedman portrays the humanity,
courage, and resolve of the Plains Indians. The format makes the book attractive to
elementary and junior high school students.

86. Grisham, Noel. **Buffalo ... and the Indians on the Great Plains.** Austin,
     Tex.: Eakin Press, 1985. 37p. FRL: 4. Subject: Buffalo—History.
     The relationship of the buffalo and the Indians of the Great Plains holds a
fascination for children of all ages. The great animals who once roamed freely in
large expanses of grasslands are now usually viewed only in a few national parks
and reserves or on commercial ranches. The vital story of the impact of the buffalo
on the daily lives of the Plains Indians is recounted along with historical events.
The text chronicles the Indian people's use of the buffalo for food and shelter,
clothes and ornaments, as well as tools, weapons, and musical instruments. The
entire lifeway of the Plains Indian depended on the huge, shaggy mammals.

Accounts are given of the magical "albino" buffalo and the desperate Ghost Dances held during the late 1800s.

On every page the text is reinforced by black-and-white illustrations highlighted with red accents by Betsy Warren. A glossary of sixteen specialized words "to know" aids understanding of the culture. A bibliography of ten books is also included.

The factual presentation is easy to read and well organized. The table of contents provides quick access to each area discussed, and a map illustrates the geographic extent of migratory animals. The book is an excellent choice for individual reading and will be useful with groups to supplement a history lesson on the Indians of the Great Plains and the buffalo.

87. Tannenbaum, Beulah, and Harold E. Tannenbaum. **Science of the Early American Indians.** New York: Franklin Watts, 1988. 96p. FRL: 8. Subjects: Science—America—History; Technology—America—History; Science, Ancient.

Scientific achievements of the American Indians in North and South America in the pre-Columbian period cannot be separated from their philosophical and religious beliefs. In this relationship, science was considered a "natural philosophy." The American Indians made use of science by developing skills needed to adapt to their environment. Providing a brief general overview of the scientific skills necessary for their way of life, the authors acknowledge the contributions of the American Indians to scientific technology.

The easy-to-read text gives readers information on architecture, astronomy, agriculture, and artistic innovations of the pre-Columbian people in the Americas. The black-and-white illustrations, although interesting, do not always relate to the accompanying text. A glossary, books for further reading, and index provide easy access to information.

88. Weiss, Malcolm E. **Sky Watchers of Ages Past.** Boston: Houghton Mifflin, 1982. 84p. FRL: 6. Subject: Astronomy, Prehistoric.

Although this children's book on prehistoric astronomy does not limit its focus to the Americas, the content does include specific information on Indian archaeoastronomy. The study of the heavens by ancient people is the oldest science. To begin his discussion, Weiss focuses on Chaco Canyon, the site of an abandoned Pueblo settlement that was a great trading center. Interested in the art of the people of this area, modern artist Anna Sofaer discovered a rock Anasazi "calendar." All over the world, ancient people built "observatories" and "instruments" to record the mysteries of the skies. Southwest Indians recorded the passage of seasons. Eclipses and movements of the sun and planets were predicted by the Mayas.

Illustrations by Eliza McFadden accompany the text. The easily read content provides limited information on ancient astronomy for young readers.

600-699 Technology (Applied Sciences)

89.   Brandenberg, Aliki. **Corn Is Maize: The Gift of the Indians.** New York: Harper & Row, 1976. 32p. FRL: 3. Subjects: Agriculture; Corn.

In one of the Let's-Read-and-Find-Out Series of books, author and illustrator Aliki Brandenberg traces the farming of corn from planting to harvest, then asks the questions: "Where did corn come from? How did it start?" Scientists believe that people in South and Central America planted seeds of a tall grass that pollinated with another grass and, over hundreds of years of cultivation, became the grain the native people called maize. Soon, people in all the Americas were growing a form of maize for their food needs, in different ways best suited to their climate. The development of corn is traced through modern agricultural practices.

Children who read this attractive book, illustrated on every page by simple three-tone drawings, will learn how Indian farmers thousands of years ago developed the grain called maize. The blending of history and science offers a fresh approach for teachers of young students.

90.   Brescia, Bill, ed. **Our Mother Corn.** Seattle, Wash.: Daybreak Star Press, 1981. 79p. FRL: 5. Subjects: Agriculture; Corn.

Originating with the Curriculum Development Staff of the United Indians of All Tribes Foundation, this book provides teachers and children in the upper-elementary and middle-school grades with an excellent resource on the tall, life-giving plant, "Mother Corn." In the lives of the Hopi, Pawnee, and Seneca, as well as other tribes, corn was the central focus long ago and continues to be important today.

First, the reader learns the origin of corn, then traces it through pollination and fertilization, discovers planting and crop rotation, and is provided with the addresses where native corn seed can be obtained, as well as some farming notes. The rest of the book contains legends, games, songs, chants, and corn recipes for the Seneca, Pawnee, and Hopi tribes. The information is well documented throughout the text, and the book includes a glossary and bibliography of books used in researching subject areas. The illustrations and designs by Roger Fernandez are attractive. Not only will readers learn about corn, they will acquire insightful information about the Hopi, Pawnee, and Seneca cultures and history. This book is an excellent teaching tool for science, vocational, and social studies areas.

91.   Cox, Beverly, and Martin Jacobs. **Spirit of the Harvest: North American Indian Cooking.** New York: Stewart, Tabori & Chang, 1991. 255p. FRL: 7. Subjects: Cookery; Food; Social life and customs.

Paperback books on the cookery of individual tribal peoples are available in bookstores and museums across the United States. *Spirit of the Harvest: North American Indian Cooking* by Beverly Cox and Martin Jacob presents a different approach to Indian foods. In a large library-bound hardback book, the authors provide a carefully researched text on the traditional food preparation of the tribes from different geographic regions of North America. The focus is the distinctive cooking of North American Indians who used indigenous plants, seafood, and game.

Important foods such as corn, beans, squash, and potatoes were carefully cultivated by North American Indians before Columbus. The culture of major tribal groups determined their diets, ceremonial use of food, and historic dishes. The book is divided into five geographic regions. Experts on native cuisine introduce the chapters on each region. Clara Sue Kidwell is a member of the Chippewa Tribe of Minnesota and Choctaw tribe of Oklahoma. She wrote the opening chapter, "Native American Food," and the introduction to the chapters "The Southeastern Coast and Woodlands" and "The Northeastern Coast and Woodlands." Arthur D. Amaiotte, a member of the Ogalala Sioux Tribe, provided the introduction and notes on the recipes for the chapter "The Great Plains." Harriet Koenig provided chapter introductions and notes on recipes for "The Southwest" and "The West." An anthropologist, she specializes in American Indian cultures.

This volume contains 150 recipes selected from across the United States. Native Americans who supplied many recipes are recognized. All recipes can be easily prepared using modern kitchen techniques. Many traditional foods, such as Cherokee Red and Green Mixit, Iroquois Leaf Bread, Mohegan Succotash, and Assiniboin Game Stew, are included. Some ingredients have recently been recognized as healthy and flavorful—wild rice, corn, beans, sunflower seeds, venison, fowl, and fish.

This volume is so attractive that browsers will enjoy reading the pages. A specially created map places the tribes and their principal foods in geographic context. Fifty full-color photographs featuring historic Indian artifacts illustrate the recipes. Black-and-white Indian designs accompany the informative text. The appendix includes a section on Native American ingredients used in the recipes, a bibliography of books by geographic region, photographic prop credits with location, and a detailed index. Incorporating details about the social life and customs of native people with indigenous recipes, the volume can be used for research and units on ethnic cooking. This book is not just another cookbook; it is a book about the distinctive cookery of North American Indians from coast to coast.

92. Diamond, Arthur. **Smallpox and the American Indian.** San Diego, Calif.: Lucent Books, 1991. 64p. FRL: 6. Subjects: Smallpox—West (U.S.); Diseases— Social aspects.

History is full of disasters, stemming from a variety of causes. However, disasters cannot be viewed in isolation. Arthur Diamond's book, *Smallpox and the American Indian*, details the historical period and cultural background of the Indian people when smallpox decimated their numbers. Usually, the smallpox epidemic and its impact on American Indian populations are briefly mentioned in the study of American history, but few people realize that this disease led to the destruction of many Indian cultures.

Three hundred years after Columbus arrived in North America, Native Americans still occupied wilderness from Alaska to Mexico, from the Missouri River to the Pacific Ocean. By the early 1800s the fur trade had been established. Indian people received blankets, weapons, and other goods in exchange. In the summer of 1837, a steamboat journeyed up the Missouri River to trade with Mandan, Assiniboin, and Blackfoot tribes. The goods the native people received led to a smallpox epidemic that lasted from 1837 to 1840. An estimated 100,000 to 300,000 Indians died in the plague. Whole tribes were destroyed. Greed, heartlessness, and misunderstanding led to the spread of smallpox among many tribes. This book focuses on the tribes of the upper Missouri, but the tragedy also occurred in Alaska, the Northwest, California, and the Southwest.

A brief overview of the smallpox epidemic among Indian tribes, this small book offers an excellent introduction for junior high school students. The text is easy to read and understand. Historical and medical information about the smallpox virus and development of the vaccine is presented. Technical concepts and interesting anecdotes are explained and illustrated in inset boxes. Further reading materials for young adults, and works the author consulted, are appended. The glossary and index make the information easily accessible. Black-and-white pictures provide interest. Such an important topic deserves a broader and more scholarly approach for use by secondary students and adults.

As part of the series World Disasters, this topic is significant not for dramatic quality but for educational value. Readers will learn of the attitude toward Indian people at that time. "Once Edward Jenner discovered smallpox vaccination in 1797, the real reason for the disease's continuance among the Indians was apathy and indifference on the part of whites to the plight of the infected." By reliving this shameful event, the reader can see how indifference and greed affected the lives of Indian people. The author implies that apathy toward those suffering from disease still exists. Young readers will gain a vision that they can work together to prevent future epidemics.

93. Henry, Edna. **Native American Cookbook.** New York: Julian Messner, 1983. 94p. FRL: 6. Subjects: Cookery; Social life and customs.

Of Nipmuc and Cherokee ancestry, Edna Henry (whose Indian name We-Cha-Pi-Tu-Wen means Blue Star), offers an intimate view of Native American recipes from different Indian people, enlivened with stories, culture, history, and legend. The author's introduction tells the delightful story (excellent for use in classrooms at Thanksgiving), which is told and retold at family gatherings, about "Chief-Without-Food" and his war in the form of a challenge dance with "Chief-With-Food." The sections on maize and turkey, and those on the Nipmuc, Shinnecocks and Narragansetts, Iswa (Catawba), Seminole, Cuna natives of the San Blas Islands, Sioux, Inupiat, and Klondike and Southwest regions, each have introductory background information. The recipes, some traditional and others adapted to modern ingredients, use simple, natural components, from the tasty cattail biscuits to the easy-to-prepare Princess White Flower's winter stew.

Children of all ages and adults will find that the book is fun to read, full of tasty recipes, and a storehouse of information. The author provides a list of substitutes for native foods. Nadema Agard illustrates the book with black-and-white line drawings. The index to food, recipes, and information on legends, cultural areas, and history makes the cookbook useful for educational purposes.

94. Kavasch, Barrie. **Native Harvests: Recipes and Botanicals of the American Indian.** New York: Vintage Books, 1979. 202p. FRL: 10. Subjects: Food; Botany—North America; Cookery.

Writing from a scientific perspective, ethnobotany teacher Barrie Kavasch provides research on the extent of Amerindian influences on today's food. Wild plants, some of which were domesticated and harvested, were used extensively by native people of the Americas in every facet of their daily lives. Not only were botanicals used as food and medicine, but the natural environment also provided clothing, shelter, and tools. As people developed agriculture-based societies, they developed new species of corn, beans, squash, gourds, pumpkins, and many other edible crops. In addition to cultivated plants, their diet included fresh and saltwater foods, game, and a large variety of edible wild plants. Many Amerindian foods are the basis of classic American cuisine today. Barbeques, clambakes, chowders, gumbos, cranberry dishes, cornbreads, puddings, and other dishes originated with American Indian tribes. Just as different tribes had their own culture and language, the cuisine varied according to growing season, geographic location, and way of life.

Discussion of native plants and recipes of ancestral origin are provided for seasonings, soups, vegetables, mushrooms, game, saltwater and freshwater harvests, breads, and beverages. Topics not usually included in books are wild medicines and cosmetics, smoking mixtures, and natural chewing gums. A very valuable chapter gives guidelines for poisonous plants. The author has profiled or illustrated most of the plants used in the recipes that are unfamiliar to users.

Unlike other books on Native American cuisine, the author's primary emphasis is on native flora; she also includes introduced species used by Amerindians. The well-researched information on plants and their preparation encourages the enjoyment of wild harvests. Many recipes, such as yellow squash soup, use ingredients readily available in gardens or markets; other botanicals must be gathered from the natural environment. For tasty, creative, salt-free recipes, home economics teachers will appreciate the opportunity to include unique American cuisine in their units. Students of science who are interested in cookery and the use of wild plants will find the scholarly approach applicable to scientific research and projects.

95. Lavine, Sigmund A. **The Horses the Indians Rode.** New York: Dodd, Mead, 1974. 78p. FRL: 7. Subject: Horses.

For readers who love horses and history, *The Horses the Indians Rode* will convey an accurate portrayal of the cultural impact of the horse on Indian life. Drawing on early chronicles, trader and trapper diaries, and tribal lore, as well as contemporary sources, Lavine records the background of the horse in North and South America. Beginning with the origin of the horse in North American and its mysterious disappearance, the story shifts to the introduction of the horse into South America by the Spanish. The South American tribes overcame their worship and fear of the horse and became skilled horsemen. The acquisition of the horse spread to the northern tribes between the Rocky Mountains and the Mississippi River through trade, raids, and capture of wild horses. The mastery of the horse by the Plains Indians brought liberty, wealth, and status. On the eastern seaboard, colonists introduced the horse to the native people of that area.

Young people will be fascinated with the "Horse Plains Culture," the story of the mustang, and the development of the colorful Appaloosa and Pinto breeds. The excellent, brief treatment is highly readable and will not only appeal to horse lovers but also can be used to support history and agricultural science curricula.

Numerous illustrations, photographs, and old prints enliven the text. The book includes an index but has no bibliography. *The Indian and His Horse* (Morrow, 1960) by Robert Hofsinde is also recommended for children.

96. Vogel, Virgil J. **American Indian Medicine.** Norman: University of Oklahoma Press, 1970. 583p. FRL: 10. Subjects: Medicine; Botany—Medical; Medicine men.

Vogel's book points out the valuable contributions Indian cultures have made to the worldwide practice of medicine. Most of the literature on Indian medical practice emphasizes the ceremonial and shamanistic aspects of healing rites. While ritual healing has indeed played a major role in the treatment of illness, the utilization of indigenous ethnobotanical drugs was frequently of equal importance. Western culture was quick to recognize the importance of these plants, and "Indian cures" and many treatments were adopted in both professional and folk medicine.

Although this book approaches Indian medicine from a historical viewpoint, the main theme of the book is that modern medicine is deeply indebted to Indian medicine. The treatment of illness is a dynamic process, and Indian medicine progressed as well as Western medicine. The author notes that Indian medical practices were no more strange than early Western practices such as bleeding. Vogel also recognizes that some effective Indian drugs such as cocaine were used for centuries before adoption by Western medicine because of ethnocentric attitudes. An excellent chapter on American Indian therapeutic methods provides a comprehensive outline of historical and contemporary Indian medicine relating to specific ailments.

Because this book is not written in medical terms, middle and secondary school students will not have any difficulty reading and understanding the material. Teachers in social studies and English will be able to recommend this subject as a relevant and interesting research topic. Over half of the book is devoted to the appendix, "American Indian Contributions to Pharmacology." A complete index of the text, an index of botanical names, and a comprehensive bibliography of the subject make this book a basic text for any research on Indian medicine.

97. Weslager, C. A. **Magic Medicines of the Indians.** Wallingford, Pa.: Middle Atlantic Press, 1973. 161p. FRL: 9. Subjects: Medicine; Herbs; Botany—Medical.

Weslager has written a very readable and informative account of the use of medicines by American Indians. The book is written on a level that can be easily understood by the general reader and is not intended to be a comprehensive or technical text on Indian pharmacology or ethnobotany. The author points out that Indian healers had a long history of utilizing such medical practices as poulticing, sweating, setting broken bones, and using plants as purgatives, vermifuges, diuretics, and emetics. Indian cures were not limited to herbs, although the world has profited from the contributions the Indians have made in this area.

Ceremonies have played a large role in healing for the Indian people, and this book discusses healing ceremonies among the Delawares as representative of these rites among all Indian tribes. Several chapter divisions are devoted to the listing of herbs that have been used by various tribes. Weslager indicates that specific herbs used by various tribes are constantly changing, depending on availability and results.

Because the book has been written primarily to entertain, readers will enjoy it both for recreation and as an excellent resource on Indian healing ceremonies and medicine. The emphasis is on subjects that will appeal to the young adult reader. Library professionals should be aware that most of the material is written using the Delaware tribe as the primary source of information.

98.   Whitney, Alex. **American Indian Clothes and How to Make Them.** New York: David McKay, 1979. 114p. FRL: 6. Subject: Clothing.

The well-researched text of Alex Whitney and excellent drawings and diagrams of Marie Ostberg and Nils Ostberg offer readers a firsthand look at attractive, durable, and practical clothing of North American Indians. Apparel varied according to environment, available materials, and use, which included everyday, ceremonial, or for war. The first seven chapters offer information supported by illustrations on native materials used to make and decorate clothing: skinwork and weaving used for clothing construction, and bead, quill, feather, shell, bone, and horn used for adornment. A section not included in most other books on Native American clothing discusses sewing equipment and techniques used in making the items. The remaining chapters incorporate easy-to-follow instructions for constructing apparel and adornment, accompanied by drawings and diagrams. The clothing includes dresses, shirts, vests, moccasins, and accessories such as jewelry, belts, and pouches. Directions are included for making specific tribal items such as a Salish owl pendant, Plains link belt, and Navajo two-piece dress.

For students in elementary through high school, this compact book can serve as a source of information on American Indian clothing as well as an instruction manual for making and adorning a variety of items. A map and list of major Indian tribes of the North American continent, list of suppliers, selected bibliography, metric conversion table, and index make the book useful as a reference.

700-799 Arts and Recreation

99.   Amsden, Charles Avery. **Navajo Weaving: Its Technic and Its History.** Glorietta, N. Mex.: Rio Grande Press, 1974. 261p. FRL: 10. Subject: Weaving.

In 1929, Charles Amsden, born and raised on the edge of the Navajo tribal range, began research on the technical aspects of Navajo weaving. This book, first published in 1932, covers two major areas: techniques of Navajo weaving and history of Navajo weaving. The first section describes and illustrates in detail the various weaves used by the Navajo, records the processes employed in making their native dyes, and discusses types and uses of Navajo textiles. The second division traces the beginning of the weaver's art through archaeological knowledge of the development of the loom and its prototypes in the prehistoric Southwest. The history of the origin of the Navajo craft and its mutations begins with the introduction of sheep by the Spaniards and the adopted art of weaving from captive Pueblo women around the middle of the eighteenth century. The history is researched from its earliest historical references in old Spanish documents and brilliant "Bayeta period" to 1932. This period encompasses the transformation from a native craft of blanketry into a rug-making industry.

Not only is the text comprehensive, but the illustrations are also unusual in that they are authentically dated plates of more than 100 blankets dating back to the Civil War and earlier that illustrate every phase of blanket making. The endpapers of the book contain nine colored photographs of rugs.

This thoroughly documented volume contains an excellent index and a bibliography of works cited. The material should be of value in American history, ethnic studies, and art.

100. Baldwin, Gordon C. **Games of the American Indian.** New York: Grosset & Dunlap, 1969. 150p. FRL: 8. Subject: Games.

In simple language, Baldwin discusses ten major categories of games played by Indian children from prehistoric times to the present. Using short paragraphs and a fairly easy vocabulary, the author selected choices from tops, dolls, and whistles through games of skill to tell us a story. Children of all ages and cultures enjoy the skill of creating string figures as described in the book.

The introduction provides a good basis for understanding that games were instruction through play, providing practice for warfare, hunting, farming, and keeping house. Information on demeanor, physical stereotyping, and diversity of language and culture is included. Although individual tribal games are mentioned in the text, the author treats most of the specific games as part of the nine geographic regions identified by anthropologists as having similar cultural lifestyles.

The extensive photographs and line drawings will appeal to young adult readers, especially if they do not enjoy reading text. Physical education and child development classes for all school-age children will find the material valuable.

101. Barry, John W. **American Indian Pottery: An Identification and Value Guide.** Florence, Ala.: Books Americana, 1984. 214p. FRL: 15. Subject: Pottery.

Having carefully and thoroughly researched the ceramic arts of American Indians, the author presents an authoritative guide to assist the reader in the identification and appreciation of American Indian pottery. Well established in North America by 2500 B.C., pottery was an integral part of the Indian lifeway. Following the role of ceramic arts from prehistoric to historic and into the contemporary period allows the reader to understand that pottery provides the archaeologist with clues to the unwritten record of Indian culture. Clay figures, canteens, urns, and bowls were used as utilitarian, commercial, social, and ceremonial objects. The author contends that the continued pursuit of ceramic arts by Native Americans will help preserve their cultural past.

In contrast to the many technical books on the subject, this guide is easily understood and will be enjoyed by young people as well as adults. The 400 full-color plates of exceptional quality and detailed information on the pottery forms of twenty-seven tribes illustrate the styles and designs of pottery developed in the significant pottery regions of the country. The introductory chapter will be especially valuable to potters who are interested in the traditional methods of the Indian people. The book will be popular with students interested in this art form, teachers and potters looking for information on handbuilt methods, and admirers and collectors appreciative of Pueblo and other Indian pottery.

The appendix provides (1) a glossary to explain definitions used within the context of the book that apply to ceramics, (2) references for further research into the development of pottery and the personalities associated with it, (3) a list of pottery collections in private and public institutions, and (4) a pricing index of trade prices (in 1984) of contemporary wares, based on their artistic worth. No prices are provided for prehistoric or museum pottery.

102.   Baylor, Byrd. **When Clay Sings.** New York: Charles Scribner's Sons, 1972. unpaged. FRL: 4. Subjects: Art; Pottery.

Young readers of this artistic account by Byrd Baylor and illustrator Tom Bahi will be encouraged to respect the pottery shards that lie scattered near the remains of the homes of the prehistoric people of the Southwest. The poetic simplicity of the title refers to bits of pottery as a piece of someone's life, created with care and song for use in the home or ceremony.

Capturing the sandstone reds, desert browns and tans, and stark black and whites of the ancient pottery, artist Bahi uses designs derived from prehistoric cultures of the Anasazi, Mogollon, Hohokam, and Mimbres. Feeling kinship with the Indian child in the text who finds the ancient bits of clay, young readers see that the designs can take a thousand shapes: horned toads and lizards, butterflies and turtles and leaping fish, deer and mountain goats and antelope flashing across a canyon, and even scary things called monsters. For pure enjoyment, for study of an ancient art, or for raising social consciousness about the intrinsic value of ancient artifacts, *When Clay Sings* presents a solid rationale for teaching children the value of ancient pottery.

103.   Bedinger, Margery. **Indian Silver: Navajo and Pueblo Jewelers.** Albuquerque: University of New Mexico Press, 1973. 264p. FRL: 10. Subjects: Silversmithing—Navajo Indians; Silversmithing—Pueblo Indians.

Based on historical evidence, Margery Bedinger's authoritative account traces the acquisition of metals from the Spanish to the contemporary silverwork of the Navajo and Pueblo Indians. The author relates how the Indians gained skills in metalwork and learned different techniques. The origins of the basic forms and decorative designs for conchos, crosses, najas, and pomegranates are included. Of interest also is the preference of various tribes for different styles. Navajo silversmiths prefer plain areas of silver with stones as accents, as opposed to Zunis, who use silver settings for elaborate stonework.

The book has some distinctive features that will be especially valuable to aspiring silversmiths. The 155 photographs and drawings, nine in color, are very distinct, and the designs on the pieces of jewelry can be clearly seen. The trend away from the traditional designs toward the development of highly individualistic, unique silverwork should inspire creativity among young metalworkers. Concern about the effects of commercialization, tourism, imitation of original forms, and use of inferior metals is expressed.

This scholarly and very complete book is presented in a useful, readable form. The author includes detailed notes, an extensive bibliography, and an excellent index. Those interested in Indian silverwork should find the text and illustrations of significant value.

104.   Bennett, Edna Mae. **Turquoise and the Indian.** Chicago: Swallow Press, 1970. 152p. FRL: 11. Subjects: Turquoise; Silversmithing; Mining.

Found in the arid regions of the Southwest where many American Indians live, turquoise is an integral part of the life of the American Indian. Edna Mae Bennett provides the first comprehensive treatment of the gem in fifty years. She studied many sources and samples of turquoise lapidary to gather information. In New Mexico, Arizona, and the southern portions of Colorado, Utah, Nevada, and California, the beautiful blue-green stone influences many aspects of Indians' lives.

All tribes made use of the stone, but some were more influenced by it than others. Many rites and celebrations may require its use. The gem is also highly prized as an ornament. Because turquoise is native to the area and occurs near the surface, Indians were able to mine it with primitive tools. The mineral is soft and easily worked in its natural state.

The book's contents trace the early records of the Spanish reports of the gem, mining activity, lapidary work, contemporary jewelry, and pawn, and concludes with the significance of the gem in ceremonies, mythology, and archaeology. The book is well illustrated, containing black-and-white photographs and maps, fourteen color reproductions of turquoise settings, and the author's own drawings of Indian motifs. An extensive bibliography and an adequate index are provided. This popular account, based on technical research, with extensive illustrations, should have value to lapidaries, silversmiths, anthropologists, and readers interested in the significance of turquoise in the culture of the Southwest Indian people.

105.   Bierhorst, John. **A Cry from the Earth: Music of the North American Indian.** New York: Four Winds, 1979. 113p. FRL: 5. Subject: Songs and music.

Offering a wide variety of American Indian music and dance from the major geographic regions of North America, Bierhorst selected songs from noted collectors to illustrate music from the late eighteenth century through the mid-twentieth century. Music of the Eskimo, Northwest Coast, Yuman, Navajo, Great Basin, Plains, Pueblo, and Eastern woodlands is included to destroy the myths that all Indian songs sound alike. An integral part of life, the songs and dances are distinguished by their purpose, whether for pleasure or need, in daily life or ceremony. Much of the informative text, which includes thirty songs, describes music created for the very young and for storytelling, for prayer and magic, of love and war, and for new life in the modern age. The use of instruments—drums, rattles, and flutes—as accompaniment is discussed as well as the structure of the music and the unique vocal techniques that use speech and body rhythm.

Note should be made by public and school librarians that a record album of native performances of most of the songs can be purchased from Folkway Records (FC7777 *A Cry from the Earth*). The book and album may be used together or separately. The descriptive text develops appreciation of the diversity of American Indian music. The combined study of a unique music style and the culture and history of the American Indian will captivate singers and dancers as they participate in a cultural experience.

106.   Blood, Charles L. **American Indian Games and Crafts.** New York: Franklin Watts, 1981. 32p. FRL: 3. Subjects: Games; Handicraft.

One of the Easy-read activity book series, this games and crafts book offers a double-page spread for each activity. The illustrations by Lisa Campbell Ernst depict "The People," as Columbus called the Indians in 1492. The accompanying text furnishes accurate general information explaining similarities and differences by using the words, "Some made ..., Some danced...." On the opposite page, each activity is outlined in a box that provides (1) the materials needed and (2) simple direction for completing the project. The materials required are common objects of minimal or no cost. The attractive format allows incorporation of reading, art, and recreation.

The simplified activities and handcrafts in the book can promote an appreciation for the culture of the American Indian. Librarians and teachers can use this information as a springboard to develop an interest in other aspects of American Indian culture and promote the reading of additional information books on American Indian culture.

107. Brody, J. J. **Indian Painters and White Patrons.** Albuquerque: University of New Mexico Press, 1971. 237p. FRL: 11. Subjects: Art; Painting.

Although this book was written primarily as a reference book on the influence of the white market on Indian painters, the main value to the public and school library will be in the author's description of the evolution of Indian art from prehistoric times to the present. An additional service to readers is the excellent selection of illustrations showing the development of stylistic Indian paintings of the last century. The book may be a little technical for the younger reader, but it should be helpful to young adults seeking material on both early and present-day Indian art.

Dr. Brody surveys the archaeological evidence of prehistoric Indian art throughout the United States and analyzes the effects of the whites on Indian art in the nineteenth and twentieth centuries. Because Indian-white relationships had such a profound influence on Indian art, the background of government social and economic policy is also reviewed. The book centers primarily on the effect of Anglo cultural domination on Indian art in the Southwest. Indian painters of the first half of this century are given some well-deserved recognition.

The transition of traditional Indian painting to modern Indian painting is, in a sense, a representation of the modern Indian's social change. The illustrations of modern painting range from a new wave of impressionism to those Indian artists who are striving to maintain the styles of the past. The book will have value to those who are interested in studying the evolution of the simple graphic Indian painting. Of equal importance is the criticism of governmental policy toward Indians. Young adults and teachers will find this volume helpful in social studies research.

108. Culin, Stewart. **Games of the North American Indians.** Lincoln: University of Nebraska Press, 1992. 846p. FRL: 10. Subjects: Games; Gambling.

In 1891, astute researcher Steward Culin and noted historian Frank Hamilton Cushing began a joint project to research the games of American Indian culture. Cushing died at an early age and Culin finished a comprehensive one-volume study in 1907. This two-volume set, republished in 1992, is by far the most definitive study of the games of North American tribes. The introduction by Dennis Tedlock of the 1992 First Bison Book printing discusses his experience with Indian games. He verifies that those described by Culin are as much a part of American Indian culture today as they were before the time of Columbus.

Volume 1 delves into "Games of Chance." Many different tribes played games with dice made of various materials. The section on guessing games details use of sticks, hands, or moccasins to play games such as four-stick and hidden-ball. Culin found that the method and purpose of the tribal games were very similar. One hundred thirty tribes belonging to thirty linguistic groups played these games. For each game, information about the different tribal practices is included. Also, popular guessing games involving sticks, wooden disks, and hidden objects are revealed. Volume 2, "Games of Skill," elaborates games such as archery, snow-snake, hoop and pole, and ring and pin. Ten different types of games using balls are explained. With few exceptions, the ball used in a game is never touched with the hand. Thirteen types of amusements that can be regarded as games of dexterity entertained adults and children, including cat's cradle, popgun, shuttlecock, quoits, and bean shooter.

For each game of chance or skill, Culin includes the words and bibliographic sources of primary observers. More than 11,000 illustrations identified by tribe and location accompany the detailed instructions for playing the games and sports. The extensive index in volume 2 provides ready access to the text.

Groups of Indian people gather today to play games of chance and skill, a side of American Indian culture that few outsiders are privileged to share. Some games figure prominently in the myths and ceremonies of tribal people. This classical study was published in 1907 by the Bureau of American Ethnology. For sports and games that are as deeply rooted in American Indian life today as in their long past, this two-volume set is the best comprehensive reference available.

109. Fichter, George S. **American Indian Music and Musical Instruments: With Instructions for Making the Instruments.** New York: David McKay, 1978. 115p. FRL: 6. Subjects: Songs and music; Musical instruments.

Fichter's children's book is an excellent choice for libraries looking for coverage of both the music and musical instruments of the American Indian. Authentic American Indian music was collected and recorded in the late 1800s and early 1900s. The music presented in this discussion is based on selections in the *Bulletin of the Bureau of American Ethnology*. The author notes that the poetry of the original songs and the rhythmic beauty are lost when translated into English and transcribed on paper.

The discussion focuses on why the Indians sang. Although tribes spoke different languages, music formed a kinship among the people. Indian music was created for a purpose: joy and sorrow, war and healing, hunting and harvest, love and death, and lullabies. For each category of songs, there is both general and specific tribal background, as well as words for many songs.

A special feature of this book, which sets it apart from other volumes, is the large section on the making of native musical instruments. Materials, instructions, and illustrated diagrams are provided for creating and decorating many types of instruments, including the ornamental gourd rattle, clapper, musical rasp, bull roarer, jingler anklet, double-headed drum, drumstick, and bamboo flute. The drawings and diagrams of Marie and Nils Ostberg enhance the compact text and are valuable for promoting cultural understanding as well as for describing craft production. Clear, simple, black-and-white designs for decorating the instruments, a selected bibliography, and an index support the text.

110. Fox, Frank. **North American Indian Coloring Album.** Los Angeles: Price Stern Sloan, 1978. 31p. FRL: 11. Subject: Social life and customs.

In a very attractive format, this softcover books offers a brief introductory overview of fifteen North American Indian tribes. Using a 12½-by-9½-inch format, Frank Fox gives a brief summary of each tribe in a one-page review. On the opposite page, detailed line drawings by Rita Warren capture the clothing, dwellings, family units, and arts and crafts in a natural setting.

A written and visual capsule of the lifeways and history of the Iroquois, Seminole, Chippewa, Sioux, Pawnee, Cherokee, Blackfoot, Nez Perce, Haida, Pomo, and Rio Grande Pueblos, as well as the Zuni, Apache, Hopi, and Navajo, is offered as a source of quick information. Although the title implies that the book was written as a "coloring album" for young readers, its more difficult reading level may limit the use of the text to middle and secondary school students. The finely detailed drawings present a wide scope of information. This book will be helpful for professional libraries in school districts. The sheets are glued, not stapled. The lack of a table of contents and index limits use, and the tribes are not introduced in alphabetical order.

111.   Furst, Peter T., and Jill Leslie Furst. **North American Indian Art.** New York: Rizzoli International Publications, 1982. 236p. FRL: 12. Subject: Art.

For an authoritative source on art of the North American Indian people, ethnologists Peter T. Furst and Jill Leslie Furst offer an informative text, lavishly illustrated with full-color photographs of representative artifacts. The reader gains an understanding of the environmental factors and cultural traditions integral to the development of these creative works. The art is presented as an expression of Indian beliefs in magic, myth, and ritual.

The art of six major tribal areas is examined. Kachinas, pottery, weaving, and silverwork dominated the Southwest area. The California region was known for feather basketry and rock paintings, while the Pacific Northwest tribes carved totem poles, masks, and ornaments. The Eskimos of Canada and Alaska created animal sculptures and incised weapons and utensils. On the Plains, bead and quill work were exquisite, and painted hides and pipes were noted for their symbolic meaning. The embroidered garments and carved masks of the Eastern woodlands were highly developed arts and served both utilitarian and ceremonial needs.

The illustrations have well-written captions that explain the historical and cultural significance of the art. The highly informative text and superb reproductions of the artifacts make this book valuable as a general reference, as a book of art, and as a resource for understanding the form and function of visual arts in six major tribal areas in North America.

112.   Grant, Campbell. **Rock Art of the American Indian.** New York: Promontory Press, 1967. 178p. FRL: 11. Subject: Rock drawings, paintings, and engravings.

Campbell Grant, a research associate in archaeology at the Santa Barbara Museum of Natural History, has written and illustrated an overview of Indian rock art in America. The author visited most of the sites he describes while photographing, copying, and taking notes during a 12,000-mile journey. The text identifies the motifs and their probable meaning and correlates them with regional and tribal cultures and migrations. All major sites of rock art in North America are identified (approximately 15,000). The drawings are especially numerous in the western United States. In addition to visiting numerous sites, the author reviewed the literature about Indian rock art and explains how it is dated and the best ways of recording and preserving it. The volume includes summaries of some material in the author's classic work, *The Rock Paintings of the Chumash* (University of California Press, 1965).

Sixteen pages of color reproductions and 150 excellent black-and-white photographs and drawings provide excellent visuals. Through these illustrations the reader can gain insight into the ways of life of early people by viewing symbols for hunting, fertility, spirits, clans, and power, as well as depictions of migrations. Rock art shows great diversity in form—some is stylized, some abstract, some naturalistic.

The site locations and picture material should be useful to those interested in art, archeology, and travel. Another value of the record of this early form of Americana is that much rock art has been destroyed by both natural and human forces. The written record of the variety of subjects, styles, and techniques of early American Indians is carefully preserved in this survey for young adult readers.

113. Highwater, Jamake. **Many Smokes, Many Moons: A Chronology of American Indian History Through Indian Art.** Philadelphia: J. B. Lippincott, 1987. 127p. FRL: 12. Subjects: Art; History.

Entwining art and history, a chronology of events affecting Indian history and social events is recreated from early times through 1973. Indian author Jamake Highwater uses the art and artifacts of the highly diversified Indian cultures of the North American tribes to provide a view of their respective worlds. This approach, which he terms "one land, two worlds," looks at events from a different perspective. Through the use of unique illustrations he recreates historical and social events. The opening chapter does not begin with a dated episode, but with the Navajo creation story of First Man, First Woman, and Coyote. The chapters proceed from prehistoric times through 1973 A.D. and the Wounded Knee incident.

Young adults who are interested in art and history will find this approach unique and intriguing. The format could be adapted as a holistic learning approach by teachers of Indian students. Young adults searching for a different approach to research or multimedia will be drawn to examine history through art. The book includes a selected bibliography and an index.

114. Highwater, Jamake. **Song from the Earth: American Indian Painting.** Boston: New York Graphic Society, 1976. 212p. FRL: 12. Subject: Painting.

The examination of American Indian painting by the eloquent Indian writer Jamake Highwater develops the theme of "the otherness of Indians," the Indian concept or way of seeing the world. An integral part of native culture, Indian art is traced from the pre-Columbian sources through the work of the traditional painters of the early twentieth century to the productions of present-day artists. Ten notable painters are profiled: Bear's Heart, Fred Kabotie, Allan Houser, Oscar Howe, Blackbear Bosin, Fred Beaver, Archie Blackowl, R. C. Gorman, T. C. Cannon, and Fritz Scholder.

The final chapter will be of particular interest to young artists, as it probes the question: "What is Indian about Indian art?" This attractive book has innumerable color and black-and-white reproductions of paintings, including informative text on the painter, tribal affiliation, title, year, medium, location, and description of the work.

The appendix guides the reader to museums, galleries, and annual exhibitions. The chronology of Indian painting; the selective bibliography; and the index of people, tribes, and subjects, including captions, make the volume useful for the researcher as well as for the general reader. This beautiful volume will attract all patrons, especially the developing Indian artist who experiences individual expression through the medium of painting.

115. Hilger, Michael. **The American Indian in Film.** Metuchen, N.J.: Scarecrow Press, 1986. 196p. FRL: 7. Subject: Motion pictures.

Many public and school libraries contain video collections to enhance their services to students and the public. *The American Indian in Film* by Michael Hilger provides a vital reference that educators and librarians can consult to evaluate films that focus on the American Indian.

Reviews of 830 films are organized in four major chapters: silent films, early sound films, films of the 1950s and 1960s, and films of the 1970s and 1980s. The introduction to each period uses representative films to reflect the content of the time. Films reviews are arranged chronologically by number from 1903 through 1984 to illustrate the development and sometimes strange mixture of images and themes in the historical period. Hilger selected films in which American Indians are a significant part of the film, in terms of either character or plot. Each entry lists the film title, releasing company, date, and director. A brief plot summary follows based on information from periodicals, reference books, and viewing. The summaries focus on the actions of the Indian characters, with their names and those of the actors who play them, if available. References to film reviews and newspapers and magazines are parenthetical in the text.

References are cited. The name index indicates an Indian actor playing an Indian and a non-Indian actor playing an Indian. Some categories in the topical index are Bad Indians (bloodthirsty, vengeful, threat to progress), Bad Whites (Indians as victims), Ethnic Groups (cultural and character contrasts), Good Indians (noble savage), Good Whites (paternalism), Historical Events, and Literary Sources.

Two chapters, "The Fictional Indian" and "Beyond the Fictional Indian," deserve the special attention of educators. Unfortunately, many films do not receive careful screening and send the message to young people that "Indians, be they noble or bloodthirsty, are inferior to whites." Today, as in the past, producers frequently portray the "fictional" American Indian as they take liberties with biographical information and romanticize American Indian history and culture. This book can be helpful in identifying films that offer little or nothing of value about Native American history and culture.

116. Hofmann, Charles. **American Indians Sing.** New York: John Day, 1967. 96p. FRL: 6. Subjects: Music; Poetry; Rites and ceremonies; Musical instruments.

Music, dances, song-poetry, and ceremonies of Indian nations demonstrate the wealth of the culture of the American Indian. Hofmann makes available a wide range of Indian songs and ceremonies from his long experience in teaching and working with Indian people. By blending past and present, the text presents a survey of why and how the Indians made music.

Songs and ceremonies were integral in the lives of American Indians. The first section of this book deals with Indians and Indian music, using the typical characteristics of Indian songs and ceremonies: health, fertile crops, rainfall, hunting, the spirit world, and war and peace. The remainder of the text illustrates and explains specific ceremonies: the Sun Dance, False Face Society, Snake Ceremony,

Green Corn Dance, Deer Dance, and others. The importance of dance is emphasized for the rituals. Musical instruments are introduced and their significance is explained. Many of the songs and dances are ancient in origin and are important in modern-day Indian culture.

Special features of this book are numerous. Frederick Dockstader, Director of the Museum of the American Indian, offers an informative introduction. Photographs and illustrations by Nicholas Amorsi, in addition to songs transcribed in notation, enhance the text. A recording (bound in the endpapers) of seven different tribes demonstrates the variety of American Indian musical expression. The appendixes include a bibliography of other recordings of Indian music and reading lists for students, teachers, and parents.

Hofmann emphasizes the diversity of the Indian nations by recognizing the similarities and differences in their music. The variety of sound in the collection of melodies should provide enrichment for music classes. Social studies classes and other interested readers can become better acquainted with the world of the American Indian through an awareness of the universality of music in all cultures.

117. Houston, James. **Songs of the Dream People: Chants and Images from the Indians and Eskimos of North America.** New York: Atheneum, 1972. 82p. FRL: 9. Subjects: Songs and music; Eskimos.

James Houston, whose major interest since childhood has been Native Americans, provides a record of the text to songs, speeches, and dances in the words of Native Americans and Eskimos. The rich and varied songs depict the various aspects of American Indian and Eskimo life. The celebrations of culture have grown out of each specific tribe's way of life and depict the movement and vitality of the people.

The diverse selections are grouped regionally. The author not only recorded the selections but also provided graphic color illustrations on each page. The striking drawings depict artifacts, art objects, and weapons of the individual people. Although the book contains no table of contents or index, the material could be used by teachers of music or literature to help students appreciate the complexity and beauty of Native American celebrations. Many selections can be read to younger children, while others are better suited to adults.

118. Hoyt-Goldsmith, Diane. **Totem Pole.** New York: Holiday House, 1990. 30p. FRL: 5. Subjects: Tsimshian Indians; Clallam Indians; Northwest coast of North America; Totem poles.

Author Diane Hoyt-Goldsmith, using her knowledge of the art and traditions of the Pacific Northwest Coast Indian people, offers a photographic essay on contemporary totem pole carving. As a collector of Northwest Coast tribal art, she recognizes the importance of modern carvers and artists. Photographs by Lawrence Migdale present visual documentation for a private glimpse into the lives of Tsimshian carver David Boxley and his son. The thoughtful narrative unfolds through the eyes of the young boy.

David and his family live in a small town in Washington state. David's father is a leading Northwest Coast Indian artist brought up in the old ways and traditions by his grandparents. His mother, who is not Indian, is adopted in a ceremony by the Eagle Clan. David's father shares his heritage with his son. For the first time, David is old enough to help his father carve a totem pole for the nearby Klallam Indians.

Through the imagery of words and photographs, readers follow David as he helps select the cedar tree, sees the design for the totem figures created, and carves and paints the pole. At the special ceremony and feast, David and his father perform the Carver's Dance and the Salmon Dance. The cultural bond between father and son is the dominant theme of this carefully documented experience. "As I listen to the chanted songs and move to the ancient music of my ancestors, I am proud. I am proud to have a father who can transform a straight cedar log into a magnificent totem pole.... I am proud to be the son of a Tsimshian carver."

For youngsters of multicultural families, this book provides information not usually discussed in children's literature. If shared as a valuable life experience, a parent's heritage creates pride in the child. Young Indian readers will gain cultural pride as they understand the value of extended family and community.

Public and school librarians can recommend this book to all children, but especially to children of varied ethnic backgrounds. Pride in heritage and the importance of learning and respecting cultural dignity is the central theme of the story. The writing is simple and direct. The inclusion of a glossary and index make the book useful as a reference. Children will enjoy sharing the experiences of a family who values their culture.

119.   Irwin, R. Stephen. **The Native Hunter Series.** Blaine, Wash.: Hancock House, 1984. 5 vols. FRL: 7. Subject: Hunting.

119.1.   **Hunters of the Buffalo.** 52p.

119.2.   **Hunters of the Eastern Forest.** 52p.

119.3.   **Hunters of the Ice.** 52p.

119.4.   **Hunters of the Northern Forest.** 52p.

119.5.   **Hunters of the Sea.** 52p.

Stephen Irwin's original book, *The Providers*, was the source for this series, which was adapted for young readers. This collection of five books offers an insight into the hunting and fishing skills of the North American Indian and Eskimo. To provide food and shelter for their daily lives, the native people relied on different hunting, trapping, and fishing techniques, depending on their locale.

To dispel the stereotypical views perpetuated in much of the literature of the North American Indian and Eskimo, a realistic view of the hunting style for five geographic areas is recorded in words and graphic illustrations. Following a set format, each book provides a description of the geographic area; tribal populations; and the game animals, fowl, and fish.

The set of books is inexpensive and profusely illustrated with historical photographs and drawings of scenes and artifacts. The illustrations by J. B. Clemens, created for this series, enhance the understanding of the text. This informative and easily read series will appeal to a wide variety of readers at elementary school through secondary school levels. Each volume includes an index for locating specific information.

120.   Katz, Jane B., ed. **This Song Remembers: Self Portraits of Native Americans in the Arts.** Boston: Houghton Mifflin, 1980. 207p. FRL: 11. Subjects: Biography; Art.

Through the medium of oral interviews, this collective biography provides intimate portraits of twenty-one Native American creative artists. Combining the tape-recorded interviews with information gathered from other sources documented in the endnotes, the author presents the work and lives of contemporary Indian, Eskimo, and Aleut men and women from all sections of the country practicing many diverse art forms. In the field of visual arts, the reader is introduced to graphic artists, woodcarvers, sculptors, painters, pipecarvers, basketmakers, and potters. Practicing composers, dancers, actors, and directors are featured in the performing arts. The literary field includes writers, poets, and novelists. By using the words of the creative artists, Katz has presented an unusual type of biographical sketch. The text goes beyond the usual factual data and provides open and meaningful dialogue about their work as exciting and innovative approaches to traditional and modern Native American art forms.

This significant anthology offers young adults a glimpse of the satisfaction and achievement of contemporary Indian artists who share their personal view of the Indian world. Photographs of all the artists and examples of their work accompany the text.

121.   Kennedy, Paul E. **North American Indian Design Coloring Book.** New York: Dover Publications, 1971. 46p. FRL: N/A. Subjects: Art; Design.

Fifty North American Indian designs were selected and rendered for coloring in this paperback. Each rendering is a fine example of an Indian craft: masks, beadwork, and pottery and works from metal, stone, and wood. The designs are from the Eskimo, Northwest Coast, Pueblo, Navajo, Chippewa, and Plains Indian people. Each black-and-white design is on an 8-by-11-inch page and is identified as to type of design, tribe, regional location, and historical data. Some are modern designs and some are centuries old. Kennedy also includes the medium on which the design was produced. All of the information on the background of the drawings is based on material from museum collections and technical books.

School and public libraries will find demand for these designs, which were selected to show the richness and diversity of North American Indian art, by all school-age children as well as art classes, especially pottery and silversmithing. The Dover Pictorial Archive Series grants permission to make up to four duplications of each design for any one project, or in any single publication, free and without special permission.

122.   La Farge, Oliver. **Introduction to American Indian Art.** Glorieta, N. Mex.: Rio Grande Press, 1973. 212p. FRL: 11. Subjects: Symbolism; Poetry; Art; Painting; Sand painting; Pottery; Sculpture; Carving; Masks; Basketmaking; Weaving; Beadwork; Bibliography—Indians of North America—Art.

In 1931, Oliver La Farge and twelve other leading authorities on American Indian art produced two paperbound volumes containing brief essays and pictorial plates as an introduction to the art of Native Americans for the Exposition of Indian Tribal Arts in New York. In 1973, the Rio Grande Press published the two volumes in one magnificent hardback reprint edition as part of their classic series of distinguished Western Americana. The thirty-three plates were selected entirely with consideration for their aesthetic value. The accompanying essays are considered miniature masterpieces of popular writing by scholarly authorities.

Oliver La Farge and John Sloan succinctly state that the intent of the exposition was an opportunity for Americans to view fine Indian work exhibited as art. The exposition provided the Indians with a means of being seen not as the makers of cheap curios and souvenirs, but as serious artists worthy of making cultural contributions to enrich modern life. The works presented are both classic and modern in style. Indian art objects included in the book are noteworthy because they are useful and highly decorative. The collection includes American Indian symbolism, poetry, painting, sand painting, pottery, sculpture and carving, masks, basketry, weaving, and porcupine-quill and beadwork. One of the most notable chapters is the bibliography of books on Indian arts north of Mexico, by Ruth Gaines of the Huntington Free Library in New York.

The original engravings included a few color plates, but in replication all were reproduced in black-and-white halftones. Although the material is written in a more scholarly style than many other books of similar content, the essays are accurate, authentic writings of professional scholars who did thorough research in each specialized area. Art teachers should find the material excellent as an introductory text. Aspiring Indian artists and scholars of Indian art will gain respect for American Indian culture and history.

123. Nashone. **Where Indians Live: American Indian Houses.** Sacramento, Calif.: Sierra Oaks, 1989. 38p. FRL: 3. Subject: Dwellings.

This book offers drawings and information on the houses that American Indians have lived in for generations. The author complements this information with pictures showing that present-day American Indian people also live in modern houses. The brief information on the many different types of Indian houses includes the early cliff dwellers, who used ladders to enter their houses; the Papago, who made their homes of plants and earth; and the Miwok, who wove thick mats for walls. Other types of housing are the Navajo hogan, Apache wickiup, Sac-Fox bark house, and Iroquois longhouse. Shapes varied from the wigwam to the tipi to the pueblo villages. Building materials included mud (the large mud houses of the Mandan) and mat (the mathouses of the Palouse). The author explains that houses varied in shape, size, and materials depending on the location and climate.

The text is sparse, but it is adequate enough to acquaint children of all ages with the concept that American Indian houses are of many types and to dispel the notion that all Indians live in tipis. Either a drawing of an Indian house by Louis Smith or a photograph with explanatory text is included on each page. The author provides a glossary and photograph credits.

124. Naylor, Maria, ed. **Authentic Indian Designs: 2500 Illustrations from Reports of the Bureau of American Ethnology.** New York: Dover Publications, 1975. 219p. FRL: N/A. Subjects: Art; Basketmaking; Pottery; Masks.

American and Indian art expert Maria Naylor selected 2,500 illustrations of authentic Indian designs from all over North America. Designs were selected from prehistoric times to the end of the nineteenth century, from the first forty-four annual reports of the Bureau of Ethnology. In 1897, the bureau began collecting artifacts, recording tradition, and making scholarly studies of the way of life of the American Indian, which was rapidly changing. Any particular art form, no matter how traditional, can quickly be lost as native people substitute trade goods for native articles. American Indians also quickly realized that native articles might need to be radically changed to capture a commercial market; consequently, the traditional methods could be forgotten.

Content is arranged by geographic areas: prehistoric art of the Eastern woodlands with concentration on arts of the culture around the Mississippi and Ohio valley river networks; art during the historic period of the Eastern woodlands; art of the Plains area; art of the Northwest Coast, Alaska, and the Arctic regions; Pacific Northwest; and Southwest. The illustrations show designs and objects of many materials such as woven wools, beaded buckskin, basketry, pottery, and carved stone. Of special interest are masks from two areas, the Northwest Coast and the Southwest. Many of the objects were collected from original owners or original craftsmen. The designs are authentic and antedate the period of white influence. Even though many are colorful and ornamented, they were made to be utilitarian objects, such as weapons, utensils, or clothing, or were intended for ceremony, ritual, or totemic purposes. If the designs had symbolic meaning that could be determined with any degree of certainty, the details are given in the caption. The black-and-white illustrations are large enough for detail to be clearly seen, and the captions contain information such as dates, use of objects, tribe, region, and other details condensed from the Bureau of Ethnology reports.

As part of the Dover series of pictorial archives, individual items in the book are copyright free and may be used up to ten items per occasion without further payment, permission, or acknowledgment. Students in art classes looking for authentic Indian designs or readers interested in the art of the North American Indian will find this book an invaluable resource.

125. Newman, Sandra Corrie. **Indian Basket Weaving: How to Weave Pomo, Yurok, Pima and Navajo Baskets.** Flagstaff, Ariz.: Northland, 1974. 91p. FRL: 8. Subjects: Basketmaking; Pomo Indians; Yurok Indians; Pima Indians; Navajo Indians.

Interested in crafts created by American Indians, Sandra Corrie Newman has thoroughly researched and mastered the crafts of basketry of the Pomo, Yurok, Pima, and Navajo Indian people. Travels through the West provided an intimate knowledge of gathering, preparation of natural materials, and weaving techniques. She wrote the book not only to help preserve native culture but also for collectors and admirers of Indian crafts to ensure that they gain an appreciation of the meaning of the craft. Each tribe produces baskets suited to its unique social, religious, and geographic environment. She notes that basketry has changed as culture has changed; however, the craft maintains its cultural significance or sign of lineage.

This small book contains excellent directions, a glossary, and a bibliography. The numerous photographs of Indian women by Daniel Corrie, her husband, are as descriptive as the text. For craft or art classes, as well as for young adult readers interested in basketry, this book provides history, uses, materials, designs, and weaving techniques of basketmaking.

126. Orchard, William C. **Beads and Beadwork of the American Indians: A Study Based on Specimens in the Museum of the American Indian.** New York: Museum of the American Indian, 1975. 168p. FRL: 10. Subject: Beadwork.

Beads have been used since primitive times for adornment and as a medium of trade. The American Indians developed beadwork as a specialized skill using a variety of procedures. In 1929, William C. Orchard published a study on beads and beadwork of the American Indian based on specimens in the Museum of the American Indian organized by the Heye Foundation. Reprinted in 1975, his work is considered a classic reference.

Beadwork is an art practiced by American Indians today. This technological study incorporates the history, use, and distribution of New World beadwork from prehistory to the twentieth century. Shell, pearl, bone, and stone beads, and the drilling techniques of native materials are discussed, as well as more unusual bead forms and materials incorporating seeds, basketry, and dried otter's liver. A fascinating section traces the effect of European trade beads on the economy. The processes of woven beadwork, sewing, edging, inlay, and bead basketry required skilled craftspeople. All beadwork is illustrated in over 174 color and black-and-white plates and figures incorporated within the text. The information is carefully footnoted. The table of contents and index of illustrations provide access to type of beadwork. However, the lack of an index makes it difficult to locate tribal affiliation of the art. The variety of materials, design motifs, and methods of craft will be of special value in areas where people are making traditional beadwork, as well as for collectors and those interested in developing an appreciation of the art.

127. Reno, Dawn E. **The Official Identification and Price Guide to American Indian Collectibles.** New York: The House of Collectibles, 1988. 394p. FRL: 9. Subjects: Art; Artifacts; Basketmaking; Weaving; Clothing; Dolls; Games; Biography; Jewelry; Leatherwork; Pottery; Tools; Weapons.

In the 1980s, retail stores across the United States began to feature "the Southwestern look." Soon, public interest turned to collecting Indian art, weaving, and pottery. Dawn E. Reno offers an identification and price guide to American Indian art and artifacts. The guide offers advice on avoiding cheap replicas and encourages collectors to collect only items crafted by Native Americans.

Most handbooks look at only one aspect of Indian art or artifacts. However, this thick paperback volume explores thirteen different types of collectibles. The more common ones are baskets, blankets and rugs, jewelry, pottery, and artifacts. The chapter on Indian art includes brief biographies of Indian artists and those artists whose work includes scenes of Indian life. Other collectible areas reviewed are dolls, games and sports, tools and weapons, and wooden items. The discussion of ephemera and advertising includes photography, Indian women in advertising, the Indian in fiction, and biographies of Indian writers and those who specialize in Indian stories.

Each section opens with a general introduction and essays on subtopics. A listing of specific collectibles with price range follows; some are illustrated in black-and-white. A full-color, eight-page insert highlights examples of superb artistry. The concluding chapter addresses the modern artisan and recognizes that work being produced today is highly collectible. The appendixes list addresses of dealers, auctioneers, and collectors. Bibliographic sources are noted. The detailed index is a valuable tool in locating specific items.

The range of art and artifact collectibles spreads from modern silkscreens and bronze sculptures to mortar and pestle used by ancient Indian people. Antique Indian items are generally expensive. Modern American Indian artists earn their living through their work and buyers will find their art more accessible and usually less expensive. Reno's book on American Indian collectibles offers guidelines to those purchasing items and an incentive to younger artists to produce quality art.

128. Turnbaugh, Sarah Peabody, and William A. Turnbaugh. **Indian Baskets.** West Chester, Pa.: Schiffer Publishing, 1986. 264p. FRL: 10. Subject: Basketmaking.

Baskets, from prehistoric specimens to modern handwork, have been an integral part of native North American culture. Serving both as utilitarian objects for transportation and storage and as containers during ceremonies, baskets were created from a multiplicity of materials in endless, diverse forms. Drawing heavily on the resources of the Native American Indian Basket Collection in the Peabody Museum of Archaeology, the authors contribute a compendium on basketry that includes both common and less well known forms.

As Native American baskets are a part of their maker's ways of life, basketry is explained as a functional yet decorative art based on ecological and anthropological data. The reader learns how the baskets are made, how raw materials are used, and the variations that occur in form and decoration. The first section of the book provides a visual "Showcase of Basketry," with more than 120 color photographs and captions identifying native containers. The following section, "Introducing Native North American Basketry," serves as a guide to the history, distinctive features, care and conservation, and beauty of these cultural artifacts. The last section, "Identifying Native North American Baskets," is a manual to the native baskets of eleven cultural areas. Each geographic section is introduced by a map of the original tribal basketmaking groups, and over 150 black-and-white photographs complement the text.

This handy reference book expands the subject of basketry with keys to methods of manufacture and decoration, a glossary, a bibliography, and an index. The identification guide offers readers over 174 regional and tribal basket styles. The book can serve as an encyclopedic reference to basketry, a reference for basketmakers, a history of Native American handcrafted containers, an identification handbook for collectors, and a resource to aid in the development of the appreciation of this distinctive art form.

129. Villasenor, David, and Jean Villasenor. **Indian Designs.** Happy Camp, Calif.: Naturegraph, 1983. unpaged. FRL: no text. Subjects: Decoration and ornament; Pattern making.

Indian Designs contains forty-eight 8½-by-11-inch full-page designs adapted from Greater Southwest pottery, basketry, and ceremonials. Indians and non-Indians alike will find the excellent, clear line drawings valuable for decorative and ornamental art projects. The colorful designs can also be useful as patterns in sewing craft items. Each design is accurately titled and described, ranging from the Hopi Rain Bird Spirit representing the vortex of energy to the ancient Hohokam Load Carrier to a depiction of Father Sky from whence the source of Navajo life springs.

The figures are black-and-white line drawings. Although the descriptive notes are the only text, this softcover volume can be widely used by all ages for a variety of art and craft projects.

130. Wade, Edwin L., and Rennard Strickland. **Magic Images: Contemporary Native American Art**. Norman: University of Oklahoma Press, 1981. 128p. FRL: 10. Subject: Art, Contemporary.

Magic Images, a study of contemporary Native American art, provides some "magic moments" for the reader. Certainly, the definition of good art is controversial and the definition of good Indian art is even more debatable. However, in this paperback volume, the authors manage to give an excellent representation of most types of art currently being produced by Indian artists. Not only are the illustrations representative of the vastly differing styles that are emerging in Indian art, but the essays and text written by the authors also give acceptance to the broad range of contemporary Indian art. All types of Indian art, ranging from the traditional to the expressionistic to the modernist to what the authors term as individualistic, are presented with equal enthusiasm.

Several format techniques are used by the authors to enrich the book. Illustrations range from full-page color spreads to small black-and-white reproductions placed in juxtaposition to demonstrate contrasts or similarities in style or subject matter. These small reproductions also enable the authors to provide a wide variety of subjects in a limited space. With an excellent text, a superior choice of representative Indian art, and illustrations and graphics, this beautiful volume can make a good addition to the fine arts collection of school and public libraries. This book is also helpful in demonstrating the differences in primitive and modern art. Because art reflects life, social studies teachers may find the illustrations and text helpful in understanding the cultural changes in the lives of the Indian people. The visual impact of the book should attract readers of every grade level and could well serve as an inspiration to broaden their interest in different types of Indian art.

131. Weatherford, Elizabeth, and Emelia Seubert, eds. **Native Americans on Film and Video, Volume II.** New York: Museum of the American Indian, 1988. 112p. FRL: 10. Subjects: Motion pictures; Videotapes.

Films and videos continue to grow in importance as teaching and learning tools. Teachers, students, and others interested in American Indian life frequently seek this type of media to supplement research. *Native Americans on Film and Video, Volume II* can assist school media specialists and public librarians in meeting the needs of these individuals. This guide continues the work of volume I that reviewed films made before 1980. Volume II includes 200 films and videos produced after volume I, arranged in alphabetical order for easy access.

The expressed role of the selected films and videos is to combat stereotypes so often communicated in modern commercial films and to fill the need for accurate information on Native American life. Most films feature Native Americans of the United States and Canada; a few dozen are about the Southern Hemisphere. The works included in this volume are selected on the basis of accuracy, technical quality, and uniqueness. Technical information is provided on each review including format, running time, language versions, distributors, and a content summary.

Although some films reviewed are produced primarily for adult viewers, many productions, such as the excellent Spirit Bay series, are appropriate for all age levels. Complete indexes are included by subject, tribe, and region. Addresses for distributors in both volumes I and II are provided.

Over the past ten years, Indians have begun to reclaim their native oral and visual traditions. Native performers, writers, and artists are taking active roles in writing, directing, and acting. The next volume of this guide will include even more motion pictures and videotapes that reinforce the cultural heritage, address political issues, and focus on land rights and sovereignty of Native Americans.

132. Whiteford, Andrew Hunter. **North American Indian Arts.** New York: Golden Press, 1970. 160p. FRL: 7. Subjects: Art; Basketmaking; Pottery; Textiles; Leatherwork; Stonework; Woodwork; Shellwork; Metalwork.

This compact pocketbook, a Golden Science Guide on North American Indian arts, provides a comprehensive presentation of Indian arts and crafts. The material culture of the North American Indian offers the key to understanding the rich diversity of the native cultures. The skills and techniques for making tools, implements, and ornaments are explained, from the methods of gathering and preparing raw materials to the making of the object, which requires the knowledge of several crafts. Some of the arts included are well known, but many are little known because they are not practiced today. By presenting the arts in their historical context, the artifacts of the various tribes can be viewed in cultural patterns.

This handbook can be purchased in both paperback and inexpensive hardcover. A key is given by Owen Vernon Shaffer for the present location of most of the extensive, authentic color illustrations of artifacts on each page. The volume can serve as an introductory reference to the material arts of the Native American. The authenticity of the artifacts, comprehensive text, and excellent index by tribe as well as craft can be very useful for understanding traditional arts.

133. Wolfson, Evelyn. **American Indian Tools and Ornaments: How to Make Implements and Jewelry with Bone and Shell.** New York: David McKay, 1981. 111p. FRL: 6. Subjects: Handicraft; Jewelry.

This compact volume serves a twofold purpose: (1) it is a reference to the American Indian cultures who made tools and ornaments of bone and shell, and (2) it is an instruction manual for creating bone and shell implements and jewelry in the tradition of the Indian people. American Indian cultures valued tools and ornaments made from animal and shellfish skeletons for their unique characteristics, availability, and workability. Bone tools were used for hide preparation, sewing and weaving, and hunting and fishing. Although shells were used as containers or for making tools, most groups prized and traded them for making ornamental and ceremonial objects.

In the first section of the book, the author devotes a short chapter to each of the seven geographic areas in which major tribes were located and details the utilization of natural bone and shell sources in daily life. The second part includes crafter's projects for making shell knives, containers, fishhooks, tools, and jewelry, as well as bone scrapers, awls, hoes, and breastplates. Materials are listed for each craft, and instructions with diagrams are provided. The book is profusely illustrated with black-and-white photographs and drawings and diagrams by Nancy Poydar. Unique features of the instructional guide are the information on location and cleaning of shells and bones and a directory of shell distributors with addresses. Appended are a selected bibliography, common metric equivalents and conversions, and a subject index to both tribal groups and crafts. This book is an excellent addition to both children's and young adult collections. The information will be useful in social studies as well as art classes.

134. Yue, David, and Charlotte Yue. **The Tipi: A Center of Native American Life.** New York: Alfred A. Knopf, 1984. 77p. FRL: 5. Subjects: Dwellings; Great Plains.

Charlotte Yue and architect-artist David Yue combine their talents to present an intriguing book on the tipi, the Great Plains Indian dwelling. Dispelling the popular belief that a tipi is simply a tent, they characterize the carefully designed structure as a "sophisticated dwelling," designed and built to meet the demands of the nomadic hunting culture. Although the origin of the tipi is obscure, over time it grew in size and was carried by horses rather than by dogs. Complemented by fine detailed drawings, the design of the tipi is carefully explained. The way the dwelling could be adapted to meet the rigors of weather on the Plains is especially interesting. Tipis were made, set up, and usually owned by the women, who also took great pride in furnishing and making the interior comfortable.

The tipi played an important role in the life of the Great Plains Indians as they followed the buffalo in their search for food. Serving not only as a home, the tipi was the center of cultural, social, and spiritual life. Some dwellings were designated for special purposes, such as the lodges for tribal leaders, council, and special societies. Small tipis were used for children's playhouses while other lodges with decorative patterned covers were designed for use by the spiritual leaders of the people.

This topic will appeal to young readers and will fascinate young adults. The information about the history, people, customs, and dwellings of the Great Plains Indians can be accessed through the index. The book does not have a bibliography. For young adults wanting additional information on daily life in a tipi, the second edition of *The Indian Tipi: Its History, Construction, and Use*, by Reginald Laubin and Gladys Laubin (University of Oklahoma Press, 1977), is also highly recommended.

800-899 Literature

135. Allen, T. D., ed. **The Whispering Wind: Poetry by Young American Indians.** Garden City, N.Y.: Doubleday, 1972. 128p. FRL: 9. Subject: Poetry—Collected works.

American Indian young adults at the Institute of American Indian Arts in Santa Fe, New Mexico, wrote the poetry featured in this anthology. The poems cover many historical topics as well as contemporary events, the Vietnam War, and conflicts within the lives of these young people. The youthful poets use sensitive, lyrical, and sometimes earthy language.

In the introduction, Mae Durham comments that the poems are natural expressions from the specific American Indian culture from which each of these students originated. Although the poems are simple in form, they have inherent depth. The students have reached outside their immediate and traditional world to speak with the poetic vision of youth.

There is a short introduction for each student author and then a selection of several poems by that person. The poems are short selections with diverse topics. The authors' tribal affiliations include the Papago, Palouse, Navajo, Colville, Ute, Blackfeet, Cherokee, Suquamash, and Nez Perce.

The selections are appealing and will inspire other young people to write poetry. The topics are so diverse and stimulating that the anthology can be read quickly and understood easily. Many of the poems will provide good discussion material and serve as excellent examples of the depth and range of feelings that can be expressed using this medium.

136. Beidler, Peter G., and Marion F. Egge. **The American Indian in Short Fiction: An Annotated Bibliography.** Metuchen, N.J.: Scarecrow Press, 1979. 203p. FRL: 8. Subjects: Fiction—Bibliography; Short stories—Bibliography.

This annotated bibliography of short fiction including American Indian subjects will be useful for librarians and teachers, but will be of limited use for students. The annotations cover 880 short stories located in books and magazines appearing from the late nineteenth century through the 1970s. American short stories about the Indian have had a profound effect on public opinion. Many include short stories that convey information about the native people of America. Each entry, alphabetized by author and title, provides publication information and a brief plot summary.

Most of these modern short stories about Indian people were written by non-Indians. Those written by Indian authors are designated by tribal affiliation. Following the bibliography are two indexes: the "Indian Tribes Index" lists more than 150 tribes, and the "Subject Key Words Index" lists over 50 concepts to identify recurring themes.

This reference volume is targeted for scholars. The short story is a popular form of fiction for adolescents and a genre included in most literature anthologies. This volume of short story annotations featuring the American Indian can guide the reader to location. However, the stories will need to be read to determine quality and suitability. Large libraries will find the volume valuable to researchers.

137. Bierhorst, John. **In the Trail of the Wind: American Indian Poems and Ritual Orations.** New York: Farrar, Straus & Giroux, 1971. 201p. FRL: 9. Subjects: Poetry—Collected works; Oratory.

Editor and translator Bierhorst, who specializes in American Indian literature, has limited his collection of poems and ritual orations to the best examples of representative types. One hundred twenty-six selections are translated from over forty languages, representing the best-known native cultures of North and South America. A few examples of Eskimo poetry are also included.

This cross-cultural anthology calls attention to similarities and differences between peoples as widely geographically and linguistically separate as the Sioux and the Cherokee and the ancient Maya. The thematic arrangement develops universal aspects of Indian thought: the power of words, the significance of dreams, the personifying spirits of animals and objects, the dualism of expression, Father Sky and Mother Earth in creation stories, the cult of the four-world quarters, the anonymity of the poet, and the influence of alien gods.

The author's translation is primarily a literal version in which words are rearranged, with only those additions and subtractions from the original needed to make the text comprehensible in English. The excellent introduction, detailed notes on origin, and translation of each selection; glossary of tribes and languages; and period engravings are special features. Although the author recommends the anthology be read as a progression to gain a sense of continuity from start to finish, individual selections could be used in social studies, language arts, and speech classes. Primary school-age children will enjoy listening to some of the selections. This collection of oral literature includes song-texts, prayers, incantations, myths, legends, chronicles, and speeches; it is an accurate and objective introduction to a body of literature that deserves attention. Author's notes, a glossary, and suggestions for further study conclude the work.

138.   Bierhorst, John, ed. **Lightning Inside You and Other Native American Riddles.** New York: William Morrow, 1992. 104p. FRL: 4. Subjects: Riddles—Indian; Humor; Folklore.

Riddle books appeal to children of all ages. John Bierhorst is the first editor to compile the riddles of Native American culture, dispelling a common belief that there are no American Indian riddles. Bierhorst piques the reader's interest in native riddles in the excellent essay, "Native Riddling in the Americas," that introduces the volume.

The variety and richness of this Native American tradition encompass a broad spectrum of social and cultural life. In Indian tradition, some consider riddling a game. To others, riddles are quite serious. Both attitudes are correct. In hunters' riddles, most native cultures avoid naming game animals out of either respect or fear. The Maya of Yucatan may have used riddle tests to decide whether chiefs were fit for office. The Comanche remember riddles that involved gambling. A tribe of the Northwest Amazon region, the Muinane, held nighttime riddling games that took the form of dances. In Peru, the Quechua used riddling in courtship. Among the Arapaho of Oklahoma and the Kekchi of Belize, the people tell riddles solved in stories.

Seven categories of riddles compose the body of this volume. Riddles about the natural world, the human body, and animals are perhaps the most common and easiest to answer. Readers familiar with Indian culture may be more responsive to the riddles about things that grow and things that are made to be used. The last two chapters relate "Stories of Speak-Riddles and Wise-Spirit" and the "Story of the Fox and the Thrush."

The discovery of Indian riddles continues. Presently, Bierhorst notes that at least thirty tribes or cultures have some type of riddling tradition. Most of the riddles in the volume are from central Alaska, southern Mexico, and western South America, with a few from three Great Plains tribes. A list of tribes serves as a riddle index. An annotated source list is appended. Louise Brierley's illustrations capture the humor and spirit of this American Indian tradition.

One hundred forty riddles comprise this carefully researched collection. Answers in small print at the bottom of the page can be covered with the hand. This unique source can be used for exercises in higher-level thinking skills or as an introduction to a unit on writing riddles. Important for Native American folklore collections, this volume offers an understanding of the meaning riddling has in the life and customs of Indian people of North and South America.

139.   Bruchac, Joseph, ed. **Songs from This Earth on Turtle's Back.** Greenfield Center, N.Y.: Greenfield Review Press, 1983. 295p. FRL: 10. Subjects: American poetry—Indian authors; American poetry—20th century.

Usually, anthologies of American Indian poetry include non-Indian translations of native oral literature. This is not the case with *Songs from This Earth on Turtle's Back*. The collection offers selections written in English by fifty-two contemporary poets representing thirty-five different Native American groups. Many widely recognized and published poets such as N. Scott Momaday, Wendy Rose, Leslie Marmon Silko, James Welch, and others less well known offer an excellent cross-section of American Indian poetry in many different forms. The vitality of the selections flows from the deep roots of traditional literature and culture to the fresh stems of political and social issues. With great respect for the written word, the poets create an awareness of the past and a sense of the reality of the present for Native Americans.

Each writer is presented in alphabetical order, with a black-and-white photograph of most contributors and biographical information in many formats, from a brief sketch to information in the poet's own words. This broad and varied sampler of work by a new generation of Native American writers offers a clear portrait of contemporary American Indian experience. Public libraries and school media centers will find the volume an excellent addition for use by young adult readers and language arts teachers. Young aspiring Indian poets will find the contributions excellent for study and inspiration.

140. Coltelli, Laura. **Winged Worlds: American Indian Writers Speak.** Lincoln: University of Nebraska Press, 1990. 211p. FRL: 10. Subjects: American literature—Indian authors—History and criticism; Authors, Indian—Interviews; Indians in literature.

For many years, fiction and information books on American Indians were written by non-Indians, from scholarly anthropological works to romanticized and stereotyped novels. By the late 1960s, a generation of articulate, talented Native American writers emerged, defining their own literary traditions. Laura Coltelli presents a series of interviews with eleven recognized American Indian poets and novelists on the critical issues related to their works.

Each author is introduced in a biographical essay that clarifies their tribal and historical background. Coltelli had two purposes in her interviews. First, she wanted to provide cultural perspective and learn how the writers experience being Native Americans in "their modern homeland." Second, she wanted to provide an opportunity to discuss critical issues related to their works: interrelation of different Native American cultures in the past and present, Native American contributions to contemporary fiction and poetry, and the possible influence of Anglo-American authors on indigenous writers. Paula Gunn Allen, Michael Dorris, Louise Erdrich, Joy Harjo, Linda Hogan, N. Scott Momaday, Simon Ortiz, Wendy Rose, Leslie Marmon Silko, Gerald Vizenor, and James Welch were interviewed.

The interviews follow a conversational format in the form of an autobiography. The authors candidly discuss their lives and works. Erdrich and Dorris speak of their marriage and unique literary collaboration. Paula Gunn Allen traces her feminist beliefs back to the woman-centered Pueblo society. Momaday speaks of the power of naming, Ortiz of the Coyote figure, and Vizenor of the trickster. A bibliography of each writer's works is appended.

Winged Words: American Indian Writers Speak serves as a biographical reference to contemporary Native American poets and novelists. The format of the interviews and captivating information provides excellent examples for journalism classes. The volume is laudable for its serious consideration of Native American writers, often ignored by high school students and teachers.

141. Cronyn, George W., ed. **American Indian Poetry: The Standard Anthology of Songs and Chants.** New York: Liveright, 1934. 360p. FRL: 10. Subjects: Poetry—Collected works; Music; Anthropology.

Originally published in 1918 as *The Path of the Rainbow*, this collection of songs and chants forms a poetry anthology of American Indian classics. The author selects notable translations and interpretations of verse from many areas: Eastern woodlands, Southeast, Great Plains, Southwest, California, Northwest Coast, and the far North.

All Indian verse is either sung or chanted; therefore, the areas of poetry, music, and dance of the American Indian are recognized. Songs and chants signify an occasion in the life of native people. The ceremony centers around a story, carried by symbolic rite and dance. Most of the material refers to clans, a familial relation with which readers, both Indian and non-Indian, can easily identify. There are also personal songs that resulted when a great moment in a person's life inspired the creation of verse.

Most of the material originated before the influence of white civilization. The verse is beautiful and useful in the areas of anthropology, creative writing, and Indian history. Poetry teachers will find selections to inspire students of all races. Mary Austin's excellent introduction explains why the songs were written as verse.

142. Dodge, Robert K., and Joseph B. McCullough, eds. **New and Old Voices of Wah'Kon-tah.** New York: International Publishers, 1985. 139p. FRL: 9. Subjects: American poetry—Indian authors; American poetry—20th century.

In the third edition of *New and Old Voices of Wah'Kon-tah*, forty-six Native American poets write about their spiritual and historical heritage. Many names, such as the Dakota word *Wah'Kon-tah* used in the title of this poetry book, refer to the "Great Mystery" or spirit through which Indian people gain power and wisdom. Sharing their Indian heritage, the contemporary Native American poets offer 107 selections. In the foreword, Vine Deloria, Jr. invites the reader "to savor the Indian experience."

The selections range from the historical, such as "Tribute to Chief Joseph" by Duane Niatum, to the realism of "Havre, Montana: Just Off the Reservation" by James Welch. Many authors are well known and others are fledgling poets. The poems bespeak power as they delve into the themes of Native American experience.

This comprehensive poetry anthology is useful both for individual reading and as a classroom text. Many of the selections have notes explaining cultural and historical background, which aids understanding. The contemporary poets are presented in alphabetical order. Biographical sketches, especially difficult to locate for new poets, are appended.

143. Hirschfelder, Arlene, and Beverly R. Singer, eds. **Rising Voices: Writings of Young Native Americans.** New York: Charles Scribner's Sons, 1992. 131p. FRL: 6. Subject: Poetry—Collected works.

Arlene Hirschfelder and Beverly R. Singer carefully selected poetry, letters, and essays written by young Native Americans from 1887 to 1992. Some writings are unpublished and others garnered from copyrighted material. Drawing on their Native American past, present, and future, the young writers express their strong emotions about the richness, sorrow, and conviction of being Indian.

The selections were narrowed to those poems and essays that Hirschfelder felt "set the record straight about their identity, their families, communities, rituals, histories, education, and harsh realities." Selections are arranged according to these six subjects. An introductory essay for each topic provides the reader with a sensitive portrayal of the world of young Native Americans, many of whom are in grade school. For each of the sixty-two poems and essays, the author's name, tribe, and publication data are noted.

Every selection is unique. Nora Naranjo Morse, from the Santa Clara Pueblo, writes a poem reflecting her family's grief when her brother dies during the Vietnam War. In the poem "Rising Voices," Carla Wiletto, a Navajo student at Rough Rock Community High School in Arizona, testifies that the voice of her people will be heard soon. A letter written in 1883 describes the high school experience of Frank Keokuk, of the Sac and Fox tribe, at Hampton Institute in Virginia. A fifth-grade Crow student from Montana states in her poem "As I Dance" that she is happy she is Indian and taking on the heritage of her people. These young people reflect the strength and feelings of their people. Expressions of protest against prejudice, oppression, and loss of identity are eloquently stated.

Readers of all cultures will have little trouble relating to the thoughts expressed in this collection. A table of contents and author/title index are included. These writings by young Native Americans are especially valuable to share with other young Indian students who want to express themselves in writing. This anthology, also available in paperback from Ballantine Books, belongs on the library shelves and in the classroom.

144. Jones, Hattie. **The Trees Stand Shining.** New York: Dial Press, 1971. unpaged. FRL: 4. Subject: Poetry—Collected works.

A most attractive poetry collection, *The Trees Stand Shining* blends American Indian literature and art in a harmonious relationship. In a beautiful format, a double-page spread offers a full-page color painting by Robert Andrew Parker accompanied by a page of short selected poems by Hattie Jones. The selections offered in this anthology are really songs from many different tribal people. The simple and deeply meaningful words of prayers, stories, lullabies, and a few war chants express how different tribal people felt about their world and their lives.

The words were passed from generation to generation and translated from Indian languages. Each song in poetic form is identified by tribe. A list of the sources from which they were gathered is provided. The words in these selections lend themselves to oral reading. School-age students of all grade levels will enjoy this anthology.

145. Momaday Natachee Scott. **American Indian Authors.** Boston: Houghton Mifflin, 1972. 151p. FRL: 9. Subjects: Literature—Collected works; Short stories; Legends; Biography; Speeches; Poetry.

One of four anthologies of multi-ethnic literature from Houghton Mifflin, this collection contains high-interest writings by historic figures as well as contemporary Indian authors. Short stories, legends, biography, oratory, and poetry are included. Many of the authors are well known to the public and others are only known locally. The selections by Chief Joseph, Two Leggings, D. Chief Eagle, Black Elk, Charles A. Eastman, Thomas S. Whitecloud, Alonzo Lopez, Emerson Blackhorse Mitchell and T. D. Allen, Patty Harjo, Juanita Platero and Siyowin Miller, Durango Memdza, Grey Cohoe, Littlebird, N. Scott Momaday, James Welch, and Vine Deloria, Jr. feature a photograph and a brief biographical sketch of each person. Discussion questions are included at the end of each selection.

The twenty-six works by American Indian authors were selected by Natachee Scott Momaday, teacher, artist, and author of books for young people, who is of Cherokee, French, and English descent. From traditional legends to contemporary creative works, all the authors maintain distinctive features of their culture in their literature. The selections are short and will be enjoyed by middle and secondary readers, with special appeal to adult education students.

146.   Sanders, Thomas F., and Walter F. Peek. **Literature of the American Indian.** Beverly Hills, Calif.: Glencoe Press, 1973. 534p. FRL: 8. Subject: Literature—Collected works.

Thomas Sanders, whose Indian name is Netacomet, and Walter Peek, whose Indian name is Nippawock, compiled this large anthology as a testimonial to the pride they feel in their Indian heritage. One hundred fourteen literature selections, which represent twenty-eight tribes and noted contemporary authors, include songs, legends, history, oratory, contemporary poetry, and fiction. The first chapter is a historical overview of the Indian's origin, ethnicity, and endurance. The authors conclude that, despite the beliefs of missionaries, anthropologists, and archaeologists, American Indians are an ancient people with an infinite variety of cultural patterns.

Each chapter is provided with an introduction by the authors. Many obligatory selections are included, such as Chief Joseph's surrender speech, the noteworthy epic of Dekanwida, and text of the Law of the Great Peace of the Roundhouse. The cross-section of material ranges from the creation stories and mythology of pre-Columbian poetry, through the orations and speeches of protest to assimilation and, finally, contemporary critical literature.

This major work has a title and author index, but no reference to tribal affiliation. The only method of locating the sources from which the selections were taken is through the acknowledgments. Even then, the original source and translator are not available.

The text is not difficult to read and can be enjoyed by children from grades four through twelve. As with most anthologies containing material on the American Indian, there is some romanticism as well as truth. With careful introduction by teachers knowledgeable about the purpose of traditional storytelling, this major work should provide Native Americans and non-Indians with a sense of Indian identity. This volume will be a good addition to libraries and useful to teachers of literature.

147.   Sneve, Virginia Driving Hawk. **Dancing Teepees: Poems of American Indian Youth.** New York: Holiday House, 1989. 32p. FRL: 4. Subject: Poetry—Collected works.

Virginia Driving Hawk Sneve chose a variety of poetic works for this collection. The selections from the oral traditions of North American Indians and from contemporary tribal poets mark the passages from birth through adolescence.

Stories, chants, and songs were handed down through generations of leaders and storytellers to preserve cultural values.

The spoken words are drawn from a variety of tribal sources. The birth of a child receives meaning through the words of the Lakota Sioux, Black Elk. Other selections include an Omaha newborn ceremony, the poetry of Driving Hawk Sneve, a Hopi "lullabye," a Paiute cradle song, a Zuni corn ceremony, and the verse of the Makah people. As children grow, they learn about nature in "I Watched an Eagle Soar," "We Chased Butterflies," and "The Black Turkey-Gobbler." Other poetic passages paint vivid pictures of joy and heartbreak with scenes of blue elk, dancing teepees, an elder brother, and cold winter's snows. The sources from which the material is reprinted are provided.

A catalog of designs by Stephen Gammell depict works from the Northwest Coast totems, Great Lakes beadwork, Navajo sandpainting, and the motifs of Southwestern pottery. Gammell gives life to the words as he represents the scenes in detailed, childlike drawings. Printed on heavy paper with sewn pages, the collection will withstand heavy use by children.

Elementary children will delight in the drawings and words. Oral traditions of American Indians contain words carefully chosen and meant to be spoken. This book, with its vivid illustrations and carefully selected stories and poetry, offers the storyteller words to inspire children.

148. Tapahonso, Luci. **A Breeze Swept Through.** Albuquerque, N. Mex.: West End Press, 1987. 51p. FRL: N/A. Subject: Navajo Indians—Poetry.

Poetry books by a single adult are often of little value to the curriculum and are not very appealing to young adult readers. However, the variety of poems in Luci Tapahonso's collection makes this small book a valuable addition to libraries. Assistant professor of English, women's studies, and American Indian studies at the University of New Mexico, Tapahonso offers an intimate glimpse of her strong elemental Navajo roots as she writes of the harmonious relationship between her traditional values and the modern world of "shades," a low 280-ZX, and pink heart-shaped earrings. She relates through poetry, through the language she chooses, and through the free verse style. She speaks to older teens, especially young Indian women, with pathos and humor in "Feast Days and Sheep Thrills," with feeling for her children in "For Misty Starting School," and of death and life in "Dear Alvin." The medley of topics brings a freshness to modern poetry.

Selections from this small poetry compilation of thirty-three poems with four themes will be valuable to teachers wishing to expose young people to a modern American Indian poet.

149. Turner, Frederick W., ed. **The Portable North American Indian Reader.** New York: Viking Press, 1973. 628p. FRL: 9. Subject: Literature—Collected works.

The primary reason for the selection of the articles included in this collection was to paint an accurate picture of the American Indian for the reader. The author selected both traditional and historical materials to portray the part the American Indian has played in America's past and present. Turner's insightful introduction provides a smooth transition from the beginning of oral literature through the contemporary Indian world.

In the first division, eleven myths and tales from different tribes reflect on the rich world of oral literature. Some of the tales explain natural phenomena, such as the Cherokee tale "How the Deer Got Its Horns." The Oglala Sioux history "Ben Kindles Winter Count" records the life of the people. The creation story of the Navajo leads the reader through the Four Worlds of no sun to the Fifth World, in which we presently live.

The poetry and oratory selections of the second division are sometimes simple and often profound. The powerful speeches of the Indian orators are examples of the recorded speeches made to white men. The third division, on cultural contact, includes selections of exploration, captivity, and Indian autobiographies. All relate the views of two differing societies and describe the impact of a technologically oriented culture on a traditional culture. The last division, on image and anti-image, includes selections by writers with an ethnocentric view of the American Indian, writers who try to portray the American Indian objectively, and Indian authors who are speaking for themselves. Excerpts from the works of Luther Standing Bear, N. Scott Momaday, Vine Deloria, Jr., James Welch, Hyemeyohsts Storm, Ray Young Bear, and Simon Ortiz reflect their assessment of the Indian world.

The great diversity of the selections will provide the reader with a comprehensive insight through literature into the traditions and history of the North American Indian. The book can serve as a single source for students and teachers in language arts and American history classes. Young adult librarians and school media specialists can recommend this volume as a balanced and straightforward collection of Indian materials. A bibliography of sources is included.

150. Vanderwerth, W. C. **Indian Oratory: Famous Speeches by Noted Indian Chieftains.** Norman: University of Oklahoma Press, 1971. 292p. FRL: 10. Subject: Oratory.

Indian Oratory not only presents many of the historically significant speeches made by the Indian chiefs of the last century, but also includes brief biographical sketches of these great men. Because the great leaders did not have a written language, their speeches were representations of their oral history. Unhampered by notes, the chiefs relied on their memories and natural speaking abilities to convince their listeners. The structure was simple and poignant, and the speeches were generally speeches of survival. In most cases, heroic acts on the battlefield were not enough. The Indian had to rely on his oral skills to wrest the best possible results from situations that offered very little hope for his people. These men were leaders with a high degree of dignity and intelligence, well trained in oratory by their experience and positions. As a result, the speeches are classics and well deserving of a place in American history.

An added bonus in the book is a complete speech by Chief Joseph of the Nez Perce, "An Indian's Views on Indian Affairs," which should be required reading for every young adult. This book belies the typical history accounts of Indian wars. Chief Joseph relates a story of the government soldiers murdering women and children, scalping the dead, and mistreating prisoners, none of which the Nez Perce did in the Nez Perce War.

The history of oratory among the Indian chiefs is a history of the Indian people. This information is an important addition to research on the American Indian. Teachers of American history should make an effort to present the Indian perspective on American history, and these speeches are an excellent start for this worthwhile goal. In addition, these selections can be used by speech teachers as outstanding examples of historical oratory.

151. Witt, Shirley Hill, and Stan Steiner, eds. **The Way: An Anthology of American Indian Literature.** New York: Alfred A. Knopf, 1972. 261p. FRL: 11. Subjects: Literature—Collected works; Oratory.

This literature anthology presents the oratory of Indian leaders, students, authors, poets, organizations, publications, and documents. As an antidote to the ethnic stereotype about the American Indians' inability to express themselves, the anthology presents two kinds of writing. The ancient speeches of honored leaders and orators are recorded for the thoughts they contain rather than the way they are written. Because many of them have been translated at least once, and some more than once, the flowery old English probably was not the most accurate version. The second part of the book contains contemporary writings, both speeches and written articles. The authors' purpose, states Witt, is to "meet Indian thoughts as they were meant to be understood and have not been." Without outside interpretation, Indian people can speak to the reader directly.

The anthology begins with selections of better-known orations of great leaders, followed by legends of the Indian people. Contemporary literature ranges from the irreverent to the serious, from selections on education to culture, from war to peace, and from past tragedies to optimistic predictions for the future. Length ranges from one paragraph to five pages.

Because the book is available in hardcover and paperback, language arts teachers should find many uses for the material. American Indian students will find the selections delightful and recognize that there are many voices and many ways to express themselves.

900-999 Geography and History

152. Baldwin, Gordon C. **Indians of the Southwest.** New York: Putnam, 1970. 190p. FRL: 10. Subject: Southwestern states.

Anthropologist Gordon Baldwin, who has excavated prehistoric ruins and been on archaeological expeditions in the Southwest, relates the culture and life-style of the Southwestern Indians. Speculating that some 30,000 years ago the ancestors of the Southwestern Indians migrated to the New World from Siberia, Baldwin traces the archaeological discoveries of the ancient cultures in the region extending from central Utah and southwestern Colorado southward through Arizona and New Mexico to the northern Mexican states of Sonora and Chihuahua, and from the Pecos River in eastern New Mexico westward to and slightly beyond the Colorado River into southeastern Nevada and California. Three major physiographic divisions—mountain, plateau, and desert—contained abundant bird and animal life, much different from the desert region today.

Some of the ancient cultures disappeared and others are ancestors of today's southwestern tribes, many of whom still live on reservations on their ancestral grounds. The Navajo, Pueblo, Mohave, and other smaller tribes survived the Spaniards in their search for gold and later the settlers in search of land. Baldwin details the differences in language, agriculture, hunting, war, arts, and crafts of the numerous tribal groups, some of whom were nomadic and some of whom lived in permanent villages. The last chapter deals with the changes that have come with modern life.

Because many of the Southwest Indian tribes have successfully retained the essence of their native culture, interest in their history and life should make this book valuable for library collections. A glossary of unfamiliar words; a bibliography; a list of southwestern museums, parks, and monuments; and an index are appended.

153. Batherman, Muriel. **Before Columbus.** Boston: Houghton Mifflin, 1981. 32p. FRL: 4. Subjects: Cliff dwellers and cliff dwellings; Archaeology; Anasazi Indians.

Author-illustrator Muriel Batherman presents young readers with the fascinating story of an Indian people who flourished for a thousand years in the Southwest and then mysteriously disappeared. A group of hunters from Asia crossed the land bridge to North American and settled in the southwestern part of the continent. Given the name Basketmakers because of the remnants of baskets they left behind, these people's lives are traced through their clothing, tools, weapons, pottery, and crops. Their lives changed dramatically as they moved from caves to pit houses and then to pueblo-type villages and large cities. Although the author calls these people "Pueblo," most sources refer to the people as the "Anasazi" or "Ancient Ones," which is less misleading. The term "Pueblo" generally refers to tribes that still inhabit the southwestern part of the United States.

The simple watercolor pen-and-ink drawings are visually attractive to children and effectively illustrate the archaeological evidence on which conclusions are based about this ancient people. The text is clearly written and focuses on a topic of special interest for young readers living in the states of Utah, New Mexico, Arizona, and Colorado.

154. Baylor, Byrd. **Before You Came This Way.** New York: E. P. Dutton, 1969. unpaged. FRL: 3. Subjects: Cave drawings; Art.

Byrd Baylor and illustrator Tom Bahti, both American Indians, combine their talents to present the intriguing mystery of the rock art drawings of prehistoric Southwestern Indians. The artistic renditions of pictographs and petroglyphs on handmade bark paper stir the reader's imagination about life during the time when the drawings were made. The lyrical language of the text is presented in poetry form. Language and illustration together present a record of the lives of the ancient people and depict the animals, battles, feasts, and beliefs. Humor is subtly introduced in a manner that will help children understand that these ancient artists were real people.

This is an excellent book to be read aloud and to provide information for children on the historical significance of cave drawings. Teachers and librarians can also use the drawings to illustrate art in its earliest, simplest form.

155. Bealer, Alex W. **Only the Names Remain: The Cherokee and the Trail of Tears.** Boston: Little, Brown, 1972. 88p. FRL: 5. Subject: Cherokee Indians.

Originally created as a television drama by the author, *Only the Names Remain* is a moving narrative of the Cherokee people who lived among the rich woodlands of the southern mountains a thousand years or more before Columbus "discovered" America. Bealer's well-written book responds to the need for a simple account of the history of the Cherokee Nation for primary school and middle school readers.

The book traces the confrontation of the Cherokee with the Spanish, French, English, and American invaders. During the Revolutionary War, the Cherokee sided with the English and were defeated. The Cherokee signed a treaty that forced them to live on a small portion of their original homeland. Here the Cherokee learned the white man's ways and prospered in peace. While maintaining their culture, they developed a great civilization, a constitution, and a republican form of government. They even declined to join the Indian confederation led by Tecumseh and helped General Jackson to defeat the Creeks, acts they believed would show their loyalty to the United States and protect their sovereignty.

The development of the Cherokee alphabet by Sequoyah allowed the people to read and write in their own language. New treaties forced them to give up land until they remained on a small part of their homeland in the Appalachian Mountains of Georgia. Under the leadership of John Ross, the Cherokees reached their highest point of development. However, the discovery of gold and the development of the cotton gin brought further encroachment to their lands. Betrayed by the governor of Georgia and President Jackson, they were again deprived of their rights and land. In the spring of 1838, the weary people were forced to march to Arkansas. "The graves of the dead were like teardrops falling on a sandy trail," and to the Cherokee the journey is still known as the Trail of Tears.

Illustrator William Sauts Bock has created detailed black-and-white pen-and-ink drawings, which are found on almost every page. They add a sense of realism usually available only in photographs. A bibliography of sources is not included, but the index makes the book useful as a reference. This stirring and tragic drama portrays an important historical event, one that all American children should remember as a tragic part of American history.

156. Bernstein, Alison R. **American Indians and World War II.** Norman: University of Oklahoma Press, 1991. 247p. FRL: 10. Subjects: World War, 1939-1945—Participation, Indian; United States Armed Forces—Indian troops.

Alison R. Bernstein summarizes the impact of World War II on American Indian people. Information on the Indian wartime experience between 1941 and 1947 is very difficult to obtain. This well-documented volume fills the void.

On the eve of World War II, the Indian New Deal faced opposition. For the first time, Indian people were citizens and eligible for the draft when registration efforts began on the reservation. Over 25,000 Indian people served in the armed forces. They distinguished themselves on the battlefront, increased their incomes, and were in closer contact with other ethnic groups than ever before. On the homefront, men and women left the reservation to take jobs created by military and war industries. The Bureau of Indian Affairs no longer was involved in or controlled the lives of 65,000 tribal people who left the reservation.

Besides information on the war years, Bernstein provides valuable research on the aftermath of the war. Traditional life was interrupted. Job opportunities were limited. A policy of termination that encouraged Indian people to leave the reservation was adopted by the Democratic administration, which assumed that the wartime experiences made Indians able and willing to assimilate. Indian people entered the political mainstream and favored self-determination. Bernstein labels her last chapter: "The War's Aftermath: Turning American Indians into Indian Americans."

The text provides interesting incidents that vividly illustrate this period. Extensive annotated footnotes document the facts. The bibliographic sources include oral history transcripts, newspapers, transcripts and reports from congressional hearings, correspondence, and literature. The index consists mainly of proper names and tribal groups. Some information included in the body, such as the Navajo Codetalkers, is not easily located through the index.

This reference is the most comprehensive synthesis available on Indian affairs during the 1940s. Information on the difficulties that Indian people faced when they left the reservation and tried to adjust to off-reservation life and the effects of termination is limited. This synopsis of Indian involvement during the war years will be invaluable to students of American Indian history. American history teachers, noting that little is devoted to this subject in their textbooks, will benefit from this research. Bernstein provides Indian students with the best source currently available and with viable research topics on a period of great impact on their parents' and grandparents' lives.

157. Bjorklund, Karna L. **The Indians of Northeastern America.** New York: Dodd, Mead, 1969. 191p. FRL: 9. Subjects: Algonkian Indians; Iroquois Indians.

Karna Bjorklund and her father, Lorence F. Bjorklund, a noted illustrator, have produced a readable account of the woodland Indians who inhabited the vast northeastern part of the United States. In carefully researched words and black-and-white pen sketches, the Bjorklunds weave a colorful tale of the Algonkians and Iroquois from the time of their first encounter with Europeans through the succeeding centuries. As the history is told, the author includes the folklore of the people, which provides the Indian perspective.

The Algonkian tribesmen lived in scattered bands that depended on a family-centered way of life to meet the needs of survival in a harsh environment. The Iroquois, more powerful and aggressive, also moved into the eastern woodlands. The Algonkians moved away to avoid conflict and adopted different tribal names, still retaining the basic Algonkian language. The Iroquoian language family also included many tribes, but usually referred to the five tribes that lived on adjoining territories throughout central New York State. Numerous other small tribes also lived in this northeastern area.

As the author tells the history of these related but diverse tribes, information is included on tribal life, dwellings, food, home industry, arts, handicrafts, customs, and communication. The chapter on religion, mythology, and folklore is delightful because of the oral stories related. The later chapters deal with the Northeast Indians' relationships with the white man—some good and some bad.

Simply and entertainingly written, this book shows signs of extensive research. The lively accounts and numerous illustrations will interest young readers. Supplementary materials are a list of museums having woodland Indian collections, selected readings, and an index.

158. Brown, Dee. **Bury My Heart at Wounded Knee.** New York: Holt, Rinehart & Winston, 1970. 487p. FRL: 10. Subjects: West (U.S.); West (U.S.)—History; Wars.

Every teacher and student of American history should read this book, which provides an Indian perspective on American westward expansion. *Bury My Heart at Wounded Knee* is a documented narrative of the incursion of the white man into the sacred homeland of the Dakota, Nez Perce, Cheyenne, Ponca, Apache, Utes, and others. American history textbooks generally glorify the American military leaders who systematically slaughtered, plundered, and exploited the Indian people, who were reduced to a remnant of once proud peoples. This is a historic tale of American heroes such as Chief Joseph, Geronimo, Sitting Bull, and Red Cloud, who are generally portrayed as blood-thirsty savages in textbooks.

The book recounts this quarter century of infamy from the Indian viewpoint as the American government sought to take tribal groups and incarcerate them in unfamiliar reservations and distant reserves. Words spoken by the leaders of the Indian nations give the Indian perspective on the grim details of such encounters as Sand Creek and Wounded Knee.

Available in both hardcover and paperback, this book should be an essential acquisition for public and school libraries. Adding value to the book are the carefully selected photographs of the great leaders, their wives, and warriors. A chronology of parallel United States and European events heads each of the chapters.

159. Brown, Dee. **Wounded Knee: An Indian History of the American West.** New York: Holt, Rinehart & Winston, 1974. 202p. FRL: 8. Subject: West—Wars.

Adapted by Amy Ehrlich from Dee Brown's *Bury My Heart at Wounded Knee*, this version for young readers is recommended for the juvenile literature collections of public and school libraries. The editing allows young adults to be exposed to Brown's original account of the struggle of four great Indian tribes from 1860 through 1890. This account of the conquest of the American West by the white man focuses on the struggles of the Navajo and Apache tribes of the Southwest and the Cheyenne and Sioux tribes of the Great Plains. The words of Cochise, Geronimo, Red Cloud, Crazy Horse, and Sitting Bull are cited as spoken and relate the feelings of these chiefs about the destruction of their culture by the white man. The reader should be aware that this book presents this conflict from the Indians' viewpoint. The materials should be compared with books that present the same events from a different view.

Some of the original chapters were deleted, and some sentence structure and language were simplified. Black-and-white photographs of thirty leaders or historical events accompany the text. The inclusion of maps, bibliography, an index, and a list of Indian moons makes this book valuable as a reference to the chronology of the Indian struggle during this historic time.

160. Brown, Virginia Pounds, and Laurella Owens. **The World of the Southern Indians.** Birmingham, Ala.: Beechwood Books, 1983. 176p. FRL: 8. Subject: Southern states.

A valuable resource on the history and culture of the Indian tribes of the southeastern United States, this attractive book makes the world of these people come alive to the reader. The South was populated with more Indian tribes before the arrival of the Spanish in 1513 than the rest of North America, with the exception of Mexico. Brown and Owens trace the prehistory of the Southern Indian people and their first encounters with white men. The relationship of clans and families as well as the spirit world and natural world are presented as vital to the Indian way of life. The story of the five major Indian tribes known as the Choctaw, Chickasaw, Creek, Cherokee, and Seminole is related in separate chapters including information on customs, white encounters, famous leaders, loss of land and removal, and reestablishment of their heritage. Information on the Timucuas, Natchez, Alibamos and Koasatis, Shawnee, Catawbas, and Yuchis, who were important but lesser known tribes, is recorded.

This scholarly yet easily read book is well organized, clearly written, and fast-paced. The detailed black-and-white illustrations of historical events and maps by Nathan H. Glick add interest and authenticity. The special section on the South's Indian heritage, organized by state, provides a dictionary of place names of Indian origin. Another special feature is a chronology of important dates from 1535 to 1840. The index indicates illustrations, maps, and captions, and there is a list of references and recommendations for further reading.

In one volume, the authors have compiled an absorbing account of Southern Indian life for both young people and general readers. This informative, basic book is an excellent resource in the area of social studies for an appreciation of the role of the Indian tribes inhabiting Alabama, Florida, Georgia, Mississippi, North and South Carolina, and Tennessee.

161. Burnette, Robert, and John Koster. **The Road to Wounded Knee.** New York: Bantam Books, 1974. 332p. FRL: 11. Subjects: U.S.—History—1973; American Indian Movement.

In a controversial book, Robert Burnette, the tribal chairman of the Rosebud Sioux Reservation, and John Koster, a journalist who has covered Indian activism, write the story of Wounded Knee II in 1973. The greater part of the book is concerned with the events from the beginning of the Indian's relationship with whites to the present. Two events—the November 2, 1972, seizure of the BIA building in Washington, D.C., by a band of American Indians, and the February 27, 1973, declaration of war by AIM activists and supporters against the United States on the site of the last big massacre of Indians—are chronicled by the authors, who were eyewitnesses.

Each chapter deals with an important issue that led to the spawning of Indian activism. For three generations, the genocide of Indian people, including children, was accomplished through theft of land, resources, and money; murder by whites and other Indians; starvation; termination through relocation programs; and even the destruction of culture by denying religious freedom. The Bureau of Indian Affairs failed to provide adequate Indian education, health and welfare programs, law enforcement, and protection for treaties and land. Corruption in Indian affairs by tribal and federal governments led to a trail of broken treaties. By the 1960s, young Indians in the cities and on reservations were ready to renew the struggle against the destructive elements of the white society symbolized by the BIA. Wounded Knee II, according to the authors, proves that the Indian people have courage and faith; some would rather die than submit to another century of disgrace and penury.

The authors appeal to all Americans to become students of Indian affairs, so that, through popular demand and due process of law, the American Indian can be respected and treated as other American citizens. Nine major correctives are advocated. Although the activists' actions, particularly those of AIM, may be distasteful to some, the book addresses a critical problem that unfortunately has yet to be solved.

The paperback book should be available in libraries for young adult readers. Excellent appendixes include an American Indian population graph from 1492 to 1973; traditional tribal council and tribal government charts; Pine Ridge and Rosebud Reservations and Wounded Knee maps; the Sioux Treaty of 1893; Termination Resolution of 1953; a glossary of names and abbreviations; and a chronology of events.

162. Campbell, Liz. **Powwow 1992.** Summertown, Tenn.: The Book Publishing Company, 1994. 68p. FRL: 4. Subject: Rites and ceremonies.

Published yearly as a paperback, this small volume contains information on powwows, rodeos, canoe races, festivals, art shows, stick game tournaments, and other American Indian gatherings. Many American Indian individuals and families travel every year to these gatherings and participate in the dances. Celebrations renew traditions and reinforce native heritage.

An introduction to the history of the powwow is provided in the preface. The contemporary powwow links Native Americans to the past. The original dances, frequently called Grass Dances, were held by members of elite warrior societies. As Indian tribes were forced to live on reservations, the dances became increasingly important. Powwows were social events until the 1920s. Later, "contest" dancing, where performers compete for prizes, became increasingly popular. Typical powwows begin on Friday evening and conclude Sunday, with final competitions in the afternoon. Contest dancing is divided into categories by age and style, beginning with Tiny Tots category, for five-year-old children, through the Golden Age category, for men and women over fifty. Some categories are Fancy or Shawl Dancing, Jingle Dress, Traditional Dancing, Grass Dancers, and Gourd Dancing.

The calendar provides a monthly list of events by weekend. Addresses for the events include phone numbers. Those planning to attend are advised to call to ensure that changes or cancellations have not been made. The price of the calendar is reasonable. Published annually as a service, there is no charge to organizations for the calendar listing. An annual *Powwow Calendar* will be useful in libraries that serve American Indians of all ages who participate in these events.

163. Cantor, George. **North American Indian Landmarks: A Traveler's Guide.** Detroit, Mich.: Visible Ink Press. 409p. FRL: 9. Subjects: Museums; Reservations; Rites and ceremonies.

Popular journalist and travel writer, George Cantor, explores 300 historic sites relevant to American Indian history and culture. The author discovered that the Native American presence permeates both rural and urban areas. He highlights both the injustice to and achievements of Native American civilizations.

The travel guide is organized in seven geographical regions: Northeast, Southeast, Great Lakes and Ohio Valley, Great Plains-North, Great Plains-South, Southwest and Great Basin, and Pacific Coast and Arctic. Each section is organized alphabetically by states, then by site and location. A map of the states and selected sites introduces the geographical area. The unique feature for each site is a fascinating historical sketch of the native people of the area, including important leaders, literature, and artifacts. Practical information provides the exact location, hours and season, admission fees, and special exhibits at the site. Scattered liberally throughout the guide are photographs and illustrations. As an armchair traveler, the reader will enjoy a fascinating introduction to these historic cultural areas.

Additional features include an extensive timeline, map of tribes before European incursion, and sections on tribes and their sites. A special feature of the book is the foreword, "A Native American Guide to Indian Country" by Susan Shown Harjo, president and director of The Morning Star Foundation. Harjo's narrative, a culturally sensitive guide for visitors to tribal lands, should be read before attending Native American ceremonies. Readers will also find a glossary of terms used in the essays and an index to the sites. The travel guide complements *A Guide to America's Indians: Ceremonies, Reservations and Museums* by Arnold Marquis.

164. Capps, Benjamin. **The Indians.** New York: Time-Life Books, 1973. 240p.
 FRL: 7. Subject: History—West of the Mississippi—Mid-1800s.
 Included in the Time-Life Books Old West series, this widely read book presents an Indian point of view. The material covers the mid-1800s and the lifestyle of the Indian tribes west of the Mississippi to the Great Basin. More than thirty tribes, each with a distinct language, culture, and lifestyle, were being pressured by the whites to end their way of life.

The book includes extensive illustrations and a well-written text that covers relationships between tribes, wars with aggressors, the world of the horse culture, the value of the buffalo, the importance of religious ceremonies and social life, the invasion of the white man, and the impact of betrayals and battles. The detailed index also includes the page numbers for the profuse illustrations.

The author presents an objective viewpoint of historical facts without bias and does not stereotype the Indian people. The strong stand for independence and the struggle to maintain the native lifestyle during this difficult period inspire a feeling of pride. The historical events are presented accurately, and non-Indian young people can become better acquainted with Indian heritage in an educational and interesting manner.

165. Coe, Michael, Dean Snow, and Elizabeth Benson. **Atlas of Ancient America.** New York: Facts on File, 1986. 240p. FRL: 16. Subject: Antiquities.
 The history of ancient America is presented as an atlas containing maps, text, and pictures. Based on research by historians, anthropologists, and art historians, the subject is treated in six divisions. Part one, the new world, covers the geography and environment of the native cultures, the discovery and conquest by Europeans, and the development of interest in the culture. The second section traces the origin of the native cultures in the Americas. The next three divisions, on North America, Mesoamerica, and South America, examine the major cultures that developed after Paleo-Indian groups adapted to differing environments. In the last section, on the living heritage, the authors give examples of surviving native cultures and the influence of their beliefs and practices today.

The volume is lavishly illustrated and offers a bibliography, a gazetteer, and an index. The book is recommended for large collections as a companion to the *Atlas of the North American Indian* by Waldman (Facts on File, 1985).

166. Council on Interracial Books for Children. **Chronicles of American Indian Protest.** rev. ed. New York: Fawcett, 1979. 392p. FRL: 9. Subjects: History; Treatment.

This compilation of documents written by and about American Indians covers the struggle for survival from 1622 to 1978, the time of Columbus to the Red Power movement. Information about each major historical event concerning the American Indians' battle for human and equal rights is provided, with notes of explanation about the sources. Then all documents concerned with the event are included in the chapter.

Because American history textbooks may not deal honestly with history, the Council on Interracial Books for Children has published this book for the public "in the hope of countering some of the terrible distortions perpetrated in the name of 'American' history." The Indian viewpoint is presented in the documents, but the Indian experience cannot be fully expressed. The goal of the council is for American Indians to present their own image in their own books.

American history teachers should incorporate the documented events into their curriculum. The council printed *Chronicles of American Indian Protest* as a paperback so that anyone, regardless of economic status, could have access to primary sources. A list of some American Indian newspapers and journals is appended.

167. Debo, Angie. **A History of the Indians of the United States.** Norman: University of Oklahoma Press, 1970. 386p. FRL: 12. Subjects: History; Culture.

This in-depth survey of Indians of the United States, including Eskimos and Aleuts of Alaska, is unusual because the emphasis incorporates the social environment and history of the Indian people. Debo analyzes the problems of the Indian people since their first contacts with Europeans. The early meetings of Indians with explorers, the colonial expansion and usurpation of Indian lands, the involvement of Indian tribes with foreign powers, the relationships with the new American nation, and the century of war and encroachment show the research and scholarly background of the author. The latter section of the book is concerned with the Indians' relationship with the United States government and the policies to which they are and have been subjected.

Angie Debo, whose career and research in writing about Indian people and their problems has culminated in this book, provides a comprehensive and objective account of the ethnocentric United States government administrative policy dealing with American and Canadian Indians. For the future, she advocates protection of Indian land, vocational and educational training, voluntary relocation, awareness on the part of governmental agencies of the Indian value system and social organization, and self-determination.

Persons who work with Indian youth and adults will find this volume unique in its optimism about the future of Indian people. Students of Indian culture should gain new perspectives. Although the work is not documented, because of the author's extensive knowledge of the subject, selected readings are listed on the basis of her personal preference. A detailed index, illustrations, and maps are provided.

168. Denig, Edwin Thompson. **Five Indian Tribes of the Upper Missouri: Sioux, Arikaras, Assiniboines, Crees, Crows.** Norman: University of Oklahoma Press, 1961. 217p. FRL: 10. Subjects: Sioux Indians; Arikara Indians; Assiniboine Indians; Cree Indians; Crow Indians.

John C. Ewers edited and published the manuscript of Edwin Thompson Denig because he felt that this material would provide an authentic account of the history and ethnology of the Indian tribes of the Upper Missouri from the 1830s to the 1850s. The book comprises individual manuscripts that were first published in Bureau of American Ethnology bulletins.

A fur trader on the Upper Missouri from 1833 until 1858, Denig needed knowledge of Indian culture and language to conduct business at Fort Union in what is now North Dakota. He also recognized that information he had gathered and observations he had made of Indian life and customs would be of interest to others removed from Indian country. Denig was very concerned that the American Indians be portrayed as human beings in a positive manner. He knew the people intimately and recorded a short history of each tribe, its geographical position, peculiarities such as manners and customs, distinguishing significant differences as well as basic similarities among neighboring tribes of the same cultural area.

The book provides an excellent source of material for classroom studies of the Sioux, Arikaras, Assiniboines, Crees, and Crows. He records with accuracy the origins and migrations of the buffalo hunting tribes, describing the features of each tribe in detail. School-age young adults from these tribes will easily identify with this material.

169. Dillon, Richard H. **North American Indian Wars.** New York: Facts on File, 1983. 256p. FRL: 11. Subjects: Wars; History—1492-1891.

Tracing the annals of North American Indians from the first contacts with the conquistadors in 1492 through their famous battle with General Custer in 1876, this large volume is a well-written account of an exciting era in American history. As Europeans advanced commercial enterprises and seized control of land in the New World, conflicts with American Indian cultures led to altercations. The Spanish, Portuguese, English, and French forced their will on the native people and relentlessly pushed them from their homelands. When the Indian people resisted this encroachment on their tribal lands, massacres, broken treaties, and brutal warfare inevitably followed.

As settlers pushed to the frontiers of the West, "their manifest destiny," they again ignored the rights of the Indians to their native lands. During the period from 1860 through 1890, the Indians continued to fight back to preserve their way of life. Even though the Indian nations were defeated, the names of the great leaders and the battles have become legend. American history students will enjoy accounts of the battles of Little Big Horn, Wounded Knee, and Rosebud as well as the lesser-known engagements at Adobe Walls, Blue Licks, and Kildeer Mountain. The deeds of famous leaders such as Sitting Bull, Crazy Horse, and Geronimo are recounted as well as the strategies of the American officers who led forces against them.

The numerous color and black-and-white illustrations, which are captioned with historical information and dates, provide an extra appeal for readers. Artists' renditions and photographs of historical events and people provide visual impact. Brightly colored, full-page maps accompany the text. An index, graphs of the Indian populations by state in 1890 and 1980, and a chronology of historical events are appended.

170. Foreman, Grant. **The Five Civilized Tribes.** Norman: University of Oklahoma Press, 1972, c1934. 455p. FRL: 12. Subjects: Choctaw Indians; Chickasaw Indians; Creek Indians; Cherokee Indians; Seminole Indians; Sequoyah; Ross, John; McIntosh, Roley; Bowlegs; Government relations.

Although first published in 1934 in hardcover and in 1972 in paperback, Grant Foreman's account of the history of the Choctaws, Chickasaws, Creeks, Cherokees, and Seminoles as they started a new phase of their lives in the Oklahoma Indian territory from 1830 to the beginning of the Civil War is still one of the best documentaries on this event. Because treaties with the United States government had been broken, the removal of the five civilized tribes from the Eastern coast was filled with misery, hardship, and suffering. Their settling in the Indian Territory was extremely difficult, as they were viewed with suspicion by those already living there. The five civilized tribes hoped that they were so far away from the white man that they would be rid of his interference in their lives, but they soon discovered that the United States government would continue to harass them no matter where they were located.

Although the native groups had been nomadic tribes, they adapted through necessity and achieved more success in the fields of agriculture and government than other Indian tribes who had been placed on reservations. Schools, churches, and towns were founded, and orderly development was maintained through government and laws. An accurate record of the great leaders of the period, Sequoyah, John Ross, Roley McIntosh, and Bowlegs, is provided.

The work is footnoted and scholarly in its documentation, presenting a reliable history of this period. For the Indian student, the book establishes a positive attitude toward the accomplishments of these people. For the non-Indian reader, the book develops a positive image of Indians as evidenced by the five civilized tribes who were successful in integrating both the Indian and white cultures.

171. Gilpin, Laura. **The Enduring Navajo.** Austin: University of Texas Press, 1968. 264p. FRL: 9. Subject: Navajo Indians.

An outstanding photographer, Laura Gilpin has created a visual image of the Navajo, together with an explanatory text. The beautiful photographs in black-and-white and color are accompanied by factual information about the Navajo people as of 1968. On a 25,000-square-mile reservation, the largest tribe of Indians in North America live in a barren land. Their traditional ways of life have changed rapidly. Gilpin uses photography to record and interpret these changes.

The photographic essay is divided into four parts. The first section, on the Navajo world, includes the creation mythology and the geographic conception of the world. The section on ways of the people concentrates on the lifestyles and activities of the people during the thirty years Gilpin photographed them. The third division shows the transition from the old ways to the new, using text and scenes about tribal government and affairs. The last section, "The Enduring Way," describes the traditional ceremonies that make them uniquely Navajo. The photographs in the last section are unusual because today very few outsiders are allowed to witness the sacred portions of the ceremonies.

Gilpin's respect and admiration for the people are evident as she captures the spirit and essence of the Navajo. Readers from the upper elementary grades to adults will delight in the excellent photographs and enjoy reading the accompanying text. The Navajo word pronunciation guide, bibliography, and index are useful.

172. Hamilton, Charles, ed. **Cry of the Thunderbird: The American Indian's Own Story.** New York: Macmillan, 1957. 283p. FRL: 8. Subjects: Traditions; Hunting; Sports; Religion; Warfare; White encroachment.

Charles Hamilton selected excerpts from many sources to compile this anthology of records. The anthology is interesting because it presents the words of American Indians, showing the reader a new interpretation of historical events. The situations are important because when the Indian refers to himself, he tells the truth, even though it may be unflattering. The stories are told with humor and dignity and with naïvete, and with wisdom as well.

Fifty authors give an authentic, intimate portrait of an early way of life. They represent twenty-five tribes; however, they record their observations as individuals, not members of tribes. This useful book contains information on traditions, hunting, sports, religion, warfare, and the impact of white encroachment. The Indian authors were keen critics of the white conquerors. In the 100 tales, the reader should gain a better perspective on the Indian's own story.

Hamilton includes extensive source notes as well as brief biographical information about each author. The selections cover many areas and provide positive images of the American Indian for youth.

173. Heizer, Robert F., and Albert B. Elsasser. **The Natural World of the California Indians.** Berkeley: University of California Press, 1980. 271p. FRL: 12. Subject: California Indians—History.

Research anthropologists Heizer and Elsasser have written a compact study of California Indian tribes that makes this book a welcome addition to public and school libraries. Before California was invaded by the Spanish and Americans, American Indian tribes occupied almost all of the state, from the deserts to the highlands and mountains. This book traces the diversity of the languages and cultures and provides rich information on such topics as the Indian's ability to adjust to the environment by utilizing available foodstuffs, tools, and housing.

This accurate account of primitive life relies on archaeological studies to document the devastating period when first the Spaniards and then the gold seekers sought to decimate the Indian population. The destruction of entire tribes and the appropriation of tribal lands without treaty is not a historical episode in which Americans can take pride. Even today, the California Indians are only slowly growing in numbers and regaining a small portion of the lands they once enjoyed.

The information is well documented, and the divisions of the book are such that specific information can be found easily. Three indexes provide additional information on plants used only by California Indians, displays of Indian life and artifacts, a listing of California tribes and their pronunciation, as well as an excellent reference and index section. Extensive illustrations and maps make this small volume invaluable for research purposes. Secondary students and adults should find this book a rich source of information in history, social studies, and ethnic studies.

174. Hothem, Lar. **North American Indian Artifacts: A Collector's Identification and Value Guide.** Florence, Ala.: Books Americana, 1984. 426p. FRL: 10. Subject: Antiquities.

A specialist in antiques and collectibles, the author has prepared a third edition of this sturdy paperback guide to prehistoric (before writing), historic (after European and Russian contacts), recent (from 1900-1970), and contemporary (from 1970 to the present) American Indian collectibles and their value at publication date. Twenty different types of objects are covered in detail, and each major collection area is identified and described: chipped and organic material artifacts, axe forms and stone collectibles, bannerstones and banded slate ornaments, copper and hematite artifacts, ceramics, historic trade-era items, baskets, beadwork and quillwork, pipes, clothing, wooden collectibles, kachinas, dolls, toys, musical items, blanket and rug weavings, and silver and turquoise jewelry.

Brief information on the history of the form is provided, and numerous photographs of artifacts illustrating each type are provided on corresponding pages. A unique feature is the suggested reading list at the end of each chapter. A major weakness is the lack of an index, which makes it necessary to locate items only by type rather than by tribal group. The author provides a list of professional and government agencies and a directory of businesses and further sources of information.

Although the collection of prehistoric and historic Indian artifacts has been abused by some collectors, the creation of artistic objects rooted in traditional culture by American Indian artists is a major source of revenue. For persons interested in purchasing quality Indian arts and crafts, the book gives general help in acquisition of good pieces. The book may be included as a reference in a school or public library collection, not only as a collector's guide, but as a means of acquiring knowledge and appreciation of Indian artifacts. American Indian arts and crafts should be valued and recognized just as other art forms of the world are valued and recognized.

175. **Indians of the Americas.** New York: Franklin Watts, 1989- . 64p. 26 vols. FRL: 4.

175.1. Alter, Judith. **The Comanches.** 1994. Subject: Comanche Indians.

175.2. Anderson, Madelyn Klein. **The Nez Perce.** 1994. Subject: Nez Perce Indians.

175.3. Beyer, Don E. **The Totem Pole Indians of the Northwest.** 1989. Subject: Northwest Coast of North America—Social life and customs.

175.4. Carter, Alden R. **The Shoshoni.** 1989. Subject: Shoshoni Indians.

175.5. Doherty, Craig A., and Katherine M. Doherty. **The Apaches and Navajos.** 1989. Subjects: Apache Indians; Navajo Indians.

175.6. Doherty, Craig A., and Katherine M. Doherty. **The Iroquois.** 1989. Subject: Iroquois Indians.

175.7. Doherty, Katherine M., and Craig A. Doherty. **The Zunis.** 1993. Subject: Zuni Indians.

175.8. Greene, Jacqueline Dembar. **The Maya.** 1992. Subject: Maya Indians.

175.9. Greene, Jacqueline Dembar. **The Chippewa.** 1992. Subject: Chippewa Indians.

175.10. Landau, Elaine. **The Cherokees.** 1992. Subject: Cherokee Indians.

175.11. Landau, Elaine. **The Chilula.** 1994. Subject: Chilula Indians.

175.12. Landau, Elaine. **The Hopi.** 1994. Subject: Hopi Indians.

175.13. Landau, Elaine. **The Pomo.** 1994. Subject: Pomo Indians.

175.14. Landau, Elaine. **The Sioux.** 1989. Subject: Sioux Indians.

175.15. Lee, Martin. **The Seminoles.** 1989. Subject: Seminole Indians.

175.16. Liptak, Karen. **North American Indian Ceremonies.** 1992. Subject: Rites and ceremonies.

175.17. Liptak, Karen. **North American Indian Medicine People.** 1990. Subject: Medicine men.

175.18. Liptak, Karen. **North American Indian Sign Language.** 1990. Subject: Sign language.

175.19. Liptak, Karen. **North American Indian Survival Skills.** 1990. Subjects: Cookery; Dwellings; Tools.

175.20. Liptak, Karen. **North American Indian Tribal Chiefs.** 1992. Subject: Biographies.

175.21. Myers, Arthur. **The Cheyenne.** 1992. Subject: Cheyenne Indians.

175.22. Myers, Arthur. **The Pawnee.** 1993. Subject: Pawnee Indians.

175.23. Newman, Shirlee P. **The Incas.** 1992. Subject: Inca Indians.

175.24. Newman, Shirlee P. **The Inuits.** 1992. Subject: Inuit Indians.

175.25. Powell, Suzanne. **The Pueblos.** 1993. Subjects: Prehistoric Indians of the Southwest; Pueblo Indians.

175.26. Quiri, Patricia Ryon. **The Algonquins.** 1992. Subject: Algonquin Indians.

175.27. Shepherd, Donna Walsh. **The Aztecs.** 1992. Subject: Aztec Indians.
The Indians of the Americas series, published by Franklin Watts covers the major American Indian tribes of North and South America. The attractive, full-color First Book series for middle school students includes separate volumes for twenty-two American Indian tribes. Each title is well written and informative.

Written by various authors, each book contains information about particular tribal groups of people. The volume on the Algonquian Indians describes their daily life, religion, crafts, games, and political life. It also chronicles the society's confrontation with Europeans. Each book records important historical events, such as the Trail of Tears, the forced march of the Cherokees. Geographic location is the key for including tribal groups in one volume: the Totem Pole Indians of the Northwest and the Pueblo Indians of the Southwest. Most of the books detail the destruction of tribal existence and the adjustment of Indian people to modern life.

Five volumes deal with general topics that are important in the social and cultural life of many Indian tribes. Karen Liptak authors these books on Indian ceremonies, medicine people, sign language, survival skills, and tribal chiefs. New titles of tribes not as familiar are being added, for example, two volumes on California Indian people, *The Chilulu* and *The Pomo*, by Elaine Landau.

The set is an excellent reference, providing a broad variety of subjects for individual or class projects. Five sources, some historical and some of legends, recommend further reading appropriate for middle school readers. Each book includes an index and a short paragraph about the author. These durable library books contain full-color photographs of historical events and paintings with excellent captions.

Selected titles are also available in paperback. The set is an excellent purchase. Adding individual titles will strengthen American Indian library collections.

176. Iverson, Peter. **The Plains Indians of the Twentieth Century.** Norman: University of Oklahoma Press, 1985. 277p. FRL: 15. Subject: Great Plains—History—20th century—Addresses, essays, lectures.
This anthology of articles, edited and introduced by Peter Iverson, records notable events in the history of the Plains Indians after their last formal encounter with the United States military. Iverson, a specialist in twentieth-century Indian history, acquaints the reader with the past history and the contemporary issues facing the Plains Indian people as he introduces eleven articles by leading scholars. The articles highlight water, land, and human rights; political economy and natural resources; World War II and the New Deal; and the resurgence of religious heritage. Although the materials focus on the Cheyenne, Sioux, Arapaho, Gros Ventres, Assiniboine, Kiowa, Comanche, and Crow, other tribes are included and can be easily accessed through the index.

Selecting samples of the best articles concerning modern Indian history, Iverson provides a synopsis for each article. The opening of the Kiowa, Comanche, and Kiowa-Apache reservations is chronicled by William T. Hogan. Donald J. Berthrong details the reduction of the Cheyenne-Arapaho lands in Oklahoma by profiteers who had been charged with the welfare of the Indian people. In a different light, Frederick E. Hoxie explains how the Sioux people of the South Dakota

Cheyenne River Reservation preserved some of their original homelands and survived dramatic changes. The Winter Decision, which affected the Gros Ventres and Assiniboines of northern Montana, is examined by Norris Hundley, Jr. Interviews with three politically active Indian men on the effects of the New Deal program and the ensuing termination era were conducted by Joseph H. Cash and Herbert T. Hoover.

In another selection, the World War II experiences of the Sioux, Omaha, Osage, Cheyenne, Kiowa, and Blackfoot are recorded by Tom Holm. Michael L. Lawson examines federal water projects and Indian lands, specifically the Pick-Sloan Plan and the impact on the North and South Dakota Sioux. The struggle of the Northern Arapaho tribal government to maintain an economic base and a relationship with Indian and non-Indian counterparts is explained by Loretta Fowler. Readers are informed by Donald L. Fixico of the advantages and disadvantages of economic development of natural energy resources by the Northern Cheyenne and Crow of Montana. In his article, Vine Deloria, Jr. reminds the reader of the distinctive Indian right to land, tribal government, code of conduct, and courts. The continuing importance of tradition for the Cheyenne is traced by Peter J. Powell.

Footnotes accompany each original article as an aid to research. Sixteen black-and-white historical photographs, maps of the land opening in Oklahoma and the Plains Indian lands, and an index are included. Brief biographical information for each contributor establishes the author's authority, as do citations of other major works. This collection is relevant, especially in the study of the Plains Indians in contemporary American history.

177. Jacobs. Francine. **The Tainos: The People Who Welcomed Columbus.** New York: G. P. Putnam's Sons, 1992. 107p. FRL: 4. Subjects: Taino Indians; Indians of the West Indies.

Well-documented books are a rarity for children. Francine Jacob's book *The Tainos: The People Who Welcomed Columbus* is a carefully researched piece of writing for the middle school student and teacher. The sympathetic picture of the Tainos and their treatment by Columbus and his successors relies on sources rarely used in young people's nonfiction.

The first "Indians" to welcome Columbus and his men when the three Spanish ships landed in the Bahamas were the Tainos. A peaceful, farming people, they had come from South American to islands in the Caribbean hundreds of years before. Aiding Columbus and his successors, their trust was betrayed. They were soon enslaved by the Spaniards' greed to find gold. Within fifty years, disease and domination led to their extinction. In the detailed and fairly presented account, Jacobs reveals that a few Spaniards were opposed to the treatment of the natives and tried to ensure their survival.

The story is tightly focused and readable. Maps and black-and-white illustration by Patrick Collins add interest. The author includes notes, a bibliography, an index, and a list of museums and exhibits of Taino-Arawak culture. Young people cannot truly understand Columbus and his successors unless they read this book about the devastating annihilation of the Tainos.

178.   Jahoda, Gloria. **The Trail of Tears.** New York: Holt, Rinehart & Winston, 1975. 356p. FRL: 11. Subjects: Land transfers; Government relations; History.

In a judgmental account of Indian removal of all those tribes living east of the Mississippi and their resettlement in the Indian Territory, Gloria Jahoda describes the physical suffering of the Indian tribes who died of starvation, cold, and disease. The Cherokees remember it as "the trail where we cried." The narrative begins with the war against the Indians on the East Coast and their subsequent defeat, which resulted in the Jackson-sponsored law of 1830 that sanctioned forcible removal of all tribes east of the Mississippi to Indian Territory in Oklahoma. The removal did not recognize that those lands already were occupied by other Indian tribes.

The use of dialogue with original quotations provides authenticity as well as interest. The impact of the whites, who participated in the removal and helped speed the demise of the Indians once they were in Oklahoma, is vividly chronicled. Portraits of whites who were sympathetic, such as Davy Crockett, Sam Houston, and Benjamin Petit, show a different viewpoint. The great Indian leaders of the Cherokees, Creeks, Choctaws, Chickasaws, Seminoles, Shawnees, Delawares, and Senecas tried to represent and defend their tribes with great courage.

This well-researched account uses unpublished resources as well as more familiar accounts. Grant Foreman's *Indian Removal* (University of Oklahoma Press, 1953), a scholarly account from which Jahoda drew, would also be of value in libraries for this historical period. All American history classes should include the story of the American Indian removals from 1813 to 1855 when studying the administration of Andrew Jackson. This excellent source relates the history of Indian courage in the face of expansionism during the first half of the nineteenth century and shows how the Trail of Tears led to the final massacre at Wounded Knee. The book is not footnoted but contains a bibliography and an index.

179.   Johnson, Broderick H., ed. **Navajo Stories of the Long Walk Period.** Tsaile, Ariz.: Navajo Community College Press, 1973. 272p. FRL: 8. Subject: Navajo Indians—History—1864.

Little Navajo history, as perceived by the Navajo, has been written. This collection of anecdotes and stories in the memories of the Navajo narrators brings to print many historical events relating to Navajo history, with an emphasis on the Long Walk to Fort Sumner. Since it occurred in 1864, none of the storytellers actually participated in this shameful event in American history, but all heard the tragic story from their elders. The volume is also enriched by many other stories of this era, which tell of clashes with other tribes and with the white man.

Because the stories are told by the Navajo people themselves, they give an interesting perspective to history and relate not only the many injustices of the Long Walk but also the continuing concern about the United States' failure to keep its agreements in the Treaty of 1868, particularly to provide adequate education for the Navajo people. The book is not a chronicle of historical events placed in the proper time sequence, but rather is a story of history as it was remembered by the old ones. The book contains excellent illustrations. The lack of an index limits its use for research. Navajo youth will find the stories meaningful as a Navajo perspective on history. Teachers of social studies and ethnic studies may also wish to assign readings in this book to research oral history. English teachers can use the material as examples of personal biography that can be gleaned from one's family history.

180. Josephy, Alvin M., Jr., ed. **America in 1492: The World of the Indian Peoples Before the Arrival of Columbus.** New York: Alfred A. Knopf, 1992. 477p. FRL: 10. Subjects: History; Antiquities; America—Discovery and exploration.

Commemorating the 500th anniversary of Columbus's historic journey to the new world, *America in 1492* focuses on American Indian life before the white man came. Alvin M. Josephy, Jr. gathered the writings of some eminent scholars of American Indian studies to explore this fascinating era in the history of the Americas. Brief biographies of the contributors include Standing Rock Sioux Vine Deloria, Jr., Peter Iverson, Alvin M. Josephy, Jr., Kiowa N. Scott Momaday, and Peter Nabokov.

The volume is divided into two parts: the first introduces the reader to the multiplicity of native cultures from the Arctic to South America. These ancient societies range from primitive hunting bands to the highly evolved city-states of the Inca and Aztecs. Scholars and young people will enjoy reading about the achievements of these peoples as they adapted to the diverse environments of America.

Part two delves into the creative arts of pre-Columbian societies. The reader learns that the art, music, literature, and other creative activities were second to no other civilizations. The native peoples of the Americas used artistic endeavors as an inherent component of their religion and as an important part of their daily life.

The primary goal of *America in 1492* is to dispel the prevalent stereotypes of the ancient Indian civilizations. These people were not happy, noble savages dressed in warbonnets. Many of these cultures had made extraordinary achievements in architecture, engineering, and technology. These cultures with their highly developed philosophies and religion have made significant contributions to the quality of our modern-day life.

For the high school library, this book will provide an invaluable resource for young people who wish to research the development of modern Indian cultures. The scholars have filled their articles with valuable information presented in a readable format. A special section of additional resources and a classification of languages of the Americas is included. Although there are few written materials left from this time, the illustrations are well selected and provide a good introduction to life before the arrival of Columbus.

181. Josephy, Alvin M., Jr. **The Indian Heritage of America.** New York: Alfred A. Knopf, 1968. 384p. FRL: 10. Subject: History.

The history of the Indians of North, South, and Central America from Alaska to Patagonia is detailed from the past to the present. Josephy opens this comprehensive study by examining the origins of the Indian stereotype in American folklore, the diversity of the Indian, and what "Indianness" means. The history, archaeology, and ethnology of all the major Indian cultures provide a panoramic view of the American Indians of both continents. The impact on the Indian of the early explorers and settlers of various nationalities, the destruction of the Indian tribes, and the problems facing the Indian at the time this book was written are surveyed.

This broad survey of American Indians of North, Central, and South America, written by an authority on American Indians, is an excellent reference for readers. Maps and extensive illustrations with captions are included. An excellent bibliography and a detailed index provide further readings and quick access to information.

182. Kopper, Phillip. **The Smithsonian Book of North American Indians: Before the Coming of the Europeans.** New York: Harry N. Abrams, 1986. 288p. FRL: 12. Subjects: Antiquities; Social life and customs; Archaeology.

Accompanied by excellent color pictures of prehistoric sites and artifacts, this volume explores the cultures and environments of pre-Columbian North American Indians in an archaeological context. The author explains the cultural diversity of the approximately 20 million Indian people speaking 200 different languages living in social units ranging from individual families to large cities. Remnants from the past have provided archaeologists with evidence on religions, customs, tools, weapons, arts, and the architecture of these ancient peoples. Through careful analysis of scientific evidence, the writer makes a systematic attempt to fill in the missing parts of the cultural development of the North American Indian.

The early inhabitants of America, who were given the name Indians by Columbus, lived on the American continents in many different environments and developed independent cultures, languages, and ways of life. Using geography and culture as a means of grouping, the author provides scientifically based information on nine distinct cultures. The Arctic region hunters adapted and coped with extremes of environment and great distances. In a similar manner, the lives of the people of the Subarctic were determined by seasons and animal life. In the Northeast section of North America, changing landforms determined the human activities of hunting, gathering, and agriculture. The great civilizations of mound builders in the Southeast developed large ceremonial centers and improved agricultural plants.

Although the bison was the mainstay of the Great Plains tribes, they relied on resourcefulness and adaptability to survive. The Great Basin people of the Far West lived a nomadic hunting-gathering life. With abundant resources, Northwest tribes used the verdant land and ocean wealth. In the Southwest, dedicated agriculturalists and skilled potters dwelt in pueblos and cliff dwellings. The most influential and widespread achievement, the development of corn, occurred in the highly developed civilizations in Mexico. The coming of the Europeans brought the destruction of much of the evidence of the prehistory of the North American Indians.

Providing accurate information based on archaeological finds, interesting cultural details, and innumerable photographs, this book will be enjoyed for both research and pleasure reading by youth and adults.

183. Le Sueur, Meridel. **The Mound Builders.** New York: Franklin Watts, 1974. 62p. FRL: 7. Subject: Mound builders.

Great mounds of earth are found on the surface of the North American continent along the great rivers in the present-day areas of Illinois, Ohio, and Mississippi. Little is known about the ancient people who built these structures long before the arrival of the Spanish explorers. Although many of these prehistoric ruins were vandalized or destroyed, anthropologists and archaeologists studied the sites to find answers about these advanced civilizations. Excavations of mounds and examination of artifacts have answered many questions about the cultures of the people known as mound builders. However, many questions about these mysterious people still remain.

This book for younger readers briefly introduces the four different cultures named for the regions where the first excavations were made. Although the cultures were alike in many ways, they also differed. The Adena culture, located in Louisiana from ca.1000 B.C. to A.D. 500 had an elaborate cult of the dead. In Illinois and Ohio, the people of the Hopewellian culture, 400 B.C. to A.D. 900, had long heads and were far-ranging merchants and skilled artisans. The Mississippian culture, A.D. 700 to 1700, spread from the Ohio and Tennessee valleys into an area that extends from South Carolina to Texas and from Wisconsin to Florida. The people constructed mounds used as temples and developed elaborate crafts. The Poverty Point culture, ca.1000 B.C., was located in Louisiana. The site was populated by a cluster of towns and appeared to be the center of that culture.

Numerous pictures of artifacts, maps, and ruins supplement the informative text. An index provides easy access to subjects, and a bibliography of sources for in-depth reading is provided. *The Mound Builders* by Robert Silverberg (New York Graphic Society, 1970) is recommended for collections where there is interest on the part of young adults in further information about the mound builders of eastern North America.

184. Marrin, Albert. **War Clouds in the West: Indians and Cavalrymen, 1860-1890.** New York: Atheneum, 1984. 219p. FRL: 7. Subjects: West (U.S.); Wars.

Although many adolescents are intrigued by the historical battles and out-standing personalities of the Plains Indians, few books are written specifically for younger readers. One exception is historian Marrin's account of the Indian and cavalry wars in the West from 1860 through 1890. This narrative details the struggles of the Plains natives against the never-ending westward flow of settlers seeking land. The historical and cultural events of the period affected the military campaign that led to the defeat of the Plains Indians and Apaches. By visualizing the viewpoints of both sides, the reader can readily understand the desperate struggle of the Cheyenne, Sioux, and Nez Perce, as well as the desert Apache, against United States military forces. The book brings life to this period of history, as Indian leaders Cochise and Geronimo, Crazy Horse, Sitting Bull, and the Nez Perce Chief Joseph pit their skills against the weapons and forces of Sherman, Custer, Howard, Fetterman, and other professional soldiers.

This chronicle of a period of history that dramatically changed Native American life is enlivened by liberal illustrations and captioned photographs and art, including detailed illustrations of a Plains Indian tipi and the uses of the buffalo. Pictorial maps point out the geographical locations of the defeat of Custer at Little Big Horn, the Nez Perce flight toward Canada, Apache country from 1822 to 1886, and the period during the Ghost Dance troubles on the Sioux Reservations in 1890. The author provides a bibliography of books and an index, but this book's value as a reference is diminished by the fact that neither footnotes nor other references are provided.

Among reviewers of this book there is disagreement. While some find it sympathetic toward the Plains Indians, others are concerned with the stereotypes of the Plains Indian in reference to war, fighting, prisoners, and the role of women. The author's purpose was to present the viewpoints of both sides, but the stereotypes may not be evident to a young reader unless guidance is provided by the teacher or librarian.

185. Meltzer, Milton. **Hunted Like a Wolf: The Story of the Seminole War.** New York: Farrar, Straus & Giroux, 1972. 215p. FRL: 9. Subjects: Seminole Indians—History; Osceola.

Viewing the Seminole Indian wars from 1835 to 1842 as an example of the injustice perpetrated on Indian nations by the United States government, Milton Meltzer's book is a study of the determination of a people who had been removed from their original lands to a strange land on the peninsula of Florida which they were forced to accept from the government. The Seminole Indians were not a tribe in the usual sense, but a composite of many small groups of Indians, remnants of tribes and bands. After their first war with the government, when the five civilized tribes were moved to the Oklahoma Indian Territory, the Seminoles were convinced by American agents around 1819 to move to Florida reservations. They were joined by hundreds of free blacks and runaway slaves. A highly organized government and agricultural society developed among the Seminoles and those living with them. Whites, greedy for the land of the Seminoles and slaves to work the land, soon placed impossible demands on the Indians who had the land, sheltered the slaves, and would not give them up.

The Seminoles resisted, led by the fiery young Osceola, who was betrayed and imprisoned by General Jessup. The young chief died in prison in 1838, and the other Seminoles carried on the fight, costing the lives of more than 2,000 American soldiers and between forty and sixty million dollars. Finally, many of the Seminoles surrendered and were sent west, along with their black compatriots. A number hid in the swamps, and their acestors live in the area today. The desperate fighting of the Seminoles to retain their land and freedom in the longest, bloodiest, and most costly Indian war in America's history is sympathetically chronicled by Meltzer.

Readers may feel, as did Halleck, a Seminole leader, that "I have been hunted like a wolf and now I am about to be sent away like a dog," when they read this account. American history teachers should include this historic account, which is very readable and accurate, as supplementary material. For middle and secondary school readers, this book, which includes a bibliography and an index, offers good research on a sensitive topic. A more scholarly and documented account can be found in Edwin C. McReynolds volume *The Seminoles* (University of Oklahoma Press, 1984).

186. Momaday, Natachee Scott. **The Way to Rainy Mountain.** Albuquerque: University of New Mexico, 1969. 88p. FRL: 9. Subjects: Kiowa Indians— History; Kiowa Indians—Mythology.

The Way to Rainy Mountain is Momaday's personal journey in search of his Kiowa heritage. Returning to visit his grandmother's grave, he follows the same route taken by the Kiowa tribe 300 years ago as they left their ancestral grounds at the headwaters of the Yellowstone River and journeyed to their present location in the southern Plains. Along the journey, the sacred Sun Dance doll Tai-me, the horse, and knowledge of Plains living were acquired by the Kiowa, a dominant tribe on the Plains for the next hundred years.

Momaday explains his journey in three interwoven parts of Kiowa tradition: the oral mythology, the historical journey, and his personal recollections. Beautiful illustrations by Al Momaday, his father, depict in contemporary style the mythology of the Kiowa people. The author's unique style and unusual format lend beauty to the folktales and poetry.

This book is an excellent choice if only one book can be recommended to Indian youth. Language arts classes, as well as American history classes, may introduce this book by a Kiowan Indian for enrichment, as a literary experience, and for a moving narrative. Teachers are frequently looking for books that can be read aloud to their classes. For this purpose, Momaday's beautiful book is a moving tribute to his people.

187. National Geographic Society. **The World of the American Indian.** Washington, D.C.: National Geographic Society, 1974. 399p. FRL: 10. Subjects: History; Language and languages; Handicraft; Culture.

With rich cultural detail, the lifestyle of the American Indian is depicted in this book. Written by ten scholarly authors, four of Indian descent, the text reflects anthropological research and traces the Indians' migration on the continent from 25,000 B.C. to the mid-1970s. The Bering Strait theory that American Indians are descendants of the Ice Age Asiatics is advanced by the authors, although this is not acceptable to all American Indians. The author's stated purpose is to show the Indian past and to provide an understanding of contemporary Indian culture.

The book covers the history, language, crafts, philosophy, and accomplishments of the Eastern, Southwestern, Western, and Plains Indian people. The final chapters address the clash of cultures as the Indian has dealt with the white culture through the years. An overview of the Indian today by Vine Deloria, Jr. reviews the economic and social status of the tribes and those working to better their conditions.

A part of the Story of Man Library, the book is lavishly illustrated with more than 400 fully captioned photographs, 362 in color. A detailed index provides the reader with easy access to the text. Also included are a tribal supplement and folded culture map (in the endpaper pocket) of about 600 tribes in the United States and Canada.

This excellent book about the American Indian will be useful as an introduction to American history. School and public library professionals can recommend the book to readers for a better understanding of Indian culture. The material is authentic and contains little bias or stereotyping.

188. **Native Americans.** Chicago: Childrens Press, 1991- . 28 vols. FRL: 3.

188.1. Duvall, Jill. **The Cayuga.** 1992. 45p. Subject: Cayuga Indians.

188.2. Duvall, Jill. **The Mohawk.** 1992. 45p. Subject: Mohawk Indians.

188.3. Duvall, Jill. **The Oneida.** 1992. 45p. Subject: Oneida Indians.

188.4. Duvall, Jill. **The Onondaga.** 1992. 45p. Subject: Onondaga Indians.

188.5. Duvall, Jill. **The Penobscot.** 1993. 45p. Subject: Penobscot Indians.

188.6. Duvall, Jill. **The Seneca.** 1992. 45p. Subject: Seneca Indians.

188.7. Duvall, Jill. **The Tuscarora.** 1992. 45p. Subject: Tuscarora Indians.

188.8. Fradin, Dennis B. **The Cheyenne.** 1992. 45p. Subject: Cheyenne Indians.

188.9. Fradin, Dennis B. **The Pawnee.** 1992. 45p. Subject: Pawnee Indians.

188.10. Fradin, Dennis B. **The Shoshoni.** 1993. 45p. Subject: Shoshoni Indians.

188.11. Hagman, Ruth. **The Crow.** 1992. 45p. Subject: Crow Indians.

188.12. Lepthien, Emile U. **The Cherokee.** 1992. 45p. Subject: Cherokee Indians.

188.13. Lepthien, Emile U. **The Choctaw.** 1992. 45p. Subject: Choctaw Indians.

188.14. Lepthien, Emile U. **The Mandans.** 1992. 45p. Subject: Mandan Indians.

188.15. Lepthien, Emile U. **The Seminole.** 1992. 45p. Subject: Seminole Indians.

188.16. McKissack, Patricia C. **The Apache.** 1992. 45p. Subject: Apache Indians.

188.17. McKissack, Patricia C. **The Aztec.** 1992. 45p. Subject: Aztec Indians.

188.18. McKissack, Patricia C. **The Inca.** 1992. 45p. Subject: Inca Indians.

188.19. McKissack, Patricia. C. **The Maya.** 1992. 45p. Subject: Maya Indians.

188.29. Miller, Jay. **Native Americans.** 1993, 45p. Subject: Social life and customs.

188.30. Osinski, Alice. **The Chippewa.** 1992. 45p. Subject: Chippewa Indians.

188.31. Osinski, Alice. **The Eskimo: Inuit and Yupik.** 1992. 45p. Subject: Eskimos.

188.32. Osinski, Alice. **The Navajo.** 1992. 45p. Subject: Navajo Indians.

188.33. Osinski, Alice. **The Nez Perce.** 1992. 45p. Subject: Nez Perce Indians.

188.34. Osinski, Alice. **The Sioux.** 1993. 45p. Subject: Sioux Indians.

188.35. Osinski, Alice. **The Tlingit.** 1992. 45p. Subject: Tlingit Indians.

188.36. Peterson, David. **The Anasazi.** 1992. 45p. Subject: Anasazi Indians.

188.37. Tomchek, Ann. **The Hopi.** 1993. 45p. Subject: Hopi Indians.

Childrens Press has produced a new, up-to-date edition of the series titled Native Americans. The fact-filled New True Books provide answers to basic questions about individual Native American tribal people, with material on individual tribes that will kindle the interest of children. The books are informative and packed with fascinating information that will encourage independent study.

Individual volumes describe the history, customs, religion, government, homes, and day-to-day life of various Native American tribes. A good example is the book *The Navajo* by Alice Osinski. The brief history describes customs, interactions with white settlers, and changes in traditional ways of life brought on by modern civilizations. Osinski presents facts about the Long Walk forced upon the Navajos in 1864-65. She also discusses the difficulties Navajo people face today. Some books are written by experts. For example, archaeologist David Peterson is the author of the volume on the Anasazi Indians. Other authors, such as Emile Lepthien, have a strong background in elementary education and understand the reading needs of children.

Each book is sewn in a library binding and printed on high-quality paper that will withstand hard use. The typeface is large and easy-to-read. The short, concise chapters detail information on specific topics. Each title contains a table of contents, a glossary, and a complete index. Illustrations of full-color photographs and art work support the text.

Teachers in grades two through four can use the thirty-seven different volumes to provide children with practice in fundamental research skills. While the books can be read as fascinating stories, they also contain a wealth of useful reference material, organized for easy access. The new and updated editions give elementary school children an informative and enjoyable introduction to Native American peoples.

189. Oakley, Ruth. **The Marshall Cavendish Illustrated History of the North American Indians.** New York: Marshall Cavendish, 1991. 6 vols. 64p. FRL: 7. Subjects: History; Dwellings; Food; Clothing; Social life and customs; Religion; Art.

189.1. **Art and Totems**

189.2. **Conflict of Cultures**

189.3. **Homes and Costumes**

189.4. **In the Beginning**

189.5. Religion and Customs

189.6. The Way of Life

The six-volume set, The Marshall Cavendish Illustrated History of the North American Indians, offers junior high school and high school readers an overview of North American Indian history and culture. This easy-to-read information puts the rich, arresting, and often tragic story of America's native peoples in perspective.

Each volume focuses on a different arena of tribal life. *Art and Totems* covers the dance, music, and stories of the different tribal groups. Different forms of artwork, many important in the cultural and everyday life of the people, include totem poles, pottery, jewelry, basketry, and weaving. *Conflict of Cultures,* begins with Columbus and the Spanish and continues through Wounded Knee. Recent history and the political activism of native peoples to secure quality education and civil rights illustrate the resurgence of the identity of American Indian people. *Homes and Costumes* details the diversity of Indian homes and clothing. However, the choice of the word *costumes* for this volume is not appropriate. Indian people wore clothing made of native materials, not as costumes, but as apparel appropriate to their environment. Tattooing, face and body painting, hair styles, and jewelry were part of individual tribal cultures.

In the Beginning examines the early Asiatic history of native peoples and traces the movement of tribes as they hunted and farmed, built cities, and became dependent on the horse. An important essay, "The Hollywood View of the Indian," dispels the stereotypes that young adults can easily pick up from the movies. The volume *Religion and Customs* shows the diversity of beliefs among different peoples, describing spirit gods and creators, shamans and medicine men, masks and false faces, initiation ceremonies, potlatch gift-giving, kivas, and kachinas. In the final volume, *The Way of Life,* differences among the lifestyles of groups and societies are described, including councils, leaders, laws and traditions, and relationships with the land.

Each of the six volumes has a separate glossary, index to the text, and an index of references with page numbers. The same maps of tribal areas and major linguistic areas appear in all volumes. The table of contents is not really a list of chapter headings, but boldface large-type headings that appear in the narrative. Every book has fifty black-and-white or color photographs from the Smithsonian Institute, and original artwork. The original drawings are simplistic and do not complement the historical photographs. Fact "boxes" interspersed throughout the text provide important historical data.

Young adults may not currently recognize the wide diversity among American Indian tribes. Ruth Oakley makes an effort to alleviate this problem by including a broad spectrum of specific information. She also tackles difficult issues such as disease, slums, and drunkenness. This set will fill a void for libraries needing individual books on specific topics about American Indian life and history.

190. Ortiz, Simon. **The People Shall Continue.** San Francisco: Children's Book Press, 1978. 23p. FRL: 8. Subject: History.

The back cover of this book reads: "The only existing overview of American Indian history for children written by an American Indian." In the style of a traditional narrative, Acoma poet Simon Ortiz uses words in poetry form to trace the history of the "People" from the time of creation to the present. In the last four pages he invokes a responsibility for "all People" who have suffered to share the history of the "People" and assume concern for the land and for each other in order that all "the People shall continue."

The book is best read aloud, the purpose for which it was written. If read silently, young children may have difficulty with vocabulary such as *fervor, Piedmonts*, and *artisans*, as well as with ideas such as "united strength" and "heedless and forceful men." Writing for children and giving them a sense of the entire history of the American Indian in a book with only twenty-three pages requires Ortiz to cover entire epochs in a few lines.

The vivid, graphic illustrations by Sharon Graves are appealing. On some of the double-page spreads, the depictions of scenes are not appropriate for the text, such as on pages 10 and 11, where the text refers to the arrival of the English, French, and Dutch and their God and the accompanying illustration shows a Pueblo Indian standing on the roof of a Catholic church in a Southwest desert setting. Found on several pages, this type of discrepancy provides children with inaccurate information when it is presented as a visualization of the text.

As the epic story of Native American people, this book may be useful as an introduction by teachers for all children to the story of adversity and change in the lives of the "People."

191. Peterson, David. **The Anasazi.** Chicago: Childrens Press, 1991. 45p. FRL: 4. Subjects: Pueblo Indians—Social life and customs; Anasazi Indians.

One of the New True Book series, this volume describes the culture of Native American people about 2,000 years ago. The Anasazi inhabited the area in the southwestern United States known as the Four Corners, including portions of Arizona, New Mexico, Colorado, and Utah. Author David Peterson explains this complex society in clear and concise language.

The Anasazi, called the Ancient Ones by the Navajo, lived for 1,000 years in the harsh desert mesas and canyons of the Four Corners and then simply vanished. Peterson traces 700 years of early culture, beginning with the Basket Makers, who lived in primitive pit houses. The Basket Maker period was succeeded by the discovery of the bow and arrow, pottery making, and houses built above ground. The first pueblos were built on open mesas; later, cliff dwellings were built high up in large caves. Following a chapter on daily life, Peterson tackles the question of the Anasazi mystery. Why did these people leave and where did they go?

The glossy paper and dark print provide easy reading for children. Excellent color photographs of Anasazi ruins and artifacts enhance the text. Captions explain the significance of each photograph. As a reference for children, this volume contains a list of "words you should know" and a subject index. No bibliography is provided.

Children will find this information book about the Anasazi fascinating. Teachers will note that the factual content nicely complements the recreated story *The Village of Blue Stone* by Stephen Trimble (see entry 205).

192. Poatgeiter, Hermina. **Indian Legacy: Native American Influences on World Life and Culture.** New York: Julian Messner, 1981. 191p. FRL: 8. Subjects: Civilization—Indian influences; Art; Medicine; Conservation of natural resources; Inventions; Sports; Language and languages; Agriculture.

In presenting a wealth of historical facts about the contributions of North and South American Indians to the world, Hermina Poatgeiter has provided a well-organized reference to the field of juvenile literature. She dedicates her book to "American Indian children who should know the great gifts their people have given the world." Indian influence and contributions extend into all facets of human welfare and progress.

Major influences from the Indian way of life are present in the areas of government, science, art, recreation, and language. The indigenous people living in the Americas (1) taught survival and agricultural skills to early colonists, (2) influenced government and political ideas, and (3) established a system of trails throughout the land. All three contributions unwittingly led to the conquest of the Americas.

The scientific legacy of the Indian people is particularly rich. Indian agriculturalists, through centuries of genetic selection and conservation of natural resources, developed corn, potatoes, peanuts, chocolate, beans, tobacco, rubber, and other crops used extensively today. The scope of the contributions and the beneficence with which they were originally shared makes for captivating reading.

The content of this book for young adults is presented in a manner that can serve to instill pride in Indian culture. Adults working with Indian youth will find this book to be a positive avenue for recognizing Indian contributions and counteracting the prejudices perpetuated in some literature and textbooks.

193. Porter, Frank W., III, ed. **Indians of North America.** New York: Chelsea House, 1987- . 96-144p. 55 vols. FRL: 6.

193.1. Armitage, Peter. **The Innu.** 1991. Subjects: Montagnais Indians; Naskapi Indians.

193.2. Baird, David W. **The Quapaws.** 1989. Subject: Quapaw Indians.

193.3. Bee, Robert L. **The Yuma.** 1989. Subject: Yuma Indians.

193.4. Berdan, Frances F. **The Aztecs.** 1990. Subject Aztec Indians.

193.5. Bonvillain, Nancy. **The Hopi.** 1994. Subject: Hopi Indians.

193.6. Bonvillain, Nancy. **The Huron.** 1989. Subject: Huron Indians.

193.7. Bonvillain, Nancy. **The Mohawk.** 1992. Subject: Mohawk Indians.

193.8. Bonvillain, Nancy. **The Teton Sioux.** 1994. Subjects: Teton Sioux Indians; Sioux Indians.

193.9. Brain, Jeffrey P. **The Tunica-Biloxi.** 1990. Subjects: Tunica Indians; Biloxi Indians.

193.10. Bunte, Pamela Ann, and Robert J. Franklin. **The Paiute.** 1990. Subject: Paiute Indians.

193.11. Calloway, Colin G. **The Abenaki.** 1988. Subject: Abenaki Indians.

193.12. Clifton, James A. **The Potawatomi.** 1987. Subject: Potawatomi Indians.

193.13. Dial, Adolph L. **The Lumbee.** 1993. Subject: Lumbee Indians.

193.14. Dobyns, Henry F. **The Pima-Maricopa.** 1989. Subjects: Pima Indians; Maricopa Indians.

193.15. Faulk, Odie B., and Laura E. Faulk. **The Modoc.** 1988. Subject: Modoc Indians.

193.16. Feest, Christian F. **The Powhatan Tribes.** 1990. Subject: Powhatan Indians.

193.17. Fixico, Donald L. **Urban Indians.** 1991. Subject: Social conditions— Urban.

193.18. Fowler, Loretta. **The Arapaho.** 1989. Subject: Arapaho Indians.

193.19. Garbarino, Merwyn W. **The Seminole.** 1989. Subject: Seminole Indians.

193.20. Gibson, Robert O. **The Chumash.** 1991. Subject: Chumash Indians.

193.21. Graymont, Barbara. **The Iroquois.** 1988. Subject: Iroquois Indians.

193.22. Green, Michael D. **The Creeks.** 1990. Subject: Creek Indians.

193.23. Greene, Rayna. **Women in American Indian Society.** 1992. Subjects: Women; Social life and customs.

193.24. Grumet, Robert S. **The Lenapes.** 1990. Subject: Lenape Indians.

193.25. Hale, Duane K., and Arrell M. Gibson. **The Chickasaw.** 1991. Subject: Chickasaw Indians.

193.26. Hoig, Stan. **The Cheyenne.** 1989. Subject: Cheyenne Indians.

193.27. Hoover, Herbert T. **The Yankton Sioux.** 1988. Subject: Yankton Sioux Indians.

193.28. Hoxie, Frederick E. **The Crow.** 1989. Subject: Crow Indians.

193.29. Iverson, Peter. **The Navajos.** 1990. Subject: Navajo Indians.

193.30. Kelly, Lawrence C. **Federal Indian Policy.** 1990. Subject: Government relations.

193.31. Kennedy, John G. **The Tarahumara.** 1990. Subject: Tarahumara Indians.

193.32. Lowell, John Bean, and Lisa Bourgeault. **The Cahuilla.** 1988. Subject: Cahuilla Indians.

193.33. McKee, Jesse O. **The Choctaw.** 1989. Subject: Choctaw Indians.

193.34. Melody, Michael E. **The Apache.** 1989. Subject: Apache Indians.

193.35. Merrell, James H. **The Catawbas.** 1988. Subject: Catawba Indians.

193.36. Ortiz, Alfonso. **The Pueblo.** 1994. Subject: Pueblo Indians.

193.37. Ourada, Patricia K. **The Menominee.** 1990. Subject Menominee Indians.

193.38. Perdue, Theda. **The Cherokee.** 1989. Subject: Cherokee Indians.

193.39. Porter, Frank W., II. **The Coast Salish Peoples.** 1990. Subject: Salish Indians.

193.40. Porter, Frank W., II. **The Nanticoke.** 1987. Subject: Nanticoke Indians.

193.41. Rollings, Willard H. **The Comanche.** 1989. Subject: Comanche Indians.

193.42. Ruoff, A. L. **American Indian Literature.** 1991. Subject: Literature.

193.43. Schneider, Mary Jane. **The Hidatsa.** 1988. Subject: Hidatsa Indians.

193.44. Schuster, Helen H. **The Yakima.** 1990. Subject: Yakima Indians.

193.45. Simmons, William S. **The Narragansett.** 1988. Subject: Narragansett Indians.

193.46. Snow, Dean R. **The Archaeology of North America.** 1989. Subject: Archaeology.

193.47. Tanner, Helen H. **The Ojibwa.** 1992. Subject: Ojibwa Indians.

193.48. Trafzer, Clifford E. **The Chinook.** 1990. Subject: Chinook Indians.

193.49. Trafzer, Clifford E. **The Nez Perce.** 1992. Subject: Nez Perce Indians.

193.50. Trout, Lawana. **The Maya.** 1991. Subject: Maya Indians.

193.51. Walens, Stanley. **The Kwakiutl.** 1992. Subject: Kwakiutl Indians.

193.52. Weinstein-Farson, Laurie. **The Wampanoag.** 1988. Subject: Wampanoag Indians.

193.53. Wilson, Terry P. **The Osage.** 1988 Subject: Osage Indians.

193.54. Wunder, John R. **The Kiowa.** 1989. Subject: Kiowa Indians.

In this series, written specifically for young adults, general editor Frank W. Porter III and other well-qualified scholars present the culture and history of numerous American Indian tribes. The authors include American Indian authorities. The first title of the series was published in 1987. Presently, fifty-four titles are listed under the series. The selections include well-known tribes such as the Seminole, Iroquois, Apache, and Navajo, and lesser-known tribes such as the Wampanoag, Narragansett, Tarahumara, and Nanticoke. Other books in the series are *The Archaeology of North America, Literatures of the American Indian, Federal Indian Policy, Urban Indians*, and *Women in American Indian Society*. These titles fill a void in vital subjects of importance in library reference materials. Additional books are added to the series each year.

Each volume begins with an introduction by Porter examining the problems that arise when people of different cultures come in conflict. "For American Indians, the consequences of their interaction with non-Indian people have been both productive and tragic." European religious, cultural, and materialistic views did not allow an understanding or appreciation of the native people of North America. Consequently, Europeans attempted to change the Indians' way of life. Today, American Indians are still largely misunderstood. Porter examines the myths that were and are still perpetuated by many non-Indians. Through the background of individual tribal groups, the books in the series present a comprehensive study of the issues and conflicts involving American Indians in the twentieth century.

Invitingly written and attractive, the volumes have reinforced bindings with full-color laminated covers. The text is profusely illustrated with black-and-white maps, art, and historical photographs, including scenes of modern Indian communities. Each volume contains an eight-page color picture essay featuring unique arts and crafts of the tribal people, such as the exquisite embroidery in moosehair of the Huron, the patchwork strip clothing of the Seminole, and the artistic craftwork of the Apache. Special features include a glossary, a bibliography, and an index. Each title is well organized and provides information not readily available in a format for younger readers. Paperback copies are available for some titles.

Well-documented materials on specific tribal groups are often difficult for students to locate. This comprehensive and continuing series, covering all geographical areas of North America, will appeal to junior high school and high school readers and to adults looking for general reference materials. The broad survey of the history, myth, ritual, and art of the native peoples makes the titles in the series a valuable addition to public and school libraries.

194. Powers, William K. **Indians of the Northern Plains.** New York: G. P. Putnam's Sons, 1969. 256p. FRL: 9. Subject: Great Plains.

Part of the American Indians Then and Now Series, *Indians of the Northern Plains* covers the history of the Plains Indian tribes before the Europeans came, their removal to reservations, and their struggle to maintain the ways of their forefathers while adapting to the mainstream of society. Thirteen tribes, including the Arapaho, Arikara, Assiniboine, Blackfeet, Cheyenne, Crow, Gros Ventre, Hidatsa, Mandan, Plains Cree, Plains Ojibwa (Chippewa), Sarsi, and Sioux were dependent on the buffalo for every facet of their daily lives. With the introduction of the horse in the seventeenth century, dramatic changes came to the life of the Plains Indians. In recounting the history of the Plains Indians, Powers recognizes the individuality and diversity of tribal people. He also gives basic information on dwellings, transportation, communication, food, arts and crafts, music and dance, games and sports, and language. The social organization of each tribe as a warrior nation is chronicled.

Brief biographical sketches of famous men and battles tell the tragic story of the people's removal to reservation lands. The historian ends on this note: "Positive that he is not a white man, but insecure with his Indianness, the red man follows the white man's road in constant search of the Indian way."

Excellent photographs with captions from the Smithsonian Institution accompany the text. The text is easy to read, factual, and interesting. Students and teachers who need materials on the Plains Indians should enjoy this book.

195. Quam, Alvina, trans. **The Zunis: Self Portrayals.** Albuquerque: University of New Mexico Press, 1972. 205p. FRL: 9. Subjects: Zuni Indians—Legends; Zuni Indians—Mythology; Zuni Indians—History.

This interesting addition to the oral history of the Zuni people brings to print the actual words of the Zuni storytellers who weave accounts of history, religion, and folktales. In 1968, the Zuni tribe used a federal grant to compile their oral literature. In his introduction to the book, Robert Lewis, who was governor of Zuni at that time, accurately describes the material: "Simple things—good things! ... Briefly, this is the way of my people." This simplicity, devoid of the flowery rhetoric of Western literature, provides the quality of this volume.

This book compiles the reminiscences of tribal elders, who relate their stories of historical events of the past half century. Confrontations with Navajos, Apaches, and Mexicans are recalled, including mystic occurrences and human frailty and heroism. Medicine men and high priests describe sacred creation myths and the origin of the masked rituals, which have been carried down generation to generation for centuries. Some of the stories are simply for entertainment, although almost always there is a moral for the listener. The stories were chosen by the Zunis themselves and are only a fraction of the wealth of information that was collected in the project. Photographs of some of the tribal elders who participated in the project are inserted. Alvina Quam worked as the primary translator.

Indian students of all ages will enjoy reading this book, particularly the sections on fables. The selections on history and religion are also told in a manner that is intended to intrigue the listener and reader. English teachers and ethnic studies teachers will find that the material is relevant and irresistible, even to the reluctant reader.

196. Rand McNally. **Children's Atlas of Native Americans.** Chicago: Rand McNally, 1992. 77p. FRL: 5. Subjects: Maps; Social life and customs.

The tightly organized format of the Rand McNally *Children's Atlas of Native Americans* guides young readers on a geographic journey discovering North, Central, and South America's first inhabitants. Anthropologists believe that ancestors of modern American Indians crossed the Bering land bridge into North America thousands of years ago. They spread from the cold arctic Northern region to the tip of South America. Probably as many as 100 million people with 2,000 different cultures inhabited America at the time of the first European contact around 1500. This atlas is an introduction to these diverse native cultures.

Maps, illustrations, photographs, and text present the world of American Indians as they lived in different geographic culture regions. The atlas follows a chronologic development as humans discover America during the last Ice Age. The cliff-dwelling Anasazi and the mound-building Adena and Mississippian people are discussed first, and then the reader moves south to the great civilizations of Mesoamerica: the Toltec, Aztec, Zapotec, Olmec, and Maya. The section on people of the North includes the Eskimo and the Aleut, who had a similar language and lifestyle. In the Subarctic culture area were the hunter-gatherers—the Kutchim, Chipewayan, and Cree. On the northern Pacific Coastal culture region of Canada and the United States lived the Haida, Tlingit, and Kwakiutl. The American Indians of the northeastern woodlands and the people of the Great Plains and Western tribes are addressed in separate chapters. An added bonus is material on Central and South American native peoples. The Zapotec, Arawak, Cuna, Yanomami, and Mapuche are presented in detail. As young readers see maps of the tribal locations, they will discover how and why the geographic region in which the people lived affected how they lived.

The full-color maps, authentic photographs, and colorful illustrations give life to the well-written and readable text. The atlas is highly recommended for elementary school libraries as an invaluable source for map work and reports. Relatively few atlases on Native American culture areas exist. This historical volume will not become dated.

197. Sandoz, Mari. **The Battle of the Little Bighorn.** Philadelphia: J. B. Lippincott, 1966. 191p. FRL: 10. Subjects: Little Big Horn, Battle of the, 1876; Custer, George Armstrong.

Sympathetic to the Sioux Indians, Mari Sandoz criticizes the United States government for its broken treaties with the Sioux Nation. In late June 1876, Lt. Col. George Armstrong Custer made military blunders which resulted in the massacre of his cavalry. Custer's Indian guides and even his own men saw evidence of a large gathering of Indians. The feeling of the Sioux, the concern of Custer's men, the personality of Custer, and the disbelief of the two regiments who were waiting for Custer's support come alive in this account. Custer is portrayed by Sandoz as being vainglorious, a characteristic disputed by Custer's admirers. The action in the later part of the book shifts to Reno and Benteen, the commanders of the two detachments waiting for support, ringed by Indians.

The narrative is fast-paced and informative. The tragedy caused by Custer's mistakes was a victory for the Sioux. Teachers could utilize this excellent book by reading selections to their classes or recommending it to students for personal reading.

198.   Sandoz, Mari. **Cheyenne Autumn.** New York: Hastings House, 1953. 282p.
FRL: 9. Subjects: Cheyenne Indians; Dull Knife, Cheyenne chief; Little
Wolf, Cheyenne chief.

Mari Sandoz pays tribute to a band of Cheyenne Indians who fled an
Oklahoma reservation in September 1878 to return to their homeland at the headwaters of the Yellowstone River. The journey was precipitated during the administration of President Grant by graft in administering monies meant for the Indians,
which resulted in starvation and illness for the Northern Cheyenne.

Although Little Wolf and Dull Knife, dual chieftains, were told troops would
bring them back if they left, they nevertheless started the epic journey toward their
homeland over 1,500 miles away. The 287 Cheyennes, fewer than half of them
adults, with just a few guns and horses, thwarted the efforts of more than 10,000
soldiers. Their flight led them through settled regions netted with telegraph, across
three railroads, and straight through the United States Army. Reaching their desti-
nation, the people surrendered. Only 114 had survived the desperate journey.

By using simple language, Sandoz has retained the mystical interrelations of
Cheyenne life in their flight. Based in part on talks with an old Cheyenne woman
who took part in the escape and vetertans of the frontier, and on documentary
research, Sandoz's book takes the liberty of using direct speech and other fictional
devices "for the rhythms of Indian speech." Although not considered in the strictest
sense "history," readers will be swept along in the story of one of history's cruelest
episodes.

199.   Sewell, Marcia. **People of the Breaking Day.** New York: Macmillan, 1990.
48p. FRL: 5. Subject: Wampanoag Indians.

The author and illustrator, Marcia Sewell, relates the story of the Wampanoag
people of southeastern Massachusetts as they lived before the Pilgrims landed.
Using the first-person narrative, Sewell has the people re-create their world, "We
live as our grandfathers' grandfathers have lived forever; rising each day with the
rebirth of Nippa'uus, to eat when hungry, to sleep when tired, to gather for
celebration, to glean food, and do our planting."

In full-color paintings that lend dignity and meaning to the culture of the
Wampanoag tribal people, the author tells of their joys and hardships. The nation
of several thousand people live in small settlements. They hunt, fish, plant crops,
and gather the harvest near the sea. In winter, they move inland to the woods to the
longhouse. Each family member has a role in the tribal life, from birth to death.

In a poetic narrative, the culture of the native people is explained to children.
Unusual for a nonfiction book, the text blends storytelling with information. A
glossary and list of Wampanoag/Narragansett Native American words are valuable
additions. For information on American Indian people of the eastern seaboard this
book has reference and aesthetic value.

People of the Breaking Day is a companion book to *The Pilgrims of Plimoth,*
also written and illustrated by Sewell.

200.   Sheppard, Sally. **Indians of the Plains.** New York: Franklin Watts, 1978.
88p. FRL: 6. Subjects: Great Plains; Crow Indians; Sioux Indians; Cheyenne
Indians; Blackfeet Indians.

In a brief history of the Plains Indians, Sally Sheppard has covered many
subjects in very short chapters. She describes the daily life and culture, including

specifics on the family structure, clothing, the horse, buffalo, religion, myths, and legends. She also discusses the Plains Indians' present-day life (to 1978) on the reservation. The book has numerous black-and-white illustrations with captions. The tribes covered include the Crow, Sioux, Cheyenne, and Blackfeet.

The author's use of the past tense could encourage the belief that Indians no longer live according to or believe in the old customs. She does provide good, positive information on customs, history, and religion, including an accurate and positive view of the role of Indian women. The book includes a bibliography and an index.

The book is extremely brief and very easy to read, and the information, illustrations, and format should appeal to students who find reading difficult. The volume provides a brief overview of the Plains Indians for teachers. Other books on the same subject are *The Plains Indians* by Francis Haines (Crowell, 1976) and *Plains Indians* by Jill Hughes (Gloucester Press, 1984).

201. Siegel, Beatrice. **Fur Trappers and Traders: The Indians, the Pilgrims, and the Beaver.** New York: Walker, 1981. 64p. FRL: 4. Subjects: Fur Trade—New England—History; Pilgrims (New England Colonists); Beaver.

In a question-and-answer format, Beatrice Siegel traces the intertwined story of the Indians, the Pilgrims, and the beaver as influenced by the early fur trade in North American history. She asks these questions: "What kind of animal is the beaver? What news spread through Europe? How did the Pilgrims fit into England's plans? Who else competed for the fur trade? Who did the trapping? Who became rich from the fur trade? What happened to the Indians and the beaver?"

Providing carefully researched answers with interesting details, historically accurate facts, and new insights, her account traces the greed for beaver pelts from Europe to the trade with Indians in North America. The trail follows the settlement of America by the Pilgrims, the violence between Indian trappers and European traders, and the westward migration. The special effects that the highly prized beaver pelt had on the Indian people is sensitively acknowledged. In simple, clearly understood sentences, a vivid understanding of this important historical period and the role the beaver played is provided for young readers. The fine illustrations by Lenape Indian artist William Sauts Bock support the text. As a reference, the book contains historical notes, suggested readings, and an index.

202. Stands in Timber, John, and Margot Liberty. **Cheyenne Memories.** New Haven, Conn.: Yale University Press, 1967. 330p. FRL: 12. Subjects: Cheyenne Indians—History; Mythology.

Self-elected historian of the Cheyenne, John Stands in Timber spent his lifetime in an unusual effort to collect and preserve the history of the Cheyenne. A member of the Northern Cheyenne, he was born in 1884 and died in 1967 just before his book was printed. To record the Cheyenne tradition in written form, he collaborated with anthropologist Margot Liberty for more than a decade. Her goal was to keep as close as possible to John's own speech. This fast-reading account contains lore and personal memories of the elders of the tribe.

The memories of the Cheyenne begin with creation stories and oral literature, including the contributions of Sweet Medicine, an early leader who established the tribal organization of chiefs, military societies, sacred medicine objects, ceremonies, and power. Historical vignettes of relations with the Assiniboine, Crow,

Shoshoni, and whites are given. Never-recorded stories of the Battle of the Little Big Horn and Custer are entertaining as well as historically interesting. (Stands in Timber's grandfather was killed in the Custer massacre.) The surrender of the Cheyenne, the division into the Northern and Southern tribes, early reservation life, the Ghost Dance years, and a chapter entitled "Getting Civilized," in which he recounts personal memories, including making a movie with Cheyenne Indians and whites portraying Indians, are important contributions to Cheyenne historiography.

The book is valuable as an Indian frame of reference and also for a different perspective on old materials from new sources and unrecorded materials. For the Indian reader the book fulfills Stands in Timber's dream that he can pass on to the tribe the collective memories of its past. For the non-Indian reader the book provides a rare insight into this culture. Because reading the text is like listening to an elder discuss tribal history and life, young adults will enjoy it as leisure reading. Teachers of language arts classes will find the narrative style of writing full of adventure and laughter, the oral literature delightful, and the anecdotes good examples. The information on the history of the Cheyenne and the unusual accounts of the Battle of the Little Big Horn will help history come alive. The changes in lifestyle and the social problems that developed can be studied in sociology classes. The material will build pride and appreciation in Indian history and culture. Included are twenty-seven illustrations and two maps; the genealogy of John Stands in Timber; a detailed index including incidents by people's names; detailed footnotes to show verification, addition, or inconsistencies with other accounts; and a bibliography.

203. Stein, R. Conrad. **The Story of Wounded Knee.** Chicago: Childrens Press, 1983. 31p. FRL: 4. Subjects: Wounded Knee Creek, Battle of 1890; Dakota Indians—War, 1890-1891.

For young readers from grades three through six, the author presents a simplified view of the events leading to the battle of Wounded Knee between a Sioux tribal group and the United States Cavalry. The defeat of the Western tribes, who clung desperately to their religion, led to their belief in the Ghost Dance. As the dance swept the Indian world, the Sioux felt it was a way to reach their spirits. Worried whites and Indian agents reacted and set out to seize the tribal leaders. After the death of Sitting Bull, some of his followers joined forces with Big Foot and his Sioux group, who were camped at Wounded Knee Creek. The slaughter of 200 men, women, and children horrified Americans, and the Indian dream of a land without white intruders died.

The account attempts to explain why such an event happened and how some Americans, such as poet Stephen Vincent Benét, could not forget the nightmare of the massacre. Although lacking the power of Dee Brown's book *Bury My Heart at Wounded Knee* (Holt, Rinehart & Winston, 1970), this narrative for children will serve as a reminder of a part of American history they should not forget.

204. Tiller, Veronica E., ed. **Discover Indian Reservations U.S.A: A Visitors' Welcome Guide.** Denver, Colo.: Council Publications, 1992. 402p. FRL: 9. Subject: Reservations.

The information in *Discover Indian Reservations U.S.A.* was contributed by the tribes about their reservations and rancherias. Reading this unique paperback provides an introduction to more than 210 areas in thirty-three states. The guide provides information about Indian tribal lands and activities: rodeos, tribal fairs, powwows, ceremonies, and recreation. Exploring Indian lands can provide educators and students with the opportunity to see how Indian people live today, to hear their stories, and learn about their culture.

The book lists all reservations and rancherias by state and alphabetically. A map of each state provides the general location of the reservations found there. The tribal profiles describe the reservation and the Indian tribe or band living there. A main tribal address and phone number is given. There is no history about the tribes in this book, but the profile includes cultural institutions, archaeological and historic sites, and special events open to the public. Recreational opportunities include outdoor activities, bingo halls, and casinos. Only Indian-owned and operated businesses related to recreation and tourism are listed, including Indian arts and crafts enterprises, tour operators, and accommodations. A special section provides information about respecting private homes, protecting artifacts, and the use of cameras. More than 350 Indian tribes, groups, and bands are referenced through the guide. The cross-reference chart "Location of Tribes, Bands and Communities by State and Reservation or Community" in appendix I is useful for locating particular Indian groups, especially large tribal groups like the Apache, Sioux, and Chippewa. Appendix II is a "Pow Wow Directory by State and Month." The index to the volume lists subject matter and activity.

Presently there are at least five national guides to Indian country in print. If a library already owns one of these, they probably do not need to add this title. However, this guide, published by a tribal consortium, is unique because it contains information the tribal groups want the public to know about tourist activities available. The reference provides current and accurate information about things to do and see on Indian reservations throughout the United States, except Alaska. Tourist attractions located within the physical boundaries of reservations and their communities are featured.

205. Trimble, Stephen. **The Village of Blue Stone.** New York: MacMillan, 1990. 58p. FRL: 4. Subjects: Pueblo Indians—Social life and customs; Mesa Verde National Park (Colorado); Anasazi Indians.

Through text and illustration, readers live an entire year in A.D. 1100 in a Southwest Chaco Anasazi pueblo culture. In the fictional narrative, the Butterfly and Blue Corn Clans celebrate the winter solstice, gather in the kivas for storytelling, and work together to survive the harsh environment. The author skillfully weaves threads of birth, marriage, and death through the story. Farming, weaving, pottery making, hunting, and ceremonies punctuate the panorama of activities. Trimble relies heavily upon modern day Pueblos for cultural details. His thesis, supported by many archaeologists, is that Pueblo people are the direct descendants of the prehistoric Anasazi. For those seeking verifiable information, this fictionalized account is of limited value.

The illustrators, Jennifer Owings Dewey and Deborah Reade, provide realistic black-and-white drawings. Scenes of daily life incorporate objects found at archaeological digs with traditional Hopi Indian dress and social life.

Unlike most authors who recreate stories of Native American cultures, Stephen Trimble includes vital supplementary information in *The Village of Blue Stone*. The introduction tells the story of Wetherill and Mason, the first white men to discover the large Anasazi ruins in Mesa Verde National Park, Colorado. Among the excellent visuals for teachers are maps of Anasazi country and Blue Stone village maps and a chart that shows the relationships of the main characters of the book. Trimble also provides information on Anasazi ruins that can be visited and adult and children's books for further research. The glossary gives readers accurate information to use in understanding the Anasazi culture. Children in the upper elementary grades will enjoy this book.

206.   Tunis, Edwin. **Indians.** New York: Crowell, 1979. 157p. FRL: 9. Subject: Social life and customs.

In a fascinating text supported by more than 245 drawings, Tunis creates an accurate picture of American Indian life before the arrival of the white man. The introductory chapters give general background on the daily lives of the Indian people as they developed special tribal characteristics to accomodate varying environments. Tunis has organized his material by nine major geographic groups of Indians rather than individual tribes, basing his general observations on one or two representative tribes of each major group. In each of these geographic areas the Indian groups used their ingenuity in adapting to the climate, soil, and terrain. The Iroquois and the native people of the woodlands, Southeast, Midland, Plains, western Rockies, desert, North, and coast are highlighted.

For the study of geography and the prehistory of North America, the background on the hunters, foragers, seed gatherers and farmers is presented in a format that can be enjoyed by many age levels for different levels of understanding. Every page contains black-and-white line drawings that support the text. Although the book lacks a bibliography of sources, an index makes the book useful for school and public libraries.

207.   Waldman, Carl. **Atlas of the North American Indian.** New York: Facts on File, 1985. 276p. FRL: 16. Subjects: Maps; Atlases—Historical; Social life and customs.

In a single-volume reference work, Carl Waldman provides an informational text on the Indian people of the United States, Canada, and Middle America. Believing that the study of American Indian history should be based on a proper educational foundation, Waldman's purpose is to provide an overview for understanding the American Indian and a framework for further historical and cultural study. Although the text is written for secondary school and adult readers, the more than 100 two-color maps and illustrations by Molly Braun conveying Indian-related information make the book useful for all age levels. The volume includes the prehistory of ancient Indians and civilizations, lifeways and culture prior to the arrival of European colonists, wars and land cessions, and contemporary history and change.

The book is organized by subject. An index provides easy access to specifics. Maps are located on the page with corresponding text. Almost every page includes black-and-white historical illustrations, either photographs or drawings of artifacts. Many of these illustrations, such as the drawings of dugouts and shelters, are excellent teaching materials. A wide diversity of maps is used: historical, military, cultural, contemorary, and period. Another excellent feature of the maps is that they are not cluttered with unnecessary information.

The appendix of this useful reference work is equally valuable and provides quick access to information on Indian people that is sometimes difficult to locate: a chronology of Indian history; an alphabetical list of tribes, with historical and contemporary locations; federal and state reservations, trust areas, and villages in the United States; Canadian Indian bands; major Indian place names; and museums and archaeological sites.

208. Washburn, Wilcomb E., comp. **The American Indian and the United States: A Documentary History.** New York: Random House, 1972. 4 vols. FRL: 10. Subjects: Government publications; Government policy; History—Government policy.

Director of the Office of American Studies at the Smithsonian Institution, Wilcomb Washburn has compiled a four-volume reference work of documents on the evolution of the relationship of the Indian and the United States government. The American Indians are unique in their legal status because they are the only ethnic group in the United States having a bureau of government which is concerned exclusively with them. The development of that relationship is the subject of the four volumes.

The contents include (1) reports of the Commissioners of Indian Affairs from 1826 through 1963; (2) congressional debates on Indian Affairs; (3) acts, ordinances, and proclamations; (4) Indian treaties; and (5) legal decisions. The compiler selected reports, debates, cases, treaties, and acts that seemed to illustrate most effectively the evolution of the relationship between the government and the Indian tribes. Within each of the major categories, documents are arranged chronologically.

Although comprehensive, the volumes are easy to read, the print is fairly large, and the paper will withstand heavy use. Volume 4 contains an excellent index by tribe as well as subject and government case. Anyone interested in Indian history will find that this work provides insights into the evolution of the relationship that has developed between the government and the Indian people. The original documents will aid serious research.

209. Wormington, H. M. **Prehistoric Indians of the Southwest.** Denver, Colo.: Denver Museum of Natural History, 1947. 191p. FRL: 9. Subjects: Archaeology; Indians of the Southwest—Archaeology.

Written by archaeologist H. M. Wormington, this account of the prehistory of the Indians of the Southwest is for those who are intrigued by the "ancient ones," the people who lived in and disappeared from the Southwest in ancient times. This attempt to tell the story of how these people lived in nontechnical terms describes the techniques employed by archaeologists in seeking to reconstruct the life of the Anasazi. Four cultures, the oldest of which dates to at least 25,000 years ago, are studied in the Southwest, which today usually means New Mexico, Arizona, southern Utah, and the southwestern corner of Colorado. The ruins of the prehistoric dwellings and living sites were recorded from the times of the early Spanish explorers. Since that time archaeologists have been attempting to fit the great jigsaw puzzle of their cultures together. The most ancient cultures, the Sandia, Folsom, Cochise, and others were thought to be a nomadic people living off the land. The origin of these people has never been pinpointed, although migration from Asia is a common theory. Two cultures which are recorded in the book are the Anasazi, found in the Four Corners region, and the Hohokam, located in the drainages of the Salt and Gila rivers of southern Arizona. Other less-known cultures, the Mogollon, Sinagua, and Patayan, are also presented.

Anyone who spends time in the Southwest deserts will find artifacts lying on the ground and see remnants of the architecture of these prehistoric Indian people. This book contains fifty-three illustrations that serve to satisfy readers' curiosity, stimulate their interest in archaeology, and promote a respect for these cultures. Finally, Wormington hopes that people will respect the sites and not destroy them before archaeologists can further unravel the puzzle of the prehistoric cultures.

In reconstructing the record of these particular civilizations, an appreciation can be gained for a people who built permanent homes, cultivated the land, created beautiful as well as useful objects, lived in a harsh but beautiful land, and did not seem interested in spending their lives warring against others. A popular topic for research by non-Indians, public and school librarians should be aware of the concern of many Indian people about entering or disturbing these sites. The book includes a glossary, a bibliography, an index, and the locations of exhibit sites, modern pueblos, and local museums.

210. Yue, Charlotte, and David Yue. **The Pueblo.** Boston: Houghton Mifflin, 1986. 117p. FRL: 6. Subjects: Pueblo Indians; Southwestern states; Dwellings.
The Pueblo is an excellent book of reference value for children and young adults. The Yues have carefully researched and illustrated the history, daily life, dwelling structures, and relationship of the Pueblo people to their land. They cover Pueblo Indian life in the Southwest from ancient times to the Pueblo communities today.

Struggling to master a harsh and often inhospitable environment, the different groups of people referred to as Pueblo Indians built cliff dwellings, stone masonry cities, and adobe villages, some in mountains, some by streams and rivers, and some on high desert mesas. They developed farming methods for hot, dry regions and made pottery and baskets in which they cooked and stored food. Their dwellings included ceremonial chambers and often housed large numbers of people.

The book is valuable as a reference for upper-elementary through high school-age readers. The text is easily read and supported by black-and-white line drawings. The index provides quick access to subjects; the bibliography and list of other books are useful. This intriguing topic will interest many readers, especially those familiar with the Southwest. The subject is a popular one for research and the information will be useful for curriculum units.

920 Collective Biography

211. Avery, Susan, and Linda Skinner. **Extraordinary American Indians.** Chicago: Childrens Press, 1992. 252p. FRL: 6. Subject: Biography.
Childrens Press offers the Extraordinary People series to acquaint children of all races with the accomplishments of black, Hispanic, Native, and Asian Americans. The four-volume set incorporates short, easy-to-read biographies and important historic events of each ethnic group. *Extraordinary American Indians* is the work of writer Susan Avery and Indian educator Linda Skinner. A rich diversity of biographical information about outstanding American Indian people is revealed. The tightly woven sketches are compared to the weaving of a Navajo rug by the

authors. This superb collection of biographies about native people provides a guided tour from the Iroquois Confederation to the American Indian Movement.

The biographies and historical events are interwoven in chronological order. Middle school readers will grasp the understanding that some lives and events are interlaced, and an individual's life can sometimes directly affect others. Biographies in this volume begin with the San Juan Pueblo resistance leader, Pope, who died around 1692, and continue with Odawa Military leader, Pontiac, and Cherokee leader, Nancy Ward. The priceless legacy of the Iroquois Confederacy is discussed. Sketches of Mohawk chief, Joseph Brant; Seneca orator, Red Jacket; Shawnee war chief, Tecumseh; the inventor of the Cherokee writing system, Sequoyah; Lemhi Shoshone interpreter, Sacagawea; and Duwamish orator, Seathl, complete the period of the 1700s. The chapters on Indian removal, the Dawes Act, and the Sand Creek massacres reflect the injustice and fragmentation of native life as Indian people lost their land. Courageous Indian people who stepped forward during this period include Seminole patriot and resistance leader, Osceola, and Seneca chief and Commissioner of Indian Affairs, Ely Samual Parker.

In the 1800s, Indian leaders with whom many children are familiar struggled to protect their way of life, including Apache resistance leader Geronimo Hunkpapa Lakota tribal leader Sitting Bull, Nez Perce Chief Joseph, Lakota war chief Crazy Horse, Northern Paiute religious leader Wovoka, and Lakota medicine man Black Elk. Toward the end of the 1800s, Paiute Sarah Winnemucca, Ponca La Flesche family members, Charles Eastman, and Gertrude Simmons Bonnin used education to make their contributions. The Indian Reorganization and Citizenship Acts, Codetalkers of World War II, tribal termination and self-determination, and AIM detail the history of the Indian people, their survival, and continuing vitality. A variety of professions in the biographical sketches—artists, athletes, activists, writers, and politicians—are included. The breadth of the work encompasses fifty-one biographical essays, including the La Flesche, Deloria, West, and Echo-hawk families.

Students can easily locate information on the person or historical event they are researching in this excellent reference. However, the book, if read in its entirety, has an even greater value. The stories reveal a complete picture of diverse people, varied cultural traditions, and an enduring presence in modern history. Historical issues of treaty rights, economic and educational status, and self-determination still face today's American Indian people. Historical pictures and biographee's photographs are interspersed in the text. An excellent bibliography of biographies and history, and also fiction, poetry, folktales, myths and videotapes, offers supplementary resources for educators. The detailed index to the articles makes a vital contribution to the use of the text as a reference.

212. **Biographical Dictionary of Indians of the Americas.** Newport Beach, Calif.: American Indian Publishers, 1983. 570p. FRL: 10. Subject: Biography.

A two-volume set, the *Biographical Dictionary of Indians of the Americas* lists in encyclopedic format the vital information on both historical and contemporary American Indians. The introduction, on the problems of compiling American Indian biography, should be read by library and media professionals for an understanding of the unique challenge for writers of Indian biography. Much of the material for the articles came from the twenty-volume *Encyclopedia of Indians of the Americas* (Scholarly, 1974). Additional sources, when used, are listed at the end of each citation. The article length ranges from one sentence for little-known personages such as Blackfoot Chief Little Bear to five pages for Annie Dodge Wauneka, nationally recognized for her work in modern health care and education on the Navajo reservation.

The biographees includes notable leaders as well as those in the areas of social service, fine arts, and literature. Over 1,080 names are included. The index in the second volume provides names of biographees under tribal affiliation; however, no page numbers are provided. As a quick biographical reference, the set will be very useful. Many little-known people are also included, although the information is limited on those individuals. Black-and-white biographical portraits, artists' sketches, and other historical sketches of Indian culture accompany every page.

213. Capps, Benjamin. **The Great Chiefs.** New York: Time-Life Books, 1975. 240p. FRL: 8. Subject: Biography.

No aspect of Indian history was more dramatic or picturesque than the Indian leaders of America. Working in cooperation with the editors of Time-Life Books, Benjamin Capps has written a fascinating account, not limited to narratives about the lives of the Indian leaders, but including pertinent background material about such topics as the Ghost Dance phenomenon and the peyote cult. The chiefs shared one characteristic: they were all respected by their peers. Their individualism was evidenced by the resourcefulness with which they adjusted to the circumstances of the times. Geronimo of the Apaches held the U.S. Army at bay for over thirty years. Washakie of the Shoshoni and Quanah of the Comanche were remarkable in leading their respective tribes to coexist peacefully with the U.S. government. Chief Joseph of the Nez Perce fought the U.S. Army in one of the most brilliant wars of history and continued fighting politically for the rights of his people until his death.

Perhaps the most significant value of this book to school and public libraries is the pictorial segment of this volume. Historical photographs, magnificent reproductions by Catlin, and prints from other noteworthy artists make this volume a "must" purchase. The book is handsomely bound in leather-like binding and reasonably priced.

Teachers will find this book useful in art and history classes. Children and young adults will enjoy reading the interesting text and looking at the excellent pictures. The conflict between the Indian and the government is well documented and reported. This volume is important for many curriculum areas.

214. Deur, Lynne. **Indian Chiefs.** Minneapolis, Minn.: Lerner Publications, 1973. 103p. FRL: 5. Subject: Biography.

This collective biography is a Pull Ahead Book for young people. The fourteen Indian leaders briefly profiled were involved in the American Indian struggle to defend their land and way of life against the invasion of the encroaching white civilization. King Philip, Pontiac, Joseph Bryant, Tecumseh, Sequoyah, Osceola, Black Hawk, Keokuk, Crazy Horse, Gall, Sitting Bull, Cochise, Geronimo, and Joseph tried to halt the gradual destruction of their people.

The author takes issue with history, stories, and movies that have the American Indians of that period look like bloodthirsty savages. Heads of Indian tribes are referred to as Indian patriots, and the savagery of the white invaders is discussed in the opening chapter. Deur wrote the book because she feels it is time for Indian heroes and leaders to take their rightful place in the nation's history. The struggles of the Wampanoag, Shawnee, Sauk and Fox, Sioux, Nez Perce, and others illustrate the organization, ability, and dignity of these people.

Deur strives to present a clear picture of the contributions of these leaders and the reasons they chose to fight or not fight. When facts are not clear, she makes reference to disagreements among sources. The book has extensive black-and-white illustrations, all of which have captions. Students should gain a positive image of these leaders because the text shows they were protecting what was theirs. The material is easily read and should be useful and relevant in any class studying the American Indian.

215. Dockstader, Frederick J. **Great North American Indians: Profiles in Life and Leadership.** New York: Van Nostrand Reinhold, 1977. 386p. FRL: 12. Subject: Biography.

American Indian scholar Dockstader presents biographical sketches of 300 American Indian leaders who lived between 1600 and 1977. In addition to the famous chiefs mentioned in most children's biographies and those who lives have been covered in full-length books, an effort was made to include men and women in every field of endeavor, including art, politics, medicine, and social sciences, as well as all regions and all tribes. The brief biographical profiles include authentic data, birth and death dates, translations of native names, and understanding of Indian life and customs. Readers will be able to place many of the major Indian figures in their proper perspective in history. The volume may serve as a ready reference to basic information and an excellent guide to further sources. The bibliography for further reading includes historical summaries, personal accounts, and biographical notes.

This appealing volume can be easily read. The author notes that if the book were read from beginning to end one would discover a narrative of Indian-white relations during this time period. The large book has dark type on heavy paper and many black-and-white illustrations, including photographs of the biographees and pictures of Indian art objects. For quick reference the reader can use the chronology of dates, tribal listing of names, and index of names. Libraries and school media centers will find this volume valuable to all patrons.

216. Eastman, Charles A. **Indian Heroes and Great Chieftains.** Lincoln: University of Nebraska Press, 1991. 241p. FRL: 7. Subjects: Biography; Dakota Indians—Biography.

Originally published in 1918, this collection is unusual in that Charles A. Eastman (Ohiyesa) interviewed many of the individuals about whom he wrote. A Santee Sioux, Eastman fled to Canada with his family when he was four years old, during the 1862 Sioux Uprising in Minnesota. After returning with his father to the Dakota territory, he became a government physician at the Pine Ridge Agency. Today he is recognized for authoring eleven books on Native American issues. Eastman offers a bridge to understanding the personal lives of American Indian leaders who are frequently misunderstood.

Few Native American biographies are actually based on interviews by Indian authors. Eastman's accounts provide an unusual perspective on fifteen great Indian leaders. He interviewed many friends and acquaintances during the years before

1918. The accounts come alive for readers as they follow the personal narratives of the courageous Red Cloud, the remarkable Spotted Tail, the brilliant Chief Little Crow, and the young Sioux leader, Tamahay. Eastman writes of Little Wolf, whom he knew well and of the noble Chief Joseph of the Nez Perce, whom he assisted in 1897 with a grievance document against the government. Other biographies of leaders who fought for liberty and justice are the well-known Gall, Crazy Horse, Sitting Bull, and those with whom readers may be unfamiliar: Rain-in-the-Face, Two Strikes, American Horse, Dull Knife, Roman Nose, and Hole-in-the-Day. The paperback volume includes eight portraits.

This collection is noteworthy because Eastman relies on primary sources. His personal association with these heroes cannot be duplicated by modern authors who must rely on secondary materials. The reprint of his work offers Indian students an opportunity to read a more accurate and personal account of their leaders and heroes. As Charles Eastman suggests, "The names and deeds of some of these men will live in American history, yet in the true sense they are unknown, because misunderstood. I should like to present some of the greatest chiefs of modern times in the light of the native character and ideals, believing that the American people will gladly do them tardy justice."

217. Freedman, Russell. **Indian Chiefs.** New York: Holiday House, 1987. 151p. FRL: 6. Subject: Biography.

Captivating biographical essays portray six Western Indian leaders who faced difficult decisions in the 1840s as white settlers moved west and encroached on their native lands. In each situation the leader of the Indian tribe or band was forced to make decisions that could determine the fate of his people. Some of the leaders were war chiefs and some were peace chiefs. As they led their people in a time of historical crisis, their decisions had far-reaching effects on the lives of their people. Categorized as juvenile literature, the stories are centered around interesting anecdotes and are liberally peppered with memorable quotations. Black-and-white photographs of the renowned leaders and major historical events in their lives add visual impact to the excellent text.

These six inspiring leaders met the challenge of the crisis in their own unique ways. Red Cloud, leader of the Ogalala Sioux, won the battle for the Bozeman Trail but lost the war to preserve the Sioux way of life. One of the most influential of the military Kiowa chiefs, the great orator Satanta, felt that the whites broke the Medicine Lodge Treaty, which gave his people the right to pursue the buffalo. Quanah Parker, leader of the last band of Comanches to surrender, became a successful rancher, businessman, and politician. Washakie of the Shoshonis kept his people on friendly terms with whites and negotiated a peace settlement that provided his people with a good reservation on the Wind River. Through his military genius, Chief Joseph attempted to lead the Nez Perce into Canada by seeking to avoid confrontation with American army troops. The Hunkpapa Sioux leader Sitting Bull became one of the most well-known Indians after the Battle of the Little Big Horn.

The stories are told accurately and fairly in the context of more recent historical information. The Indian leaders of the Western tribes are depicted as people who had to make decisions and take responsibility for their consequences. Perceptive readers will gain insight into the different ways of achieving goals, the importance of making decisions, and the value of cultural heritage.

218. Gridley, Marion E. **American Indian Women.** New York: Hawthorne Books, 1974. 178p. FRL: 9. Subjects: Biography; Women—Biography.

Marion Gridley offers a varied collection of informative biographies about eighteen notable American Indian women. The subjects range from historical personages to contemporary figures. The achievements of these women are inspirational for all readers. The stories of Pocohontas, the savior of Jamestown, and Sacajawea, the guide for Lewis and Clark, are well known. Less well-known are Wetamoo, Chief Massasoit's older son's wife, who led her people fearlessly after his death; Cherokee Nancy Ward; and Modoc Winema, who counseled their people to pursue peace rather than war. Many of the contemporary Indian women profiled sought to help their people in the areas of health, education, and service. During a time when it was rare for white women to enter professional fields, Susan La Flesche Picotte of the Omaha people became the first Indian woman physician. Annie Wauneka worked tirelessly to gain medical treatment for the Navajo people. Notable women in the education field are Elaine Abraham Ramos, Wilma L. Victor, and Esther Burnette Horne. In the arts, readers will recognize the talents of the renowned ballerinas Maria and Marjorie Tallchief, potter Maria Martinez, poet E. Pauline Johnson, and painter of Pueblo Indian life Pablita Velarde.

These inspiring stories of American Indian women who worked towards goals and accomplished them will provide a bond with which young Indian women can identify. The center section includes small pictures of each biographee. A bibliography of full-length books provides readers with sources for more detailed accounts. An excellent index makes this collective biography valuable for research. This book is an excellent choice to complement the biographies that highlight American Indian men.

219. Gridley, Marion E. **Contemporary American Indian Leaders.** New York: Dodd, Mead, 1972. 192p. FRL: 9. Subject: Biography, contemporary.

Highlighting the outstanding achievements of twenty-six modern American Indians, this collection of biographies represents a wide variety of viewpoints by outstanding Indian leaders of today. The leaders range from activists to conservatives, from young to elder statesmen, from traditionalists to progressives, and from rural to urban backgrounds. The author's goal is to let all individuals speak for themselves, expressing their attitudes and opinions on matters pertaining to Indian and Indian-white relationships.

The biographies not only represent a variety of tribes but also a cross-section of vocations. Included are Commissioner of Indian Affairs Louis R. Bruce, dentist George Blue Spruce, National Congress of American Indians leader Leon Cook, Navaho Community College Executive Vice President Ned Hatathli, author Vine Deloria, Jr., militant Henry Adams, Congressman Ben Reifel, crusader La Donna Harris, artist Maria Martinez, and Medal of Freedom award winner Annie Dodge Wauneka.

Readers should acquire a different concept of contemporary Indian leaders, especially concerning current situations and the growing trend toward Indian nationalism. The short paragraphs provide easy reading and promote a favorable, realistic image of American Indian people today. Each person's biography is an accurate portrayal of that person as an individual. The book contains an index, which is unusual for a collective biography, and an insert of photographs of those included.

220. Heuman, William. **Famous American Indians.** New York: Dodd, Mead, 1972. 128p. FRL: 8. Subject: Biography.

As part of the Famous Biographies for Young People Series, this collective biography provides brief, pointed, and informative biographical sketches of nine of the best-known Indian leaders on the North American continent. King Philip, Pontiac, Joseph Brant, Osceola, Tecumseh, Sequoyah, Chief Joseph, Crazy Horse, and Sitting Bull responded to the white man's encroachment and usurpation of Indian homelands. From 1639 until 1890, the Wampanoag, Seminole, Ottawa, Sioux, and Nez Perce leaders strove to protect their people and were determined to remain in their homelands.

Their stories are not pleasant to read, but they are essential for understanding and evaluating white involvement with American Indians. Although these leaders did not succeed in keeping their homelands, they are considered notable individuals, from King Philip in New England to Osceola in Florida, through the Midwest of Pontiac, across the wide Missouri to the Great Plains of Sitting Bull and the mountains of Chief Joseph. The last chapter of the book deals with the history of the Indian people from when they were placed on reservations to the present.

In an insert are photographs and old prints of these famous Americans. The author also provides a brief index. The selections have very short paragraphs and can be easily read. Young people should gain a favorable image of some famous American Indian leaders who made a contribution to their history.

221. Katz, Jane B. **We Rode the Wind: Recollections of Nineteenth Century Tribal Life.** Minneapolis, Minn.: Lerner Publications, 1975. 110p. FRL: 7. Subjects: Biography; Great Plains—Biography.

Jane B. Katz carefully selected material that she feels has been translated without bias to compile an anthology of the Indian perspective on nineteenth-century tribal life. She wanted to be faithful to the recollections of the Indian chroniclers of the past and to present a record of their knowledge of Plains Indian life. In the brief selections from other sources, many well-known Indian men and one woman reminisce about their lives: C. A. Eastman, John Stands in Timber, Two Leggings, Chief Luther Standing Bear, William Whipple Warren, Waheenee, and Black Elk.

The narratives describe the distinct history, language, and traditions of each Great Plains tribe. The tribal historians recall the diversity of the people and the richness of their heritage. Facts about broken treaties with the United States government are presented accurately and are based on historical documentation. This material should be an excellent supplement when covering the events of the 1800s.

222. Roland, Albert. **Great Indian Chiefs.** New York: Macmillan, 1966. 152p. FRL: 9. Subject: Biography.

Vignettes of Indian history are presented through the biographies of nine American Indian chiefs who struggled for their people's survival. Albert Roland provides a carefully researched and selective introduction, with pertinent details and memorable quotations. Authentic biographical detail allows an understanding of the uniqueness of American Indian leaders who faced the incursion into their homelands.

Hiawatha sought peace for the Iroquois. Powhattan, leader of 200 villages of the Algonkian, cemented peace with a marriage between his daughter and colonist John Rolfe. Philip of Pokanoket fought for freedom and independence from the British. In the Southwest pueblos, Pope led the revolt against the Spanish. Pontiac fought with the French against the British, hoping the French would help protect the traditional hunting grounds. Ships visiting the shores of the Pacific Northwest helped Maquinna and his people maintain their culture until the major overland route to the West was completed. Shawnee Chief Tecumseh dreamed of Indian unity to regain their lands. Sequoyah gave the Cherokee a written language. Sitting Bull led the Sioux brilliantly in their futile efforts to resist the invasion of Sioux territory.

In the introduction on these first Americans, the author discusses the diverse culture of the tribes in different parts of America, who found their traditional ways challenged by the British, Spanish, French, and Americans for three centuries. The conclusion traces the progress of the Indian people, who today provide many professional people, politicians, artists, and other leaders for the nation. Part of the America in the Making series, the book was written specifically for the young adult. The material contains excellent references to stereotypes and is a valuable resource for historical and biographical information.

223. Waldman, Carl. **Who's Who in Native American History: Indians and Non-Indians from First Contacts Through 1900.** New York: Facts on File, 1990. 410p. FRL: 7. Subjects: Biography—Dictionaries; Government relations—Biography—Dictionaries.

Award-winning author on American Indian history, Carl Waldman contributes an extensive biographical reference of individuals who shaped Native American history. Most collected biographies limit themselves to a specific group of people. In this unusual treatment of a neglected subject, Waldman provides information on the lives of prominent Indian and white men and women who interacted before the twentieth century. Taking a different approach, he provides a comprehensive book in dictionary format. This is the only reference of this kind published for readers interested in all of the people who had an impact on this period of Indian history.

More than 1,000 entries, covering more than four centuries, are addressed in an A-to-Z format. Each entry incorporates all variations of the subject's name, tribe or occupation, and birth and death dates. The concise biographical summary of his or her role is very detailed, and extensive cross-references make this source easy to use. If a name within the biographical sketch is printed in capital letters, the reader is cross-referenced to a summary of that person's life. This valuable feature underscores the broad interdependency of Native Americans and whites. Two appendixes give lists of Native Americans by tribe and non-Indians by their contribution.

The reader is introduced to a broad spectrum of individuals. People covered include tribal leaders, medicine men, warriors, army scouts, explorers, and traders, and the biographies examine their achievements and associations and their impact on Indian history. Relationships between American and European statesmen, army officers, scholars, and educators are noted. Artists and photographers chronicle the history and culture of notable Indians and white people.

Clearly written, *Who's Who in Native American History* is a single source that can be consulted for biographical information on people important in Native

American history. The biographies include both renowned and less familiar figures. Students from grades seven through twelve, history buffs, and teachers will find it a quick reference. Libraries need to provide biographical information on the interdependency of Indian and white men and women. Waldman's biographical dictionary is highly recommended.

224. Waters, Frank. **Brave Are My People: Indian Heroes Not Forgotten.** Santa Fe, N. Mex.: Clear Light, 1992. 189p. FRL: 8. Subjects: Biography; History.

Frank Waters is the renowned author of the novel *The Man Who Killed the Deer* and the factual *Book of the Hopi* and *Masked Gods*. Now he adds a collected biography of legendary Native Americans to his impressive array of fiction and nonfiction titles. Since 1930, when Waters' first book was published, he has been recognized for his ability to share with his readers an understanding of Native American people. In the introduction, Vine Deloria, Jr. offers this tribute: "Frank has saved his best and deepest book for the last part of his writing career...." He expresses his emotion about the vignettes, "I personally would like nothing more than to walk into Frank's chapters with a weapon and stand at the side of these noble men as they breathe their last—a second with a real person is better than a long life with people who cannot take a chance and live their dreams and ideals."

Focusing on twenty-two legendary Native Americans, Waters offers glimpses into their lives. The leaders, selected from the Atlantic to the Pacific, lived during Anglo-American expansions from the 1600s through the 1900s. Waters includes acclaimed warriors such as Powhatan, Massasoit and Metacomet, Pontiac, Red Jacket, Tecumseh, Black Hawk, Sequoyah, Osceola, and the warrior horsemen of the Great Plains: White Antelope, Santana, Red Cloud, and Crazy Horse. The brilliant tactical maneuvers of the leaders at the battles of the Little Bighorn and Wounded Knee are recounted. The profound philosophy and moving oratory as well as pain, humor, and heartbreak illuminate the lives of Deganawidah, Joseph Brant, Mangas Coloradas, Manuelito, Irataba, Chief Joseph, and Chief Seattle.

Based on careful research of the historical period, this volume includes reconstructed scenes and conversations. The bibliography provides the sources from which Waters drew his sensitive account of the Native American spiritual leaders. Artist renditions of fifteen leaders are included with credits supplied.

Although there are other collections of biographies that young people can read, Waters offers readers a personal insight into the dignity and purpose of native leaders. The portraits are realistic and do not seek to glorify the leaders, but present the struggles they faced and nobility they possessed in a changing world. Young adults, especially Indian youth, will experience the force of Water's admiration and feel a kinship with noteworthy Native Americans of the last five centuries.

225. Wayne, Bennett, ed. **Indian Patriots of the Eastern Woodlands.** Champaign, Ill.: Garrard, 1976. 168p. FRL: 5. Subjects: Biography; Massasoit; Tecumseh; Black Hawk; Osceola.

The Indian people living in Eastern America welcomed white people to their native land. Shortly afterward, the Wampanoag, Shawnee, Sauk and Fox, Seminole, and other groups found themselves being forced from their homelands, either by treaty or force. Bennett Wayne offers young readers clearly written biographical sketches of four Indian patriots who chose to remain and fight for their people's rights. The selections were written by Virginia Boight (Massasoit), James McCagne (Tecumseh), La Vere Anderson (Black Hawk), and Wyatt Blassingame (Osceola).

Befriending the Pilgrims and honoring treaties, the peaceful leader Massasoit found the English were never satisfied. The great Shawnee warrior and statesman Tecumseh dreamed of a united Indian nation where the Indian people could live free of white intruders. Black Hawk, the proud and spirited war chief of the Sauk, fought bravely on his native soil until the food supply was exhausted. The Seminole war chief Osceola provided leadership during fierce battles with English soldiers.

Each biography begins with a full-page black-and-white portrait and a notable quotation from the Indian patriot. The editor concludes each biography with brief information about the tribal people and a map showing locations of major events. Historical pictures enhance the text. The index provides access to events, names, and Indian tribes. Valuable as a reference, these well-written biographies will be appealing to all children and be of special interest to young Indian readers. This book is an excellent companion volume to *Indian Patriots of the Great West* (see entry 226).

226.   Wayne, Bennett, ed. **Indian Patriots of the Great West.** Champaign, Ill.: Garrard, 1974. 166p. FRL: 5. Subjects: Biography; Sitting Bull, Sioux chief; Crazy Horse, Sioux chief; Quanah Parker, Comanche chief; Joseph, Nez Perce chief.

In this easily read book, the heroic struggle of the Plains Indians is recounted through the lives of the great chiefs of the Western tribes. Buffalo hunters, miners, and settlers were protected by the army as they invaded the lands of the Great Plains. The great leaders Sitting Bull and Crazy Horse of the Sioux, Quanah Parker of the Comanches, and Chief Joseph of the Nez Perce fought valiantly with their people to remain on their homelands and preserve their way of life. The young reader learns of the battles they fought, the buffalo who disappeared, and the subjugation they faced.

The biographical sketches were written by LaVere Anderson, Enid LaMonte Meadowcroft, and Elizabeth Rider Montgomery. Following the same format used in *Indian Patriots of the Eastern Woodlands* (see entry 225), the editor provides leaders' portraits, famous quotations, historical pictures, tribal information, and maps of important events. The index to events, names, and Indian tribes makes the volume useful as a reference. The biographies of the four leaders of the Western tribes will not only inspire young Indian people but also serve as an introduction to others about the incredible obstacles the Indian people faced as they fought to retain their freedom.

227.   Whittaker, Jane. **Patriots of the Plains: Sitting Bull, Crazy Horse, Chief Joseph.** New York: Scholastic Book Services, 1973. 128p. FRL: 6. Subjects: Biography; Great Plains—Biography.

This collective biography is an attractive book containing many sepia-toned photographs with captions that will appeal to students. Three great chiefs chose freedom for their people rather than reservation life. Chief Joseph of the Nez Perce and Sitting Bull and Crazy Horse of the Sioux are described in the battles they fought to remain free. The author acknowledges the assistance of Rosebud Yellow Robe in preparing the information on Sitting Bull and Crazy Horse, and of the Nez Perce Tribal Executive Committee for help on Chief Joseph's entry.

The text contains very short paragraphs. Although there is no index or bibliography, the material is considered accurate and can be easily read and enjoyed by intermediate through adult levels to promote an awareness and understanding of Native Americans. The book contains little bias or few stereotypes and should promote a positive self-image. The biographies can provide supplemental material for American history classes and should also appeal to students and teachers looking for interesting biographical material.

92 Individual Biography

Black Elk

228.   Neihardt, John G. **Black Elk Speaks.** Lincoln: University of Nebraska Press, 1961. 238p. FRL: 11. Subjects: Black Elk; Sioux Indians—History.
   Black Elk, a holy man of the Oglala Sioux, recounts the story of his life in this fascinating book first printed in 1932 and currently in its eighth printing. Black Elk related his story to John Neihardt because he felt the history of the Sioux should be preserved for his people. The reminiscences of Black Elk were spoken in Sioux and translated by his son and were often supplemented by the recollections of his old friends.
   Black Elk participated in such major historical events as the Battle of the Little Big Horn and the Battle of Wounded Knee. His eyewitness accounts of these battles, his very personal accounts of his childhood and youth in those troubled times for the Sioux, and his visions of spiritual phenomena provide the main material for this classic. The lessons of history are timeless, as evidenced by the continued popularity of this book, which is available both in hardcover and paperback.
   Young adults will find this account very readable because of the intriguing narrative of familiar historical events and the mystical quality of the narrator. The book is an excellent resource for classes in American history and literature as well as leisure reading.

Cochise

229.   Sweeney, Edwin R. **Cochise: Chiricahua Apache Chief.** Norman: University of Oklahoma Press, 1991. 501p. FRL: 11. Subjects: Cochise, Apache Chief; Apache Indians—Biography; Apache Indians—Wars, 1872-73.
   This highly acclaimed biography deserves all the accolades it has received. Meticulously researched, this book is the authoritative account of the life of the greatest of the Apache chiefs. Sweeney has produced a scholarly study of an outstanding American Indian leader in a very readable form.
   Cochise was most noted for his warfare against the Arizona settlers and government troops whom he fought successfully for nearly twenty years. Although he was the chief of a small band of Chiricahau Apaches, he was highly respected by other Apache bands who frequently joined him in his expeditions. Commanding

in appearance and highly intelligent, Cochise earned the admiration of both his followers and his enemies.

Although he would be considered ruthless by today's standards, Cochise was in a desperate situation that demanded extreme measures. The victim of many broken promises by American military and government officials, he learned to survive by trusting no one. He challenged the best troops that Mexico and the United States could muster by brilliantly conceived hit-and-run tactics. At the end of his life he saw the inevitability of the settlement of Arizona by the white man and reluctantly surrendered. He died a broken man, but one whom history would recognize as the greatest of the Apache chiefs.

The book provides excellent maps and photographs that clarify the text. Also included are extensive notes, a complete bibliography, and a comprehensive index. Students in secondary schools and adults will find this book to be one of the best available biographies of American Indian chiefs.

Geronimo

230. Barrett, Steven M., ed. **Geronimo: His Own Story.** New York: Ballantine Books, 1970. 207p. FRL: 8. Subjects: Geronimo; Apache Indians—Biography.

The name Geronimo evokes a common response in most Americans. His exploits as the leader of a small band of Apaches that kept the United States Army occupied for decades are well known to fans of movies and television programs. Geronimo dictated his own life story while imprisoned at Fort Sill, Oklahoma Territory. In this book a new picture of Geronimo emerges, that of a patriot warrior and humanist primarily interested in serving his people, who were being exploited and deceived by American agents. The portion of this book that actually tells Geronimo's own story relates both his account of ancient Apache legends and his remembrance of Apache life and battles with the Mexican and American troops.

The original book was written in 1906, and an additional introduction by Frederick W. Turner III was added in 1970. The addition of editorial footnotes by the editors to add corrections and personal comments to Geronimo's account does not make the text any more relevant. The most significant value of the book lies in Geronimo's personal account of history as he saw it. The narrative is simply and beautifully told. Others who wish to read further on this episode in history can read such books as *The Truth About Geronimo* by Britton Davis (University of Nebraska Press, 1976), which gives a different account of Geronimo's life from the perspective of the traditional non-Indian historian.

Students and teachers of American history will find this book helpful in understanding an Indian perspective of the Apache wars, which have been so grossly misrepresented in screen and print accounts. Those interested in reading dramatic autobiographic literature should find the section of the book relating to Geronimo's oral history intriguing. A selected bibliography and an appendix on the surrender of Geronimo are included.

Hiawatha

231. Fradin, Dennis Brindell. **Hiawatha: Messenger of Peace.** New York: Margaret K. McElderry Books, 1992. 40p. FRL: 5. Subjects: Hiawatha; Iroquois Indians—Biography.

A prolific author of nonfiction books, Dennis Fradin traces the true story of the real Hiawatha, who was even more remarkable than the myths created by author Henry Schoolcraft and poet Henry Wadsworth Longfellow. Hiawatha is a familiar American Indian name, but few people really know the significance of his life. This short biography, written for elementary school children, outlines the historical facts and stories that the Iroquois elders handed down to their young people for years.

Thousands of years ago, the people who became known as the Iroquois lived in present-day New York State. Five separate Indian tribes who shared customs and languages were the Mohawk, Oneida, Onondaga, Cayuga, and the Seneca. These five tribes, all part of the Iroquois language group, were constantly warring with each other. An Iroquois Indian, Hiawatha lived about 500 years ago. After overcoming a terrible personal tragedy, he rose to a position of leadership in his tribe. He became friends with the Huron Indian Degandawida. The two men brought peace to the five warring tribes of the Iroquois. This union, the Iroquois Federation, flourished about 300 years. Dagandawida was called Peacemaker by the Iroquois. Little is known about Haiwatha's early years and the period after he established the Federation.

Children will gain an understanding of the Iroquois people and their customs. An excellent introduction to American government studies, this biography explains how one democratic form of government originated. Some ideas of Hiawatha and Peacemaker became part of the United States Constitution. Most biographies of early American Indian leaders written as juvenile literature use illustrations by a single artist. This biographical sketch includes ten photographs in color and ten in black and white. Some photographs, paintings, and drawings are historical. Others are by modern Iroquois Indians. A bibliography of selected works and an index make this book an outstanding addition to any elementary collection of individual biographies.

Howe, Oscar

232. Milton, John R. **Oscar Howe: The Story of an American Indian.** Minneapolis, Minn.: Dillon Press, 1972. 56p. FRL: 6. Subjects: Howe, Oscar, 1915- ; Artists; Dakota Indians—Biography.

Another of the Dillon Press series on notable American Indians, this book is a short biography of Oscar Howe, a Yanktonai Sioux of South Dakota, who has achieved prominence as a painter and college professor. The book follows his childhood on the Crow Creek reservation, his experiences in an Indian boarding school and the military, his success as an artist, and ultimately his achievement as one of the preeminent American artists.

The biography is an interesting account of the difficulties he faced in his early life: poverty, a disfiguring skin disease, and physical abuse in boarding school. However, the main lesson of the book is plainly told: a determined man can achieve success despite the frustration and discouragements of life. Certainly, this is a life story that can provide hope for every young person who reads this book, and it will have added significance for the Indian youth.

Since the author was able to submit the manuscript to Professor Howe for editing, the book can be considered accurate. As with any biography on a contemporary person, an update on the life of this unique man would be helpful for the present-day reader. Biographies of this type are useful to English teachers who are looking for literature to which young Indian students can relate.

Ishi

233. Kroeber, Theodora. **Ishi in Two Worlds.** Berkeley: University of California Press, 1976. 213p. FRL: 9. Subjects: Yahi Indians; Yana Indians; California Indians—History; Ishi.

234. Kroeber, Theodora. **Ishi, Last of His Tribe.** Berkeley, Calif.: Parnassus Press, 1964. 215p.

Ishi, Last of His Tribe is adapted from the anthropological study entitled *Ishi in Two Worlds*, both written by Theodora Kroeber, the curator of the Indian Museum at the University of California at Berkeley. Both books are the haunting story of the life of the last surviving Yahi of the Yana tribe of Northern California. Based on the life of a starving and lonely young Indian man who stumbled into "civilization" near Oroville, California, on August 29, 1921, the book narrates the tragic story that he related to several anthropologists who befriended him.

Ishi, in his childhood, was one of few survivors of his tribe's massacre by California gold seekers. Forced to subsist on the meager offerings of a hostile environment, constantly harassed and hunted by the ever-encroaching white people, the few remaining Yahi were killed or disappeared. Kroeber relates the struggle of the remaining remnant of a once strong and prosperous tribe and the tragic story of Ishi as he attempted to survive alone. Finally, in complete desperation, Ishi found a solution to survival as he entered the white world. He became well known and lived the remainder of his life telling the true story of the Yana and their culture.

The fictionalized style used in *Ishi, Last of His Tribe* is an excellent medium for several areas of instruction. Because it is an anthropological document written for a younger audience, this true story can be used for American literature classes. American history classes will find this information valuable as it relates the tragic story of California Indians.

The companion biography from which this account was adapted, *Ishi in Two Worlds*, serves as a valuable resource for research papers on Ishi, an important figure in American history, or as material for research on California Indians. This volume contains excellent photographs, many of which were taken at the actual locations in the Deer Creek country of northern California where Ishi was born and lived for nearly half a century. The author's notes, a bibliography, and an index make the volume useful for young adults.

Joseph

235. Beal, Merrill D. **I Will Fight No More Forever.** Seattle: University of Washington Press, 1963. 366p. FRL: 9. Subjects: Joseph, Nez Perce chief; Nez Perce Indians—History.

In chronicling what General Sherman called "one of the most outstanding of the Indian wars," Merrill D. Beal provides an important contribution to American history. The book not only describes an important historic event but simultaneously narrates the biography of an American Indian leader of heroic stature. Chief Joseph moved his tribe some 1,600 miles in eleven weeks and fought thirteen battles against United States troops that vastly outnumbered his small band of Nez Perce. He defeated the enemy in all encounters and would have made an escape to Canada if he had not remained to protect the children, aged, and wounded.

Even after his surrender to General Miles on October 5, 1877, Chief Joseph continued to negotiate for fair treatment for his people. Only his death prevented him from seeing them return to their sacred homeland. The book also provides an excellent history of the Nez Perce, the historical events that resulted in the encroachment of the whites on lands set aside by treaty for the Nez Perce, and the treatment of the Nez Perce as exiles following the war. Chief Joseph emerges from this account as an American hero who sought only peace and fair treatment for his people.

Because of the dramatic nature of this historical episode, students will find the book extremely interesting, especially the middle chapters, which deal with the Nez Perce War. Even more important, Indian youth will discover a leader who ranks with any white American military leader in terms of strategy and leadership. This book is one librarians can recommend for an honest perspective of American history. The author carefully documents all details, including lists of the killed or wounded. Each chapter is provided with notations, and there are a detailed bibliography and an index.

For elementary school children, the Montana Council for Indian Education, Billings, Montana, has printed *Chief Joseph's Own Story* (n.d.), as told by Chief Joseph in 1879 on his trip to Washington, D.C. The moving words of Chief Joseph offer an intimate understanding of the Nez Perce and their courageous struggle to remain free. The small paperback contains thirty-one pages and has black-and-white photographs and illustrations.

Sitting Bull

236. Vestal, Stanley. **Sitting Bull: Champion of the Sioux.** Norman: University of Oklahoma Press, 1957. 352p. FRL: 10. Subjects: Sitting Bull; Sioux Indians—Biography.

Although first published in 1932, this book remains one of the most definitive accounts of the life of Sitting Bull, one of the preeminent Sioux Indian leaders. Sitting Bull led thousands of warriors in many of the most famous Indian battles of history. This powerful biography traces the life of Sitting Bull from his childhood, through his exploits as a young warrior, to his great victories as a leader, and finally his gallant leadership of a captured nation. Sitting Bull was finally silenced by his death at the hands of Sioux military police.

A Rhodes Scholar, Stanley Vestal provides a sensitive portrait. Using witnesses of many of the events chronicled as primary sources and supplementing these accounts with years of research into the documents of this era, Vestal provides an authoritative account. Evident from the treatment of Sitting Bull and the struggles of the Sioux against the U.S. government is the author's respect for both Sitting Bull and the Sioux Nation. Vestal provides sufficient quotations from Sitting Bull to illustrate that he was not subservient to his captors and that he continued to demand fair treatment for his people until his death.

As one of the most well-known Indian leaders, Sitting Bull is a popular subject for research for middle and secondary school readers. The extensive index and bibliographical index are useful for research. As a historical figure of note, his life is worthy of study in social studies, particularly in American history. English students will find this book an excellent example of how good biography should be written. Because of the subject matter, the book will also be attractive to the student seeking good leisure reading.

Tallchief, Maria

237. DeLeeuw, Adele. **Maria Tallchief: American Ballerina.** Champaign, Ill.: Garrard, 1971. 144p. FRL: 6. Subjects: Tallchief, Maria; Osage Indians—Biography.

Fulfilling one of the vital needs of the public and school library, this short biography of a highly successful Indian woman will be enjoyed by most students. Maria Tallchief's story is prime evidence of the value of perseverance and hard work in achieving a high goal. Born of Osage Indian parents, Maria as a child dreamt of being a great dancer. With endless hours of practice and with the constant support of her parents, she achieved success as a teenager in California and was determined to become a ballerina. The book traces her frustration and heartbreak as she continued to work for her goal of stardom on the ballet stage. Remarkably, she and her sister became members of one of the most highly respected ballet companies in New York. Under the tutelage of George Balanchine, whom she later married, Maria became one of the foremost ballerinas in the world.

The book is well written and tells an inspiring story. Details of her life are accurate and reflect a pride in her Osage Indian heritage. In the later editions of this book, the brief historical account of the Osage is eliminated. Although a factual description of the Osage people would be an asset, the original account was somewhat derogatory, and the new editions are an improvement. The book contains illustrations by Russell Hoover, an index, and a glossary of ballet terms. Because of the hostility that is shown to Maria, some Indian students may relate to her experiences. However, the main message of the book is that goals can be achieved if one is willing to work hard enough. As a complementary book, children will enjoy Tobi Tobias's *Maria Tallchief* (Crowell, 1970), which has excellent, realistic illustrations by Michael Hampshire.

Wauneka, Annie

238. Nelson, Mary Carroll. **Annie Wauneka: The Story of an American Indian.**
     Minneapolis, Minn.: Dillon Press, 172. 66p. FRL: 7. Subjects: Wauneka,
     Annie; Navajo Indians—Biography.

Much of the value of adding this volume to the public and school library
biography collection lies in the fact that this is the only full-length biography written
thus far about this remarkable Navajo woman. The story of her achievements in
obtaining health and education benefits for her people should be an inspiration for
all students, particularly young Indian females. Annie Wauneka's election to the
Navajo tribal council and her subsequent success in bringing the plight of the
Navajo to the attention of the nation is an American epic.

The daughter of Chee Dodge, the first tribal chairman of the Navajo tribe,
Annie Wauneka learned of the needs and desires of her people from an early age.
Fluent in both English and Navajo, she used her language and social skills to help
bridge the cultural gap between the Navajo and the white. She was awarded the
Medal of Freedom, America's highest civilian honor, by President Johnson in 1963,
and she received many other notable awards and honors.

Although there are some simplifications of Navajo culture, this book provides valuable information on both the Navajo people and the amazing life of Annie
Wauneka. Photographs accompany the text. The book is written in very simple
language and should prove an excellent resource for teachers seeking information
on successful contemporary Indian leaders. Indian students in intermediate grades,
junior high, and high school can identify with Annie Wauneka's life story and will
find the book both readable and worthwhile.

Other Notable Individuals

239. **North American Indians of Achievement.** New York: Chelsea House,
     1992- . 104-128p. 24 vols. FRL: 5.

   239.1. Bernotas, Bob. **Jim Thorpe.** 1992. Subject: Thorpe, Jim.

   239.2. Bernotas, Bob. **Sitting Bull.** 1992. Subject: Sitting Bull, Sioux chief.

   239.3. Bland, Celia. **Osceola.** 1994. Subject: Osceola.

   239.4. Bland, Celia. **Pontiac.** 1994. Subject: Pontiac.

   239.5. Bonvillain, Nancy. **Black Hawk.** 1994. Subject: Black Hawk.

   239.6. Bonvillain, Nancy. **Hiawatha.** 1992. Subject: Hiawatha.

   239.7. Cuiklik, Robert. **Tecumseh.** 1993. Subject: Tecumseh.

   239.8. Guttmacher, Peter. **Crazy Horse.** 1994. Subject: Crazy Horse, Sioux
          chief.

239.9. Henry, Christopher. **Ben Nighthorse Campbell.** 1994. Subject: Campbell, Ben Nighthorse.

239.10. Holler, Anne. **Pocahontas.** 1993. Subject: Pocahontas.

239.11. Roman, Joseph. **King Philip.** 1992. Subject: King Philip.

239.12. Schwartz, Melissa. **Cochise.** 1992. Subject: Cochise, Apache chief.

239.13. Schwartz, Melissa. **Geronimo.** 1992. Subject: Geronimo.

239.14. Schwartz, Melissa. **Wilma Mankiller.** 1994. Subject: Mankiller, Wilma.

239.15. Scordato, Ellen. **Sarah Winnemucca.** 1992. Subject: Winnemucca, Sarah.

239.16. Shumate, Jane. **Sequoyah.** 1994. Subject: Sequoyah.

239.17. Sonneborn, E. **Will Rogers.** 1994. Subject: Rogers, Will.

239.18. Tratter, Clifford. **Chief Joseph.** 1993. Subject: Joseph, Nez Perce chief.

239.19. Wilson, Claire. **Joseph Brant.** 1992. Subject: Brant, Joseph, Mohawk chief.

239.20. Wilson, Claire. **Quanah Parker.** 1992. Subject: Parker, Quanah, Comanche chief.

Individuals with specific talents emerge in every generation of American Indian people. They assume the challenge of instructing and inspiring their people in a changing world. The biographies in the series North American Indians of Achievement covers the lives of notable men and women. W. David Baird in the introduction "On Indian Leadership" suggests that leadership is determined by culture and the unique circumstances of the time and place in which individuals live. Until the late fifteenth century, most tribes were not governed by a single individual. Various people within the group rose to leadership roles that were political, social, or religious in nature. Leaders had to earn the respect of their people.

In traditional Indian communities, men and women of great talent valiantly struggled to serve their people. Some of the biographies in this set examine the lives of great chiefs: Mohawk Joseph Brant, Apache Cochise, Nez Perce Joseph, Sioux Crazy Horse, Comanche Quanah Parker, and Sioux Sitting Bull. The white man's greed for Indian land forced leadership upon rebels who fought to retain their traditional way of life: Osceola of the Seminole, Pontiac of the Ottowa, Tecumseh of the Shawnee, Black Hawk of the Sac and Fox, Geronimo of the Apache, and King Philip of the Wampanoag. Hiawatha founded the Iroquois Confederacy and ended the war among his people. The biography of Pocahontas describes her role as peacemaker between the Powhatan tribes and the Jamestown English settlers.

Gradually, the nature of Indian leadership changed. Indian people explored new fields. Special skills and talents brought them to positions of distinction— Cherokee alphabet inventor, Sequoyah; Northern Paiute writer and diplomat, Sarah Winnemucca; Cheyenne U.S. Senator, Ben Nighthorse Campbell; Principal Chief of the Cherokee, Wilma Mankiller; Cherokee entertainer, Will Rogers; and Sac and Fox athlete, Jim Thorpe. The biographies only touch on the multitudes of strong men and women who assumed leadership roles to make Indian people a vital part of America's cultural landscape.

Chelsea House adds new biographies to this series every year. The authors of each volume tell the lives of the individuals in a straightforward, objective manner. The full-color laminated cover for each biography comes with reinforced binding. Forty black-and-white archival photographs, artwork, and maps help readers in middle and junior high school visualize the historical period in which each leader lived. The chronology of events, bibliography, and index make each title useful for reference work. Some books are available in paperback.

The biographical series recounts the life stories of North American Indians who are well known and also some who are less known but equally important. Young people from grades six through twelve can explore the varied lives of these prominent Indians and gain pride in their achievements. Biographies of contemporary Indian leaders offer encouragement to American Indian students. Librarians can strengthen the ethnic diversity of their collection with these titles.

Appendix:
Publishers' Addresses

Harry N. Abrams
110 E. 59th St.
New York, NY 10022

Alfred Van Der Marck Editions
1133 Broadway
New York, NY 10010

American Indian Publications
177 F Riverside Dr.
Newport Beach, CA 92663

American Library Association
50 E. Huron St.
Chicago, IL 60611

Arch Cape Press
15 Sherwood Pl.
Greenwich, CT 06830

Arco Publishing
219 Park Ave. S.
New York, NY 10003

Atheneum
597 Fifth Ave.
New York, NY 10017

Ballantine Books
101 Fifth Ave.
New York, NY 10003

Bantam Books
666 Fifth Ave.
New York, NY 10019
    Orders to:
    414E Gold Rd.
    Des Plains, IL 60016

Beechwood Books
Box 20484
Birmingham, AL 35216

Beyond Words Publishing, Inc.
Pumpkin Ridge Road
Rt. 3 Box 492B
Hillsboro, OR 97123

Book Publishing Company
P.O. Box 99
Summertown, TN 38483

Books Americana
P.O. Box 2326
Florence, AL 35630

Bradbury Press
2 Overhill Rd.
Scarsdale, NY 10583
    Distributed by:
    E. P. Dutton
    2 Park Ave.
    New York, NY 10016

Capricorn Books
200 Madison Ave.
New York, NY 10016

Capricorn Books
G. P. Putnam's Sons
200 Madison Ave.
New York, NY 10016
    Orders to:
    1050 Wall St.
    West Lyndhurst, NJ 07071

Carolrhoda Books
241 1st Ave. N.
Minneapolis, MN 55401

Center for Indian Education
College of Education
Arizona State University
Tempe, AZ 85201

Chelsea House Publishers
95 Madison Ave.
New York, NY 10016

Children's Book Press
1461 Ninth Ave.
San Francisco, CA 94122

Childrens Press
1224 W. Van Buren St.
Chicago, IL 60607

Clear Light Publishers
823 Don Diego
Santa Fe, NM 87501

Crestwood House
Box 3427
Highway 66 S.
Mankota, MN 56001

Crossing Press
17 W. Main St.
Trumansburg, NY 14886

Crowell
10 E. 53rd St.
New York, NY 10022

Crown
419 Park Ave S.
New York, NY 10016

Council for Indian Education. *See*
    Montana Council for Indian
    Education

John Day
62 W. 45th St.
New York, NY 10036

Daybreak Star Press
Daybreak Star Cultural-Educational
    Center
Discovery Park
P.O. Box 4100
Seattle, WA 98199

Dell Publishing
750 Third Ave.
New York, NY 10017

Denver Museum of Natural History
2001 Colorado Blvd.
Denver, CO 80207

Dial Press
750 Third Ave.
New York, NY 10017

Dillon Press
106 Washington Ave. N.
Minneapolis, MN 55401

Discus Books
(Avon Books)
The Hearst Corporation
959 Eighth Ave.
New York, NY 10019

Dodd, Mead
79 Madison Ave.
New York, NY 10016

Doubleday
277 Park Ave.
New York, NY 10017

Dover Publications
180 Varick St.
New York, NY 10014

E. P. Dutton
2 Park Ave.
New York, NY 10016

Eagle Feather Trading Post
168 W. 12th Street
Ogden, Utah 84404

Eakin Press
P.O. Box 23066
Austin, TX 73735

Facts on File
Rand McNally
P.O. Box 7600
Chicago, IL 60680

Far West Laboratory for Educational
    Research
1855 Folsom St.
San Francisco, CA 94103

Farrar, Straus & Giroux
19 Union Square W.
New York, NY 10003

Fawcett Book Group
1515 Broadway
New York, NY 10036

Four Winds
Scholastic Book Services
50 W. 44th St.
New York, NY 10036

Franklin Watts
730 Fifth Ave.
New York, NY 10019

Fulcrum Publishing
350 Indiana St., Suite 510
Golden, CO 80401

Gale Research, Inc.
835 Penobscot Bldg.
Detroit, ML 48226-4094

Garrard Publishing
1607 N. Market St.
Champaign, IL 61820

Glencoe Press
8701 Wilshire Blvd.
Beverly Hills, CA 90211

Golden Press
Western Publishing
1220 Mound Ave.
Racine, WI 53404

Greenfield Review Press
R.D. 1, Box 80
Greenfield Center, NY 12833

Greenwillow Books. *See* William
    Morrow

Grosset & Dunlap
51 Madison Ave.
New York, NY 10010

Harper & Row
10 E. 53rd St.
New York, NY 10022

Hastings House
10 E. 40th St.
New York, NY 10016

Hawthorn Books. *See* E. P. Dutton

Hayden Book Company
50 Essex St.
Rochelle Park, NJ 07662

Holiday House
18 E. 53rd St.
New York, NY 10022

Holt, Rinehart & Winston
383 Madison Ave.
New York, NY 10017

Houghton Mifflin
2 Park St.
Boston, MA 02107

House of Collectibles
201 E. 50th Street
New York, NY 10022

Indian Historian Press
1493 Masonic Ave.
San Francisco, CA 94117

International Publishers
381 Park Ave S., Suite 1301
New York, NY 10016

Johnson Books
1880 S. 57th Court
Boulder, CO 80304

Alfred A. Knopf
201 E. 50th St.
New York, NY 10022

Lerner Publications
241 First Ave. N.
Minneapolis, MN 55401

Libraries Unlimited, Inc.
P.O. Box 6633
Englewood, CO 80155-6633

J. B. Lippincott
East Washington Sq.
Philadelphia, PA 19105

Little, Brown
34 Beacon St.
Boston, MA 02106
    Orders to:
    200 West St.
    Waltham, MD 02154

Liveright Library Department
386 Park Ave. S.
New York, NY 10016

Lucent Books, Inc.
P.O. Box 289011
San Diego, CA 92198-0011

Macmillan
23 Orinda Way
Orinda, CA 94563

Margaret K. McElderry Books
Macmillan Publishing Company
866 Third Avenue
New York, NY 10022

David McKay
2 Park Ave.
New York, NY 10016

Julian Messner
Simon & Schuster
1230 Ave. of the Americas
New York, NY 10020

Middle Atlantic Press
P.O. Box 263
Wallingford, PA 19086

Montana Council for Indian
    Education
P.O. Box 31215
517 Rimrock Rd.
Billings, MT 59107

William Morrow
105 Madison Ave.
New York, NY 10016
    Orders to:
    Wilmor Warehouse
    6 Henderson Dr.
    West Caldwell, NJ 07006

Museum of the American Indian
Broadway at 155th St.
New York, NY 10032

National Congress of American
    Indians
804 D Street N. E.
Washington, DC 20002

National Council of Teachers of
    English
508 S. 6th St.
Champaign, IL 61820

National Geographic Society
17th and M Sts., N.W.
Washington, DC 20036

Naturegraph Publishers
P.O. Box 1075
Happy Camp, CA 96039

Navajo Community College Press
Tsaile, AZ 86556

Thomas Nelson
407 7th Ave. S.
Nashville, TN 37203

New Seed Press
P.O. Box 3016
Sandford, CA 94305

Nodin Press
519 N. Third St.
Minneapolis, MN 55041

Northland Press
Box N
Flagstaff, AZ 86001

Old Army Press
405 Link Ave.
Fort Collins, CO 80521

Orchard Books
387 Park Avenue South
New York, NY 10016

Pantheon Books. *See* Random House

Parnassus Press
2721 Parker St.
Berkeley, CA 94704

Price Stern Sloan, Inc.
410 N. La Cienega Blvd.
Los Angeles, CA 90048

Promontory Press
Outerbridge & Lazard
200 W. 72nd St.
New York, NY 10023

G. P. Putnam's Sons
200 Madison Avenue
New York, NY 10016

Raintree Children's Books
205 W. Highway Ave.
Milwaukee, WI 53203

Rand McNally
P.O. Box 7600
Chicago, IL 60680

Random House
201 E. 50th St.
New York, NY 10022

Rio Grande Press
La Casa Escuela
Glorietta, NM 87535

Rivola Books
Pinnacle Press, Inc.
Steck-Vaughn
P.O. Box 26015
Austin, TX 78755

Rizzoli International Publications
712 Fifth Ave.
New York, NY 10019

Rourke Publications, Inc.
P.O. Box 3328
Vero Beach, FL 32964

Schocken Books
200 Madison Ave.
New York, NY 10016

Scholastic Book Services
50 W. 44th St.
New York, NY 10036

Charles Scribner's Sons
597 Fifth Ave.
New York, NY 10017

Sierra Oaks Publishing
P.O. Box 255354
Sacramento, CA 95865-5354

Stewart, Tabori & Chang, Inc.
575 Broadway
New York, NY 10012

Swallow Press
1139 S. Wabash Ave.
Chicago, IL 60605

Time-Life Books
Time and Life Bldg.
New York, NY 10020

Todd Publications
P.O. Box 92
Lenox Hill Station
New York, NY 10021

University of California Press
2223 Fulton St.
Berkeley, CA 94720

University of Chicago Press
5801 Ellis Ave.
Chicago, IL 60637

University of Nebraska Press
901 N. 17th St.
Lincoln, NE 68508

University of New Mexico Press
Albuquerque, NM 87106

University of Oklahoma Press
105 Asp Ave.
Norman, OK 73069

University of Texas Press
Box 7819
University Station
Austin, TX 78712

University of Washington Press
American Indian Studies Program
Seattle, WA 98105

Van Nostrand Reinhold
135 W. 50th St.
New York, NY 10020
    Orders to:
    Lepi Order Processing
    7625 Empire Dr.
    Florence, KY 41042

Viking Press
625 Madison Ave.
New York, NY 10022

Vintage Book
Box 16182, Elway Station
St. Paul, MN 55116

Visible Ink Press
Gale Research, Inc.
834 Penobscot Bldg.
Detroit, ML 48226-4094

Henry Z. Walck
19 Union Square W.
New York, NY 10003

Walker & Company
720 Fifth Ave.
New York, NY 10019

Franklin Watts
730 Fifth Ave.
New York, NY 10019

West End Press
P.O. Box 87125
Albuquerque, NM 87125

World Book Childcraft International
Merchandise Mart Plaza, Rm. 510
Chicago, IL 60654

Yale University Press
302 Temple St.
New Haven, CT 06520

Author/Title Index

Numbers refer to annotations in part 2. Any number followed by (n) refers to an author or title noted in an annotation.

Abenaki, 193.11
Algonquins, 175.26
Allen, T. D., 135
Alter, Judith, 175.1
America in 1492: The World of the Indian Peoples Before the Arrival of Columbus, 180
American Indian and the United States: A Documentary History, 208
American Indian Authors, 145
American Indian Clothes and How to Make Them, 98
American Indian Games and Crafts, 106
American Indian in Film, 115
American Indian in Short Fiction: An Annotated Bibliography, 136
American Indian Literature, 193.42
American Indian Medicine, 96
American Indian Music and Musical Instruments: With Instructions for Making the Instruments, 109
American Indian Mythology, 16
American Indian Poetry: The Standard Anthology of Songs and Chants, 141
American Indian Pottery: An Identification and Value Guide, 101
American Indian Tools and Ornaments: How to Make Implements and Jewelry with Bone and Shell, 133
American Indian Women, 218
American Indians, American Justice, 36
American Indians and World War II, 156
American Indians Sing, 116

American Indians Today: Issues and Conflicts, 53
Amon, Aline, 79
Among the Plains Indians, 42
Amsden, Charles Avery, 99
Anasazi, 188.36, 191
Anderson, Jean, 81
Anderson, Madelyn Klein, 175.2
Annie Wauneka: The Story of an American Indian, 238
Antelope Woman: An Apache Folktale, 62
The Apache, 188.16
Apache, 193.34
Apaches and Navajos, 175.5
Arapaho, 193.18
Archaeology of North America, 193.46
Armitage, Peter, 193.1
Art and Totems, 189.1
Art of American Indian Cooking, 81
Ashabranner, Brent, 20, 21
Atlas of Ancient America, 160
Atlas of the North American Indian, 165(n), 207
Avery, Susan, 211
Authentic Indian Designs: 2500 Illustrations from Reports of the Bureau of American Ethnology, 124
The Aztec, 188.17
Aztecs, 175.27, 193.4

Baird, David W., 193.2
Baldwin, Gordon C., 100, 152
Barrett, Steven M., 230

Barry, John W., 101
Batherman, Muriel, 153
Battle of the Little Bighorn, 197
Baylor, Byrd, 22, 102, 154
*Beads and Beadwork of the American
Indians: A Study Based on
Specimens in the Museum of the
American Indian*, 126
Beal, Merrill D., 235
Bealer, Alex W., 155
Bedinger, Margery, 103
Bee, Robert L., 193.3
Before Columbus, 153
Before You Came This Way, 154
Begay, Shonto, 23
Behrens, June, 24
Beidler, Peter G., 136
Ben Nighthorse Campbell, 239.9
Bennett, Edna Mae, 104
Benson, Elizabeth, 140
Berdan, Frances F., 193.4
Bernhard, Emery, 25
Bernotas, Bob, 239.1, 239.2
Bernstein, Alison R., 156
Beyer, Don E., 175.3
Bierhorst, John, 7, 9, 10, 26, 27, 28, 29,
105, 137, 138
*Biographical Dictionary of Indians of the
Americas*, 212
Bjorklund, Karma L., 157
Black Elk Speaks, 228
Black Hawk, 239.5
Black Indians: A Hidden Heritage, 60
Bland, Celia, 239.3, 239.4
Blood, Charles L., 106
Bonvillain, Nancy, 193.5, 193.6, 193.7,
193.8, 239.5, 239.6
*Books on American Indians and Eskimos:
A Selection Guide for Children and
Young Adults*, 3
Bourgeault, Lisa, 193.32
Brain, Jeffrey P., 193.9
Brandenberg, Aliki, 89
*Brave Are My People: Indian Heroes Not
Forgotten*, 224
Breeze Swept Through, 148
Brescia, Bill, 90
Brody, J. J., 107
Brown, Virginia Pound, 160

Bruchac, Joseph, 30, 31.1, 31.2, 139
*Buffalo ... and the Indians of the Great
Plains*, 86
Buffalo Hunt, 85
Buffalo Woman, 46
Bunte, Pamela A., 193.10
Burland, Cottie, 11
Burnette, Robert, 161
Bury My Heart at Wounded Knee, 158

Caduto, Michael J., 31.1, 31.2
Cahuilla, 193.32
Calloway, Colin G., 193.11
Campbell, Liz, 162
Cantor, George, 163
Capps, Benjamin, 146, 213
Carter, Alden R., 175.4
Catawbas, 193.35
Cayuga, 188.1
Cherokee, 188.12, 193.38
Cherokees, 175.10
Cheyenne, 175.21, 188.8, 193.26
Cheyenne Autumn, 198
Cheyenne Memories, 202
Chickasaw, 193.25
Chief Joseph, 239.18
Chief Joseph's Own Story, 197(n)
Children's Atlas of Native Americans, 196
Chilula, 175.11
Chippewa, 175.9, 188.30
Chinook, 193.48
Choctaw, 188.13, 193.33
Chronicles of American Indian Protest, 166
Chumash, 193.20
Clark, Ella E., 12
Clifton, James A., 193.12
Coast Salish Peoples, 193.39
Cochise, 239.12
Cochise: Chiricahua Apache Chief, 229
Cody, Iron Eyes, 70(n)
Coe, Michael, 165
Cohen, Caron Lee, 32
Coltelli, Laura, 140
Comanche, 193.41
Comanches, 175.1
Conflict of Cultures, 189.2
Contemporary American Indian Leaders,
219

Corn Is Maize: The Gift of the Indians, 89
Costo, Robert, 45
Cox, Beverly, 91
Crazy Horse, 239.8
Creeks, 193.22
Cronyn, George W., 141
Crow, 188.11, 193.28
Crow Chief: A Plains Indian Story, 47
Cry from the Earth: Music of the North American Indian, 92
Cry of the Thunderbird: The American Indian's Own Story, 172
Cuiklik, Robert, 239.7
Culin, Stewart, 108
Curtis, Natalie, 34

Dancing Teepees: Poems of American Indian Youth, 147
Davis, Britton, 230(n)
De Wit, Dorothy, 38
Debo, Angie, 167
DeLeeuw, Adele, 237
DeLoria, Vine, Jr., 13, 35, 36, 37
Denig, Edwin Thompson, 168
Deur, Lynne, 214
Dial, Adolph L., 193.13
Diamond, Arthur, 92
Dictionary of Daily Life of Indians of the Americas, 80
DiGennaro, Jacqueline, 70
Dillon, Richard H., 169
Discover Indian Reservations USA: A Visitors' Welcome Guide, 204
Dixon, Ann, 39
Dobys, Henry F., 193.14
Dockstader, Frederick J., 215
Dodge, Robert K., 142
Doherty, Craig A., 175.5, 175.6, 175.7
Doherty, Katherine M., 175.5, 175.6, 175.7
Downey, Fairfax, 40
Dubois, Daniel, 70(n)
Duvall, Jill, 188.4, 188.5, 188.6, 188.7

Earth Is Sore: Native Americans on Nature, 6
Earthmaker's Tales: North American Indian Stories About Earth Happenings, 66.1

Eastman, Charles A., 216
Edmonds, Margot, 41
Egge, Marion F., 136
Elasser, Albert B., 173
Encyclopedia of Native American Religions: An Introduction, 15
Encyclopedia of North American Indian Tribes: A Comprehensive Study of Tribes from the Abitibi to the Zuni, 5
Enduring Navajo, 170
Engel, Lorenz, 42
Erdos, Richard 43
Eskimo: Inuit and Yupik, 188.31
Extraordinary American Indians, 211

Famous American Indians, 220
Faulk, Laura E., 193.15
Faulk, Odie B., 193.15
Federal Indian Policy, 193.30
Feest, Christian F., 193.16
Fichter, George S., 44, 109
Field Guide to Rock Art Symbols of the Greater Southwest, 82
Fire Plume: Legends of the American Indians, 26
First Came the Indians, 76
Five Civilized Tribes, 170
Five Indian Tribes of the Upper Missouri: Sioux, Arikaras, Assiniboines, Crees, Crows, 168
Fixico, Donald L., 193.17
Flute Player: An Apache Folktale, 62
Foreman, Grant, 170
Four Masterworks of American Indian Literature: Quetzacoatl, the Ritual of Condolence, Cuceb, the Night Chant, 9
Fowler, Loretta, 193.18
Fox, Frank, 100
Fradin, Dennis Brindell, 231
Franklin, Robert J., 193.10
Freedman, Russell, 85, 217
Fronval, George, 79(n)
Fur Trappers and Traders: The Indians, the Pilgrims, and the Beaver, 201
Furst, Jill Leslie, 111

Furst, Peter T., 111
Furtaw, Julia C., 1

Galletti, Marie, 67
Games of the American Indian, 100
Games of the North American Indians, 108
Garbarino, Merwyn W., 193.19
Gates, Frieda, 45
Geronimo, 239.13
Geronimo: His Own Story, 230
*Ghost-Dance Religion and the Sioux Out-
    break of 1890*, 18
Gibson, Arrell M., 193.25
Gibson, Robert O., 193.20
Gift of the Sacred Dog, 48
Gilpin, Laura, 171
*Girl Who Married a Ghost and Other Tales
    from the North American Indian*, 33
Goble, Paul, 46, 47, 48, 49, 50, 50.1, 50.2,
    50.3, 50.4, 51, 52
*God On Every Mountain Top: Stories of
    Southwest Indian Sacred Moun-
    tains*, 22
Grant, Campbell, 112
Graymont, Barbara, 193.21
Great Chiefs, 213
Great Indian Chiefs, 222
*Great North American Indians: Profiles in
    Life and Leadership*, 215
Great Race of the Birds and Animals, 49
Greene, Michael D., 193.22
Greene, Jacqueline Dembar, 175.8, 175.9
Greene, Rayna, 193.22
Gridley, Marion E., 218, 219
Grisham, Noel, 86
Grumet, Robert S., 193.24
Guardian Spirit Quest, 12
Guttmacher, Peter, 239.8

Hagman, Ruth, 188.11
Haida Potlatch, 73
Haines, Francis, 169(n)
Hale, Duane K., 193.25
Hamilton, Charles, 172
*Happily May I Walk: American Indians
    and Alaska Natives Today*, 55
Harlan, Judith 53

Heizer, Robert F., 173
Henry, Christopher, 239.9
Henry, Edna, 93
Henry, Jeanette, 54
Heuman, William, 220
Hiawatha, 239.6
Hiawatha: Messenger of Peace, 231
Hidatsa, 193.43
Highwater, Jamake, 14, 113, 114
Hilger, Michael, 115
Hirschfelder, Arlene, 15, 55, 143
History of the Indians of the United States,
    167
Hoffman, Charles, 116
Hofsinde, Robert, 56, 57, 79(n), 81, 95(n)
Hoig, Stan, 193.26
Holler, Anne, 239.10
Holy-Goldsmith, Diane, 118
Homes and Costumes, 189.3
Hoover, Herbert T., 193.27
Hopi, 175.12, 188.37, 193.5
Horses the Indians Rode, 95
Hothen, Lar, 174
Houston, James, 117
How the Plains Indians Lived, 44
How Raven Brought Light to People, 39
Hoxie, Frederick E., 193.28
Hughes, Jill, 200(n)
Hungry Wolf, Beverly, 58
Hunted Like a Wolf, 185
Hunters of the Buffalo, 119.1
Hunters of the Eastern Forest, 119.2
Hunters of the Ice, 119.3
Hunters of the Northern Forest, 119.4
Hunters of the Sea, 119.5
Huron, 193.6

I Will Fight No More Forever, 235
Iktomi and the Berries, 50.1
Iktomi and the Boulder, 50.2
Iktomi and the Buffalo Skull, 50.3
Iktomi and the Ducks, 50.4
*Images of a People: Tlingit Myths and
    Legends*, 70
In the Beginning, 189.4
*In the Trail of the Wind: American Indian
    Poems and Ritual Orations*, 137
Inca, 188.18

Incas, 175.23

Indian and His Horse, 95(n)

Indian Basket Weaving: How to Weave
    Pomo, Yurok, Pima and Navajo
    Baskets, 125

Indian Baskets, 128

Indian Chiefs (Deur, Lynne), 214

Indian Chiefs (Freedman, Russell), 217

Indian Costumes, 56

Indian Country, 65

Indian Designs, 129

Indian Heritage of America, 181

Indian Heroes and Great Chieftains, 216

Indian Legacy: Native American Influences
    on World Life and Culture, 192

Indian Myths and Legends, 43

Indian Oratory: Famous Speeches by
    Noted Indian Chieftains, 128

Indian Painters and White Patrons, 107

Indian Patriots of the Eastern Woodlands,
    225

Indian Patriots of the Great West, 226

Indian Picture Writing, 81

Indian Sign Language (Hofsinde, Robert),
    79(n)

Indian Sign Language (Tomkins, William),
    79(n)

Indian Signs and Signals, 79(n)

Indian Silver: Navajo and Pueblo
    Jewelers, 103

Indian Talk: Hand Signals of the North
    American Indian, 79(n)

Indian Terms of the Americas, 83

Indian Tipi: Its History, Construction, and
    Use, 134(n)

Indians (Capps, Benjamin), 164

Indians (Martini, Teri), 63

Indians (Tunis, Edwin), 206

Indians at Home, 57

Indians' Book: An Offering by the
    American Indians of Indian Lore,
    Musical and Narrative, to Form
    a Record of the Songs and
    Legends, 34

Indians of North America, 193

Indians of Northeastern America, 157

Indians of the Americas, 175

Indians of the Northern Plains, 194

Indians of the Plains, 200

Indians of the Southwest, 152

Innu, 193.1

Introduction to American Indian Art, 122

Inuits, 175.24

Iroquois, 175.6, 193.21

Iroquois Stories: Heroes and Heroines,
    Monsters and Magic, 30

Irwin, R. Stephen, 119, 119.1, 119.2,
    119.3, 119.4, 119.5

Ishi in Two Worlds, 233

Ishi, Last of His Tribe, 234

Iverson, Peter, 176, 193.29

Jacobs, Francine, 177

Jacobs, Martin, 91

Jahoda, Gloria, 178

Jim Thorpe, 239.1

Johnson, Broderick H., 179

Jones, Hattie, 144

Joseph Brant, 239.19

Josephy, Alvin M., Jr., 59, 180, 181

Katz, Jane B., 114, 221

Katz, William Loren, 60

Kavasch, Barrie, 94

Keepers of the Animals: Native American
    Stories and Wildlife Activities for
    Children, 31.1

Keepers of the Earth: Native American
    Stories and Environmental
    Activities for Children, 31.2

Kelly, Lawrence C., 193.30

Kennedy, John G., 193.31

Kennedy, Paul E., 121

Kessel, Joyce K., 61

King Philip, 239.11

Kiowa, 193.54

Klein, Barry T., 2

Kopper, Philip, 182

Koster, John, 161

Kroeber, Theodora, 233, 234

Kwakiutl, 193.51

La Farge, Oliver, 122

Lacapa, Michael, 62.1, 62.2

Landau, Elaine, 175.10, 175.11, 175.12, 175.13, 175.14
Lass-Woodfin, Mary Jo, 3
Laubin, Gladys, 134(n)
Laubin, Reginald, 134(n)
Lavine, Sigmund A., 95
Le Suer, Meridel, 183
Lee, Martin, 175.15
Legends of the Great Chiefs, 64
Lenapes, 193.24
Lepthien, Emile U., 188.12, 188.13, 188.14, 188.15
Liberty, Margot, 202
Lightning Inside You and Other Native American Riddles, 138
Liptak, Karen, 175.16, 175.17, 175.18, 175.19, 175.20
Literature by and About the American Indian: An Annotated Bibliography, 4
Literature of the American Indian, 146
Lost Children, 51
Lowell, John Bean, 193.32
Lumbee, 193.13
Lytle, Clifford M., 36, 37

Magic Images: Contemporary Native American Art, 130
Magic Medicines of the Indians, 97
Ma'ii and Cousin Horned Toad: A Traditional Navajo Story, 23
Mandans, 188.14
Many Smokes, Many Moons: A Chronology of American Indian History Through Indian Art, 113
Maria Tallchief (Tobias, Tobi), 237(n)
Maria Tallchief: American Ballerina, 237
Marrin, Albert, 184
Marriott, Alice, 16, 17
Marshall Cavendish Illustrated History of the North American Indians, 189
Martini, Teri, 63
Matson, Emerson N., 64
Matthiessen, Peter, 65
Maya, 188.19, 193.50
Mayo, Gretchen Will, 66.1, 66.2, 66.3, 66.4
McCullough, Joseph B., 142
McKee, Jesse O., 193.33

McKissack, Patricia C., 188.16, 188.17, 188.18, 188.19
McLuhan, T. C., 8
McReynold, Edwin C., 185(n)
Melody, Michael D., 193.34
Meltzer, Milton, 185
Menominee, 193.37
Merrell, James H., 193.35
Miller, Jay, 188.29
Milton, John R., 232
Mitchell, Wayne, 67
Modoc, 193.15
Mohawk, 188.2, 193.7
Molin, Paulette, 15
Momaday, Natachee Scott, 145, 186
Monster Tales of Native Americans, 74
Montana Council for Indian Education, 235(n)
Mooney, James, 18
More Earthmaker's Tales: North American Indian Stories About Earth Happenings, 66.2
More Star Tales: North American Indian Stories About the Stars, 66.3
Morning Star, Black Sun: The Northern Cheyenne Indians and America's Energy Crisis, 20
Mound Builders (Le Sueur, Meridel), 183
Mound Builders (Silverberg, Robert), 183(n)
Mud Pony, 32
Myers, Arthur, 175.21, 175.22
Mythology of North America, 7

Nanticoke, 193.40
Narragansett, 193.45
Nashone, 123
National Geographic Society, 187
Nations Within: The Past and Future of American Indian Sovereignty, 37
Native American Cookbook, 93
Native American Substance Abuse: An Anthology of Student Writings, 67
Native Americans, 188.29
Native Americans Information Directory, 1
Native Americans on Film and Video, Volume II, 131

Native Harvests: Recipes and Botanicals of the American Indian, 94
Native Hunter Series, 119
Natural World of the California Indians, 173
Navajo, 188.32
Navajo Stories of the Long Walk Period, 179
Navajo Weaving: Its Technic and Its History, 99
Navajos, 193.29
Naylor, Maria, 124
Neihardt, John G., 228
Nelson, Mary Carroll, 238
New and Old Voices of Wah'Kon-tah, 142
New Mexico People and Energy Collective, 68
Newman, Sandra Corrie, 125
Newman, Shirlee P., 175.23, 175.24
Nez Perce, 175.2, 188.33, 193.49
Norman, Howard, 69
North American Indian Art, 111
North American Indian Artifacts: A Collector's Identification and Value Guide, 174
North American Indian Arts, 132
North American Indian Ceremonies, 175.16
North American Indian Coloring Album, 110
North American Indian Design Coloring Book, 121
North American Indian Landmarks: A Traveler's Guide, 163
North American Indian Masks: Craft and Legends, 45
North American Indian Medicine People, 175.17
North American Indian Mythology, 11
North American Indian Sign Language, 175.18
North American Indian Survival Skills, 175.19
North American Indian Tribal Chiefs, 175.20
North American Indian Wars, 169
North American Indians of Achievement, 239
Now That the Buffalo's Gone: A Study of Today's American Indians, 59

Oakley, Ruth, 189, 189.1, 189.2, 189.3, 189.4, 189.5, 189.6
Official Identification and Price Guide to American Indian Collectibles, 127
Ojibwa, 193.47
Only the Names Remain: The Cherokee and the Trail of Tears, 155
Oneida, 188.3
Onondaga, 188.4
Orchard, William C., 126
Ortiz, Alfonso, 193.36
Ortiz, Simon, 190
Osage, 193.53
Oscar Howe: The Story of an American Indian, 232
Osceola, 239.3
Osinski, Alice, 188.30, 188.31, 188.32, 188.33, 188.34, 188.35
Our Mother Corn, 90
Ourada, Patricia K., 193.37
Owens, Laurella, 160

Paiute, 193.10
Patriots of the Plains: Sitting Bull, Crazy Horse, Chief Joseph, 227
Patterson, Alex, 82
Patterson, Lotsee, 83
Pawnee, 175.22, 188.9
Peek, Walter F., 146
Pelton, Mary Helen, 70
Penobscot, 188.6
People of the Breaking Day, 199
People Shall Continue, 190
Perdue, Theda, 193.38
Peyote, 17
Peterson, David, 191
Pima-Maricopa, 193.14
Plains Indians (Haines, Francis), 200(n)
Plains Indians (Hughes, Jill), 200(n)
Plains Indians of the Twentieth Century, 176
Poatgeiter, Hermina, 192
Pocahontas, 239.10
Pomo, 175.13
Pontiac, 239.4
Portable North American Indian Reader, 149
Porter, Frank W., II, 193, 193.39, 193.40

Potawatomi, 193.12
Powell, Suzanne, 175.25
Powers, William K., 194
Powhatan Tribes, 193.16
Powwow, 24
Powwow 1992, 162
Prehistoric Indians of the Southwest, 209
Pueblo, 193.36, 210
Pueblos, 175.25

Quanah, Alvina, 195
Quanah, Parker, 239.20
Quapaws, 193.2
Quiri, Patricia Ryon, 175.25

Rachlin, Carol K., 16, 17
Rand NcNally, 196
*Raven the Trickster: Legends of the North
    American Indians*, 71
*Red & White: Indian View of the White
    Man, 1492-1982*, 72
*Red Man's Religion: Beliefs and Practices
    of the Indians*, 19
Red Ribbons for Emma, 68
*Red Swan: Myths and Tales of the Ameri-
    can Indian*, 27
*Reference Encyclopedia of the American
    Indian*, 2
Religion and Customs, 189.5
Reno, Dawn E., 127
*Rising Voices: Writings of Young Native
    Americans*, 143
*Ritual of the Wind: North American Indian
    Ceremonies, Music, and Dance*, 14
Road to Wounded Knee, 161
Robinson, Gail, 71
Rock Art of the American Indian, 112
Rock Paintings of the Chumash, 112(n)
Roland, Albert, 222
Rollings, Willard H., 193.42
Roman, Joseph, 239.11
Rosenstiel, Annette, 22
Ruoff, A. L., 193.43

*Sacred Path: Spells, Prayers and Power
    Songs of the American Indian*, 10

Sanders, Thomas F., 146
Sandoz, Mari, 197, 198
Sarah Winnemucca, 239.15
Schneider, Mary Jane, 193.44
Schuster, Helen H., 193.45
Schwartz, Melissa, 239.12, 239.13, 239.14
Science of the Early American Indians, 87
Scordato, Ellen, 239.15
Seminole, 188.15, 193.19
Seminoles, 175.15, 185(n)
Seneca, 188.6
Sequoyah, 239.16
Seubert, Emelia, 131
Sewell, Marcia, 199
Shepherd, Donna Walsh, 174.27
Shepperd, Sally, 200
Shoshoni, 175.4, 188.10
Shumate, Jane, 239.16
Siegel, Beatrice, 201
Silverberg, Robert, 183(n)
Simmons, William S., 193.46
Singer, Beverly R., 143
Sioux, 175.14, 188.34
Sitting Bull, 239.2
Sitting Bull: Champion of the Sioux, 236
Skinner, Linda, 211
Sky Watchers of Ages Past, 88
Smallpox and the American Indian, 92
*Smithsonian Book of North American
    Indians: Before the Coming of the
    Europeans*, 181
Sneve, Virginia Driving Hawk, 147
Snodgrass, Mary Ellen, 83
Snow, Dean R., 193.47
*Song from the Earth: American Indian
    Painting*, 114
Songs from This Earth on Turtle's Back,
    139
*Songs of the Dream People: Chants and
    Images from the Indians and
    Eskimos of North America*, 117
Sonneborn, E., 239.17
*Spirit of the Harvest: North American
    Indian Cooking*, 91
*Spirits, Heroes, & Hunters from North
    American Mythology*, 78
Spotted Eagle & Black Crow, 25
Squanto and the First Thanksgiving, 61
Stands in Timber, John, 202

Star Boy, 52
Star Tales: North American Indian Stories About the Stars, 66.4
Stein, R. Conrad, 203
Steiner, Stan, 151
Stelzer, Ulli, 73
Stensland, Anna Lee, 4
Stiff Ears: Animal Folktales of the North American Indian, 77
Strickland, Rennard, 113
Story of an American Indian, 232
Story of Wounded Knee, 203
Stoutenburgh, John Jr., 84
Sweeney, Edwin R., 229

Tainos: The People Who Welcomed Columbus, 177
Talking Hands: Indian Sign Language, 79
Talking Stone: An Anthology of Native American Tales and Legends, 38
Tannenbaum, Beulah, 87
Tannenbaum, Harold, 87
Tanner, Helen H., 193.48
Tapahonso, Luci, 148
Tarahumara, 193.31
Tecumseh, 239.7
Teton Sioux, 193.8
This Song Remembers: Self Portraits of Native Americans in the Arts, 120
Thorne, Ian, 74
Thousand Years of American Indian Story-telling, 54
Tiller, Veronica E., 204
Tipi: A Center of Native American Life, 134
Tlingit, 188.35
To Live in Two Worlds: American Indian Youth Today, 21
Tobias, Tobi, 237(n)
Tomcheck, Ann, 188.37
Totem Pole, 188
Totem Pole Indians of the Northwest, 175.3
Touch the Earth: A Self-Portrait of Indian Existence, 8
Trafzer, Clifford E., 193.49, 193.50
Trail of Tears, 178
Tratter, Clifford, 239.18
Trees Stand Shining, 144
Tribal Scenes and Ceremonies, 75

Trimble, Stephen, 205
Trout, Lawana, 193.51
Truth About Geronimo, 230(n)
Tunica-Biloxi, 193.9
Tunis, Edwin, 206
Turnbaugh, Sarah Peabody, 128
Turnbaugh, William A., 128
Turner, Frederick W., 149
Turquoise and the Indian, 104
Tuscarora, 188.7

Underhill, Ruth M., 19
Urban Indians, 193.17

Vanderwerth, W. C., 150
Vestal, Stanley, 236
Village of Blue Stone, 205
Villasenor, Gerald, 75
Vogel, Virgil J., 96
Voices of the Winds: Native American Legends, 40

Wade, Edwin L., 130
Waldman, Carl, 207, 223
Walens, Stanley, 193.51
War Clouds in the West: Indians & Cavalry-men, 1860-1890, 184
Washburn, Wilcomb E., 208
Waters, Frank, 224
Way: An Anthology of American Indian Literature, 151
The Way of Life, 189.6
Way to Rainy Mountain, 186
Wayne, Bennett, 225, 226
Ways of My Grandmothers, 58
We Rode the Wind: Recollections of Nine-teenth Century Tribal Life, 221
We Talk, You Listen: New Tribes, New Turf, 35
Weatherford, Elizabeth, 131
Weinstein-Farson, Laurie, 193.52
Weiss, Malcolm E., 88
Weslager, C. A., 97
Wheeler, M. J., 76
When Clay Sings, 102

Where Indians Live: American Indian Houses, 123

Whispering Wind: Poetry by Young American Indians, 135

Whistling Skeleton, American Indian Tales of the Supernatural, 28

Whiteford, Andrew Hunter, 132

Whitney, Alex, 77, 98

Whittaker, Jane, 227

Who-Paddled-Backward-with-Trout, 69

Who's Who in Native American History: Indians and Non-Indians from First Contacts Through 1900, 223

Will Rogers, 239.17

Wilma Mankiller, 239.14

Wilson, Claire, 239.19, 239.20

Wilson, Terry P., 193.53

Winged Worlds: American Indian Writers Speak, 140

Witt, Shirley Hill, 151

Wolfson, Evely, 133

Woman Who Fell from the Sky, 29

Women in American Indian Society, 193.23

Wood, Marion 78

World of the American Indian, 187

World of the Southern Indians, 160

Wormington, H. M., 209

Wounded Knee: An Indian History of the American West, 159

Wunder, John R., 193.54

Yakima, 193.44

Yankton Sioux, 193.27

Yenne, Bill, 5

Yue, Charlotte, 134, 210

Yue, David, 134, 210

Yuma, 193.3

Zunis, 175.8

Zunis: Self Portrayals, 195

Subject Index to Annotations

Numbers refer to annotations in part 2. Spellings generally reflect the authors' preferences in their books.

Abenaki Indians, 193.11
Agriculture, 89, 90, 92
Alaska—legends, 39
Alcohol, 67
Algonquin Indians, 157, 175.26
  legends, 26
America—discovery and exploration, 180
American Indian Movement, 75, 161
American literature—Indian authors—
    history and criticism, 140
American poetry
  Indian authors, 139, 142
  twentieth century, 139, 142
Anasazi Indians, 153, 188.36, 191, 205
Animal ecology—study and teaching
    (elementary), 31.1
Animals—legends, 77
Anthropology, 14, 19, 141
Antiquities, 82, 165, 174, 180, 182
Apache Indians 175.5, 188.17, 193.34
  biography, 229, 230
  legends, 62
  wars—1872-73, 229
Arapaho Indians, 193.18
Archaeology, 109, 153, 182, 193.46
Arikara Indians, 168
Art, 34, 102, 107, 111, 113, 120, 121, 122,
    124, 127, 132, 154, 189, 192
  Contemporary, 130
Artifacts, 127
Artists, 232
Assiniboine Indians, 168
Astronomy, prehistoric, 88
Atlases, historical 207

Authors, Indian—interviews, 140
Aztec Indians, 175.27, 188.16, 193.4

Basketmaking, 122, 124, 125, 127, 128,
    132
Beadwork, 122, 126
Beaver, 201
Bibliography, 2, 3, 4
  Indians of North America—art, 122
Biloxi Indians, 193.9
Biography, 2, 83, 120, 127, 145, 175.20,
    211, 212, 213, 214, 215, 216, 217,
    218, 220, 221, 222, 224, 225, 226,
    227
  dictionaries, 223
Black Elk, 228
Black Hawk, 225, 239.5
Blackfeet Indians, 200
Blacks—ethnic relations with Indians of
    North America, 60
Botany
  medical, 96, 97
  North America, 94
Bowlegs, 170
Brant, Joseph, Mohawk chief, 239.19
Buffalo, 86
  fiction, 46
  history, 85
  hunters, 166

Cahuilla Indians, 193.32
California Indians—history, 173, 233, 234

Campbell, Ben Nighthorse, 239.9
Carving, 122
Catawba Indians, 193.35
Cave drawings, 154
Cayuga Indians, 188.1
Cherokee Indians, 155, 170, 175.10,
    188.12, 193.38
Cheyenne Indians, 175.21, 188.8, 193.26,
    198, 200
  government relations, 20
  history, 202
  legends, 49
Chickasaw Indians, 170, 193.25
Chilula Indians, 175.11
Chinook Indians, 193.48
Chippewa Indians, 175.9, 188.30
Choctaw Indians, 170, 188.13, 193.33
Chumash Indians, 193.20
Civil rights, 37. *See also* American Indian
    Movement
Civilization—Indian influences, 192
Claims, 65
Clallam Indians, 118
Cliff dwellers and cliff dwellings, 153. *See*
    also Anasazi Indians; Indians of
    the Southwest—archaeology
Clothing, 98, 127, 189
Coal mines and mining—Montana, 20
Cochise, Apache chief, 229, 239.12
Comanche Indians, 175.1, 193.41
Conservation of natural resources, 192
  Montana, 20
Cookery, 91, 93, 94, 175.19
Corn, 89, 90
Costumes, 56. *See also* Clothing
Courts—United States, 36
Coyotes—folklore, 23
Crazy Horse, Sioux chief, 226, 239.8
Creation—folklore, 29
Cree Indians, 168
  legends, 69
Creek Indians, 170, 193.22
Crow Indians, 168, 188.11, 193.28, 200
Crows—folklore, 47
Cryptography, 81
Culture, 167, 187. *See also* Art; Social life
    and customs; Songs and music
Custer, George Armstrong, 197

Dakota Indians
  biography, 216, 232
  legends, 25, 49
  war, 1890-91, 203
Decoration and ornament, 129
Design, 121
Directories, 1
Diseases—social aspects, 92
Dolls,127
Drugs, 67
Dull Knife, Cheyenne chief, 198
Dwellings, 123, 134, 175.19, 189, 210

Ecology, 8
Economic conditions, 55
Education, 2, 55
Encyclopedias and dictionaries, 2, 5, 80,
    83, 84
Eskimos, 117, 188.31

Fiction—bibliography, 136
Folklore, 138
Food, 94, 189
Fur trade—New England—
    history, 201

Gambling, 108
Games, 100, 106, 108, 127
Geronimo, 230, 239.13
Ghost Dance religion, 18
Government policy, 36, 59, 208
Government publications, 208
Government relations, 53, 55, 170, 178,
    193.30
  biography—dictionaries, 223
  1934-1986, 37
  sources, 72
Great Plains Indians, 44, 86, 134, 194, 200
  biographies, 221, 227
  history—20th century—addresses,
      essays, lectures, 176
  legends, 28, 50.1, 50.2, 50.3, 50.4
  social life and customs, 42
  women, 58

Haida Indians—rites and ceremonies, 73
Handicraft, 106, 133, 187
Herbs, 97
Hiawatha, 231, 239.6
History, 113, 166, 178, 180, 187, 189.190,
190, 224
1492-1891, 169
government policy, 208
sources, 72
west of the Mississippi—mid-1800s, 164
Home economics, 81
Hopi Indians, 175.12, 188.37, 193.5
Horned toads—folklore, 23
Horses, 95
fiction, 48
folklore, 32
Housing, 57
Howe, Oscar, 1915- , 232
Human ecology, 65
study and teaching (elementary), 31.1
Humor, 138
Hunting, 86, 119, 172
Huron Indians, 193.6

Inca Indians, 175.23, 188.18
Indians in literature, 140
Indians of the Southwest—archaeology,
209. *See also* Cliff dwellers
and cliff dwellings; Anasazi
Indians
Indians of the West Indies, 177
Inhalants, 67
Intermarriage, 60
Inuit Indians, 175.24
Inventions, 192
Iroquois Indians, 157, 175.6, 193.21
biography, 231
legends, 29, 30
Ishi, 233, 234

Jewelry, 127, 133
Joseph, Nez Perce chief, 226, 235,
239.18

King Philip, 239.11
Kiowa Indians, 193.54
history, 186
mythology, 186
Kwakliutl Indians, 193.51

Land tenure, 65
Land transfers, 178
Language and languages, 187, 192
Leatherwork, 127, 132
Legends, 16.22, 25, 27, 28, 31.1, 31.2, 33,
38, 40, 43, 45, 48, 51, 54, 62, 64,
66, 74, 77, 78, 145
Lenape Indians, 193.24
Literature, 193.42
collected works, 145, 146, 149, 151
Little Bighorn, Battle of the, 197
Little Wolf, Cheyenne chief, 198
Lumbee Indians, 193.13

Makah Indians, 64
Mandan Indians, 188.14
Mankiller, Wilma, 329.14
Maps, 196, 207
Maricopa Indians, 194.14
Masks, 45, 122, 124
Massasoit, 225
Mayan Indians, 175.8, 188.19, 193.50
McIntosh, Roley, 170
Medicine, 96, 97, 192
Medicine men, 96, 175.17
Menominee Indians, 193.37
Mesa Verde National Park (Colorado), 205
Metalwork, 132
Mining, 104
Minorities, 35
Modoc Indians, 193.15
Mohawk Indians, 188.2, 193.7
Monsters—fiction, 74
Montagnais Indians, 193.1
Moon—folklore, 66
Motion pictures, 115, 131
Mound builders, 183

Museums, 2, 163
Music, 34, 116, 141. *See also* Songs and
    music
Musical instruments, 109, 116
Mythology, 7, 10, 11, 16, 34, 202

Names, personal—folklore, 69
Nanticoke Indians, 193.40
Narragansett Indians, 193.45
Naskapi Indians, 193.1
Native American Church, 17
Nature in poetry, 6
Nature—study and teaching (elementary),
    31.2
Navajo Indians, 125, 171, 175.5, 188.32,
    193.29
  biography, 238
  history—1864, 179
  legends, 23
  poetry, 148
  social conditions, 68
Nez Perce Indians, 64, 175.2, 188.32,
    193.49
Nisqually Indians, 64
Northwest coast of North America, 188
  legends, 71
  social life and customs, 175.2

Oratory, 8, 72, 137, 150, 151
Ojibwa Indians, 193.47
Oneida Indians, 188.3
Onondaga Indians, 188.4
Osage Indians, 193.53
  biography, 237
Osceola, 185, 225, 239.3

Painting, 107, 114, 122
Paiute Indians, 193.10
Parker, Quanah, Comanche chief, 226,
    239.20
Pattern making, 129
Pawnee Indians, 175.22, 188.9
  legends, 32
Periodicals, 2, 5, 188
Peyote, 17
Philosophy, 6, 8

Pilgrims (New England colonists), 201
Pilgrims (New Plymouth Colony), 61
Pima Indians, 125, 193.14
Plains Indians, 47
Pocahontas, 239.10
Poetry, 6, 10, 116, 122, 145
  collected works, 135, 137, 141, 143,
    144, 147
Politics and government, 2
Pomo Indians, 125, 175.13
Pontiac, 239.4
Potlatch, 73
Potowatomi Indians, 193.12
Pottery, 101, 102, 122, 124, 127, 132
Powhatan Indians 193.16
Prehistoric Indians of the Southwest,
    175.25
Prejudice against Indians, 55. *See also*
    Stereotypes
Pueblo Indians, 175.25, 193.36
  social life and customs, 191, 205

Quapaw Indians, 193.2

Raven—legends, 71
Religion, 7, 9, 10, 11, 12, 13, 14, 17, 19,
    43, 65, 172, 189
Religion and mythology, 31.2
  encyclopedias, 14
Reservations, 2, 55, 75, 163, 204
Riddles, Indian, 138
Rites and ceremonies, 14, 24, 116, 162,
    163, 175.6
  encyclopedias, 14
Rock drawings, paintings, and engravings,
    82, 112
Rogers, Will, 239.17
Ross, John, 170

Salish Indians, 193.39
Sand painting, 122
Science,
  ancient, 87
  history—American, 87
Scouts, 40
Sculpture, 122

Seminole Indians, 170, 175.15, 188.15, 193.19
  history, 185
Seneca Indians, 188.6
Sequoyah, 170, 239.16
Shellwork, 132
Short stories, 54, 145
  bibliography, 136
Shoshoni Indians, 175.4, 188.10
Sign language, 79, 175.18
Siksika Indians
  legends, 51, 52
  women, 58
Silversmithing, 104
  Navajo Indians, 103
  Pueblo Indians, 103
Sioux Indians 18, 54, 64, 168, 175.14, 188.34, 200
  biography, 236
  history, 228
Sitting Bull, Sioux chief, 226, 236, 239.2
Smallpox—West (United States), 92
Snohomish Indians, 64
Social conditions, 21, 35, 53, 193.17
Social life and customs, 44, 55, 57, 63, 76, 91, 93, 110, 182, 188.29, 189, 193.23, 196, 206, 207. *See also* Cookery; Culture; Games; Potlatch
Songs and music, 14, 105, 109, 117, 141
Southern states, 152
Southwestern states, 160, 210
Speeches, 145. *See also* Oratory
Spiritualism, 9
Sports, 172, 192
Squanto, 61
Stars—folklore, 51, 66
Stereotypes, 4. *See also* Prejudice against Indians
Stonework, 132
Swinomish Indians, 64
Symbolism, 122

Taino Indians, 177
Tallchief, 237
Tarahumara Indians, 193.31
Technology—America—history, 87
Tecumseh, 225, 239.7
Teton Sioux Indians, 193.8

Textiles, 132
Thanksgiving Day, 61
Thorpe, Jim, 239.1
Tlingit Indians, 188.35
  legends, 39, 70
  social life and customs, 70
Tools, 127, 175.19
Totem poles, 118
Traditions, 172
Treatment, 166
Tribal consciousness, 75
Tribal government, 37
Tsimshian Indians, 118
Tunica Indians, 193.9
Turquoise, 104
Tuscarora Indians, 188.7

United States Armed Forces—Indian troops, 156
United States—history—1973, 161
Urban, 193.17

Videotapes, 111

Wampanoag Indians, 193.52, 199
Warfare, 172
Wars, 158, 169, 184
Wauneka, Annie 238
Weapons, 127
Weather—folklore, 66.2
Weaving, 99, 122, 127
West (United States), 184
  history, 158
  wars, 159
Whites
  encroachment on Indian lands, 172
  treatment of Indians, 141
Winnemucca, Sarah, 239.15
Women, 193.23
  biography, 218
Woodwork, 132
World War, 1939-1945—Indian participation in, 156
Wounded Knee Creek, Battle of (1890), 203

Yahi Indians, 233, 234
Yakima Indians, 193.44
Yana Indians, 233, 234
Yankton Sioux Indians, 193.27
Yazzie, Emma, 68
Youth, 21
Yuma Indians, 193.3
Yurok Indians, 125

Zuni Indians, 175.7
  history, 195
  legends, 195
  mythology, 195